ERIC WIBERG

JUVENILIA
Teen Books & Travel Writing

ISLAND BOOKS
New York

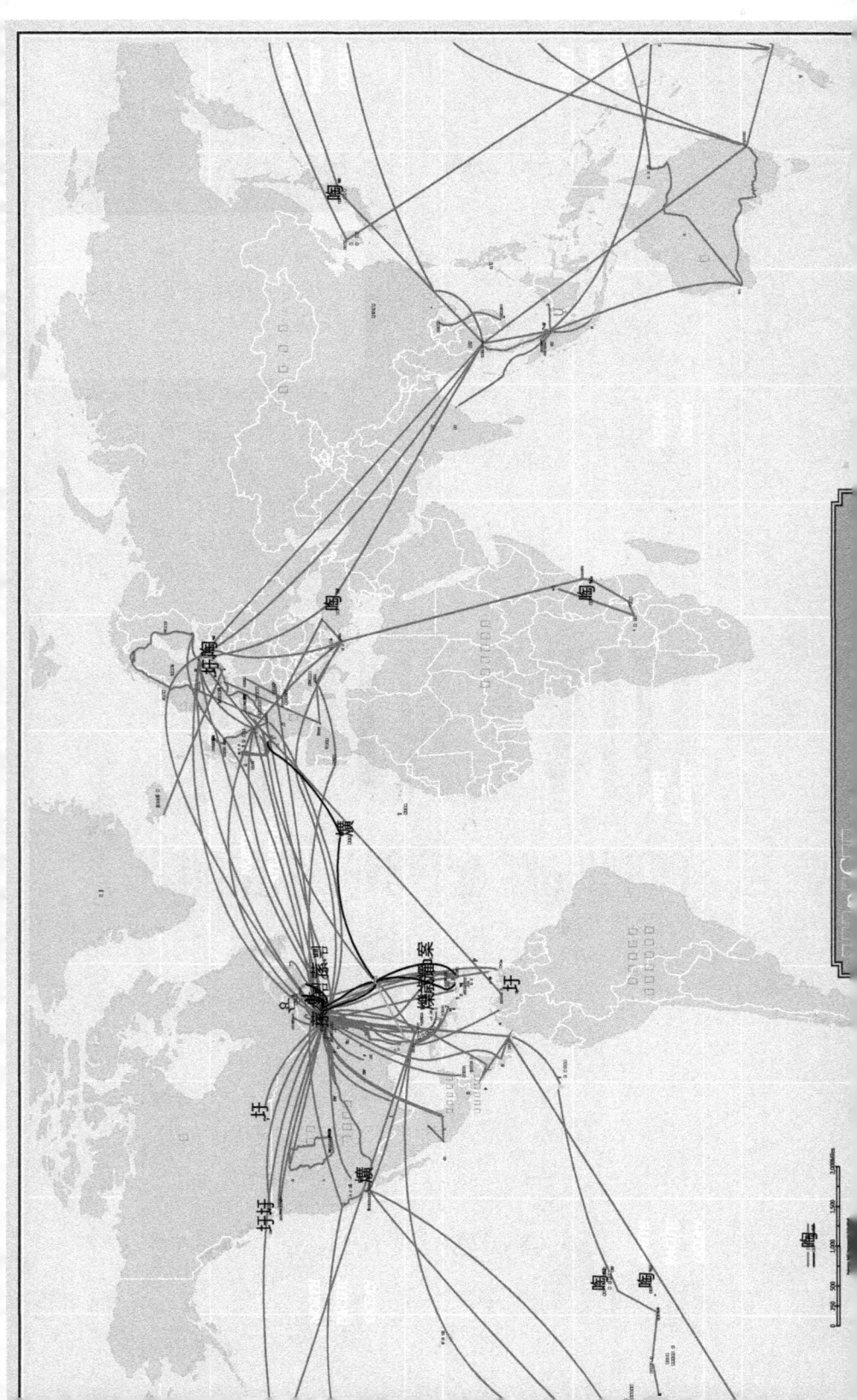

for my good friends Kent & Petra Post,
Fellow voyagers & travellers

This book is a compendium of the following four shorter titles:

Umbrae Papilionis (Shadows of Butterflies) (1988 St. George's School)
Z. (For Zarathustra) (1989 St. George's School)
Shorts (1990 Boston College)
Travel Writing (2003 Newport, Rhode Island)

by the same author:

Bahamas in World War II
Mailboats of the Bahamas
U-Boats off Bermuda
U-Boats in the Bahamas
Swan Sinks
Round the World in the Wrong Season
Tanker Disasters
Published Writing, 1976 - 2017

in production:

U-Boats in New England
Drifting to the Duchess
History of Lyford Cay International School

Published by Island Books, New York, NY, USA
© Eric Troels Wiberg, 2009 & 2017

ISBN 978-0-9843998-4-0 / 0984399844
Library of Congress Control Number: 2009914212

These are works of fiction. Any similarity to persons, living or dead, is coincidental. It is the product of the author's teenage imagination. All rights reserved. No part of this publication may be reproduced in any manner without the prior written permission of the publisher, except in the case of brief quotations embodied in articles or reviews.

For information or to contact the author please email
eric@ericwiberg.com.

Printed in the United States of America
First Edition Island Books, 2009, Second Edition Island Books, 2017

Author's Note

Leave your embarrassment at the frontispiece when you open these pages - I certainly have. These are collections of poems, essays, prose, maps, travel and miscellany from my teen years. Aside from the travel writing, they are fiction.

Juvenilia is, by definition, a retrospective of someone's early work, to discern not so much quality as direction. This writing is not meant to impress; but it is hoped that teens today might empathize with some of the rebellious anger and challenge to authority.

Umbrae Papilionis means 'shadows of the butterflies' I hoped later to write. I was a 17-year-old junior at St. George's School in Newport, RI. I was not good in spring sports (I had a habit of damaging sailboats and losing tennis matches) and took advantage of the school's little-known policy of producing a special project instead. During afternoons, I would skateboard to Purgatory Chasm to find inspiration.

Z. (for Zarathustra) was overseen on my senior year by Mrs. Janet Buell. The title derives from my study of, and flirtation with, Persian and non-Judeo-Christian religions, and a featured essay.

Shorts is, by far the loudest scream this author has put to paper. During my Freshman year, 15,000 students of Boston College was highly tumultuous and wrenchingly free. *Shorts* thus reflects my Beatnik bent.

Travel Writing has first-hand narratives of hitchhiking alone through East Africa, and voyages with untested crews across the Atlantic and Pacific Oceans; of storms, knife, shark attacks, robberies, and wrecks. It begins with reports that I filed for my parents and covers four round-the--world trips in over 70 countries and islands.

Note: Roughly a dozen short poems or essays appeared in another compendium of my writing, *Published Writing, 1976 2017*. In all instances where my writing has already been featured in a book of mine, the work was deleted as redundant and previously published. *Published Writing, 1976-2017* is available on Amazon, e-book, Kindle, etc.

ETW, NY, NY
July, 2017

Table of Contents

PART I: *Umbrae Paplionis*

Dawn	01
Long Day	02
Her Light	02
On Television	03
A School Morning	03
St. George's Whistle	04
Her	04
The Deceitful Shaft of Light	04
Wind Haikus	09
Chapel Breezes	10
A Connecticut Weekend	11
Stones	11
Death Row	12
Life	12
Shaving the Grass	12
Fog, or *Diman*	13
Fuimos de Campamento (We Went Camping)	14
Riots	14
I.L.U.	16
Secular Ode	16
Flying Home	17
Table	17
To the Televangelists	17
Fill O' Sophie (Philosophy)	18
Thoughts	18
On Writing	18
Rainfall	18

PART II: *Z. (for Zarathustra)*

Excerpt: Memory, Ambition	25
Climbing Haiku	25
The Straw Market	25
Landing in Nassau	27
Notes from a Stockholm Park	27
Don't Do Crack	27
Dazed and Running	28
Hejdå Stor Båt (Goodbye Big Boat)	29
I Saw Men Running	32
Down Fell the Bowman	33
Life Versus Limits	33
On Gender	33
So Many Things	33
My Mind is on Guitar	34
Grippsund	34
Chameleon River Haiku	42
Clang Goes the Cross	42
I Fell Silent	42
My Boat and I	43
Lean Back	44
Chapel Talk	48
At Night, While Cycling	51
Sophia	51

PART III: *Shorts*

Skull and I	55
Station	61
The Man in the Uniform	63
The Uniform in the Man	66

Two Bedraggled Men	68
What?	70
Scribbles from Saint George's	77
John Coltrane: 1926-1967	82
Thus Spoke Nietzsche	84
Zarathustrianism	92
The Stare	99
Courtney at Fourteen	100
I was killed in Mesquite, Nevada	107
The Jameson Raid in South Africa: 1895-1896	108
Fall Football	114
A Happening Hitch	116
Pensée	118
This Sea	132

PART IV: *Travel Writing 1987 2003*

John & My Travels in Scandinavia, (map)	135
EuroRail 1990 (with map)	136
Sailboat *Chebec*'s Atlantic Crossing (with chart)	154
Travels in The British Isles, France, Belgium, and the Netherlands, 1984-1991, (map)	186
A Brief Wander Through East Africa (with map)	190
You Can't Get to Mpulungu From Here	209
Yacht *Stornoway*'s Trans-Pacific Voyage 1993-94, (with chart)	219
Report on the Water Barge M/T *Titas* Round-Trip Nassau-Andros, Bahamas, April 2, 1995	241
Summary of Fourth Round-the-World Trip, 2001	248
About the author	259

PART I

Umbrae Paplionis

(St. George's, 1988)

Dawn

(1)

The sunshine is escaping
from its spherical orange mother;
through a thin, low mist
it slithers to my window
and up the wail of Arden dorm.

I face away from the sun
when I wake
I see my silhouette
grey upon the sun-tit, orange door.
Swing around on dawn hips
and lean against the pillow-padded wall,
bed upon the floor,
feet resting upon the carpet.
Vivaldi replaces Haydn
and a warm mug of coffee
Generates an emotion through my fingers.

(2)

The trees along the avenue
appeal not unlike mushrooms
looming through the mist.
The geese are heard,
the ocean seen.
A gorgeous strip of Rhode Island beach
being rinsed caressingly
before my eyes.

The misty hues of sunrise red
are slowly watered down;

weakened by the strengthening sunshine.
The rising sun radiates and enforces
the pale whites
and strong golds
of a day.
Dawn has come again.

Long Day

It's been a long day
and it's over now.
Up early,
down late.
Coffee never worked.
There's a cool mist
risING from our earth
and the farm day is done.

Her Light

The lights are quiet - unseen now.
She's gone.
That was all months ago
We've been lost for a while since.
She had been our light;
lighthouse, guidance, touchstone.
Yeah, that was the glow
it came from her
as I suppose all warmth did.

The lights are flashing now,
They've been flashing for a while
and we're confused.
We'd counted on them
for a long time.
We'd always depended on them

looked for guidance
inward the glow.

The light, which in strength
was once concentrated,
has since been dispersed
and drifted,
floated
flashing away.

On Television

    A situation wherein the Proletariat are satisfied to spend the majority of their non-working hours in submittal to the television sustains (and eventually becomes the weapon of) the Capitalist Bourgeoisie. Such a situation fosters the growth of mute, passive, and dependent working masses, which America's 1776 Revolutionaries were not.

A School Morning

Early,
as I wake,
I hear my brother
suddenly jump up.
The air conditioner rattles.
I hear the radio run on
in the kitchen, the dogs eating,
and the cat hungrily meowing.
I hear someone hitting on the
wooden batting-board,
and the rattle and screech of cars.
I hear the bus pick up a faraway neighbour
and drop off my gardener
to the dogs' tuned barks
and birds' singing.

I hear the turtles splashing happily
in their pool.
Then I hear a big Cadillac taxi
come and pick up our spoilt neighbour.
I hear someone open the screen door,
and dogs' whine.
I hear a big splash
as my dog goes for her morning swim.

St. George's Whistle

Hear my whistle echo
off these Chapel walls.
Hear my whistle wailing
down these marble halls.
They don't listen; hollow
hear my whistle fail.

Her

It seems only a few days ago
that I saw her last;
her eyes, they were quite marble-ic
and round,
like green glass.

The Deceitful Shaft of Light

Two roads diverged... and I
I took the one less travelled by,
And that has made all the difference.

- *Robert Frost*

Restlessly, the young fisherman's mate sat on the wharf with the old sailors in the early morning sun. He was listening to the tales of mysterious underwater caverns and adventures had there. Like them, he also had spent the week fishing on the Bahamian shoals, and was tired. And yet his longing for adventures, that would be worthy of their tales, made the slow wharf seem to him too quiet. With noon threatening, he set off alone in his little wooden dinghy in search of the mysterious island-caves.

The fabled underwater chasms had given him an adequate excuse to cast off the moorings from the stagnant cluster of old sailors. Leaving the murky harbour waters, he set off westward feeling relieved. The sun shone brightly upon his bars sack, and the glassy waters over which his wooden boat glided parted smoothly. The sky was cloudless, and a magnificent hue of blue was stretched over the horizon as far as the eye could see. Soon he could see the dark outline of the rooky islet featured in their tales. It lay in a chain of other tiny cays, several miles from the mainland. The caverns had been carved from out of the easternmost of the rocks, which the skiff slowly neared over the roiling swells.

He drew up to a snarl of jagged rock, barren of any fauna. Protruding from the ocean's depths, it subjected itself to the merciless surf. He watched the anchor sink silently through the waters, which, though normally turquoise, was darker so near the drop-off. The surrounding waters were deep, consuming almost all of his anchor line. The boat rose and fell slowly with the gentle swell of the ocean, a safe distance from where waves splashed lazily against the little cay.

Donning only his mask and fins, he casually slid into the warm Caribbean Sea. With the smooth movements characteristic of any spear fisherman, he swam towards an unwell coming orifice for the first time. Swimming slowly around the hollow cay, he looked for an opening in the stone. On the North side, where he had anchored the boat, he found the only entrance to the dark labyrinth and began to believe that the fishermen had been right.

Close to the ocean floor, nestled into the base of the island, there was an opening in the rock, easily large enough for him to swim through. It gaped alluringly, like the sirens of old, some forty to fifty feet below. Hovering far above, he was determined to explore any cave system, which might wind under the rock. Deciding on an exploratory dive, he took a deep breath and began his descent into the silent and shady waters.

Sliding smoothly into the depths, he reached the mouth of the system, entering the tunnel only to the length of his body. From there he was able to see that just inside the entrance the tunnel split into two smaller passageways. The small opening to the left curved towards the core of the island. From the entrance, he could see no distinct feature or light there, but at the end of the tunnel to the right could barely distinguish a shimmering shaft of sunshine.

Out of breath, he hurriedly ascended towards the bright and welcoming surface far overhead. Lungs clawing for air, he began to race against his own bubbles. With his mask pointed upwards and legs pounding furiously, he shot up. Finally, his momentum sent him bursting through the surface, where his vertical form hesitated, half submerged while his lunge sucked in their capacity of ocean air. Quickly sliding back into the possessive waters, he began again to tread water, recuperating for a second dive.

He circled slowly in the water, contemplating his next, most important dive. He had been hoping to swim through the tunnel and popped up for air in the island's hollow centre. The sailors had drawled on about a mythical blue-hole which he hoped to explore perhaps he would even become his skipper's pride. He began to dream: Who knows? Maybe Cap'n would even give me some crawfish tail to bring back to mama in fox Hill!

Having never probed into the bowels of the island, he was torn between the danger and adventure. Though on his first dive he had not seen the expected blue-hole opening in the island's centre, he felt sure of its existence. Choosing the correct tunnel would be a mortal decision. He thought of the old fishermen, not remembering which way they had directed him to swim. Having seen them in drunken criticism of other overzealous lads, he refused lo go scampering back to the harbour for advice.

Calling upon his own undeveloped sense of judgement, he decided lo act alone. He'd seen the shaft of light, which had tempted visitors to the right, and he'd looked to the left, and seen no light there. His mind raced: The opening could lay concealed behind the bend to the left. Hadn't the sailors said that the bright opening to the surface was to the left as you enter? No. Surely they must have said that the right, with its rays of sunlight, was the place of refreshment.

Many thoughts turned over in his mind. As the long week of fishing and his own hunger caught up with him, his excitement began to wane. The prospect of his home and sleep began to seem more inviting. Regardless of which direction he swam in, he decided, this would be his final dive of the day. He prepared to dive once more and probe the depths.

Making sure that the boat was secure; he took a long, deep breath, and kicked downward, toward the entrance. His legs propelled him methodically down, down, deeper, farther from the air, the sunlight, and the shrinking boat. When he reached the colder, darker, sea floor in a short time, his confidence was not as high. He looked urgently into the cavern and glanced back upward to his little boat, thinking: 'What am I doing so far away from it?'

Knowing that it was his last chance to turn back to the safety of his vessel, he turned his back and entered the caves.

For the first time, he was well within the sarcophagus surrounded by it. It was indeed darker and colder. Swimming, he reached the split, knowing that he would have to choose quickly. To the left he saw nothing but jagged, coral-lined walls; to the right he saw the shimmering ray of light, and swam toward it. Once so far within the suffocating grasp of the caves, his perspectives changed. He no longer thought in terms of making if to the surface which he had struggled to reach before. He began searching for a source of oxygen within the heart of the island;i n it's centre. He pushed forward.

He was convinced that his source lay where the rays of sunlight penetrated the silent darkness of the tunnel. His eyes became transfixed upon that magnified shaft. At first he felt as though reaching it would be a short, easy task, as they had told him it would be. Suddenly, for a brief instant, the steady, soft glow of light from the entrance was dulled. It might have been only a cloud flitting before the sun, except that the shaft of light had remained consistent. The boy whirled around; startling himself with his own panicked reaction. Nothing could be seen.

For the first time while in the cave, an element of fear began to infect his mind. He was getting very tired; his head throbbed from lack of air, and his heart began to pound furiously. He was used to open ocean, the free and rolling waves, not the suffocating encroachment of caves. Looking up, he saw no bright sunshine, no windswept crests, no placid surface awaiting his return; only cold walls of limestone.

His legs began to kick with an intense fury and his lungs rasped for air as he set an unwavering course for the distant ray of light. 'I should have reached it by now, why is it suddenly so distant?' His mind filled with frustrated questions. 'Push, push!'He told himself, 'With the sunlight will come air, and land, and safety.'

Finally, the boy came within reach of the shaft's origin. In a last, desperate attempt to be tree of the murky caverns and the unknown dangers that lurked behind him, he turned on his back, faced upward, grasped the rim of a circular opening, and pulled his face forward so that the shaft of light hit him directly in the face. When the eyes of the spear fisherman were fully adjusted, he was shattered by what he saw. He had chosen the wrong tunnel. He could never reach the point where the light hit the water. He could never make it back. The rays hit the water at sea level, a good thirty feet above where he was trapped. They had been magnified by the water through a tiny hole, through which he would have been lucky to fit his small hand, much less likely to fit his head or whole, oxygen-starved body, In the throes of death, panic clutched him with talon-like strength.

He began thrashing violently, pushing and clawing his way upward, his body tearing against the jagged sides of his cylindrical vault. With a bursting thrust, his hand broke the surface of the water and groped the air. Terror seized and pushed him. His body and arm pinned between the stones began to warm the salt water with blood. He could get no closer to the life-giving breath of air than the narrow passage would allow. Even in a frenzy he knew that it was vain, and in utter exhaustion, sank slowly downward.

His last meagre supply of air trickled slowly from his mouth upwards to meet the surface. His mask cracked slightly, and gently began to fill. As his limp form drifted back down into the tunnel and the last of his short life bubbled away, he saw two hungry sharks bearing down upon him. Then he knew what had caused the dark shadow to flit across the entrance.

The shaft dimmed; the deceitful shaft of light faded into eternal darkness.

Wind Haikus

-1-

The wind is blowing
The air around us - whipping
Hair, buffing, pulling.

-2-

Great winds blow the air
Send it hurling over us;
Strength invisible.

-3-

Push the rolling waves,
Wind; send them surging forward.
Stormy weather-works.

Capel Breezes

"Through daylight and dark I follow the bark,
I keep like a hound on her trail.
I'm strongest at noon, yet under the moon,
I stiffen the bunt of her sails."
- From *Song of the Trade Wind*

The sail as an escape
To drift away, forget;
To leave behind the times,
And schedules unmet.

To sail across the water -
Pulled across the sea;
To go against the winter gusts
And glide wherever you please.

The worries of the pressure world
Forgot when rope is cast,
But though, believe me, it is loved,
Our sailing could not last

As strong as we hold liberty,
We know that sails must cease.

Our sailing days are like breaths held
As such they need release.

A Connecticut Weekend

On a bright Easter Sunday morning in spring, an assortment of weekend companions slowly emerged from their sleepy hollows. As they gathered on a grassy slope in the sunshine, drinking coffee, I slipped, naked, into the glassy waters of the pond below, hands above my head, I slid into the cold, refreshing water; a sparkling golden retriever propelling himself alongside. Underwater I spread my eyes and watched the bottom slide beneath me, piercing that thin area between surface and sediment, moving at a pace just ahead of the stirred muck behind my kicking legs. After swimming, I paused on a shallow bank in the centre of the pond and absorbed the placid scene surrounding me.

Upon the sun-struck slope lay my friends. The girl was holding my peace symbol as my sister caught up on the goings-on of the previous night. Edward beckoned with a rotten stick for the dog to return from the pond. Everything was golden and pleasant. The tadpoles scattered outward from wherever I pushed forward, I moved toward land through the water and, feeling unobserved, unhooked my sun-warmed towel from a branch before walking airily up the knoll, wringing out my hair. I missed my necklace and the nocturnal warmth of the one who held it.

Stones

Smooth round stones
Crashing through
The brittle glass windows
Of our classroom.

Smooth, round stones
Sprout wings
And are buffed
By the winds
Or our fan.

Stones that fly
The space of this
Cubicle
Explore the perimeters
Of our cages.

Death Row

I've waited on death row,
And so will you.
Just as the bulls do.
We all do - *moo*!

Life

Life is the creation of nostalgia.

Shaving the Grass

It was summer hot, and the sun throbbed upon my back as I pushed a sputtering lawn mower around the orchard. Row after row of straight lines, like the wake of a boat, stretched behind me. Trailing lifeless behind the machine, the lines of dead grass seemed more crooked the farther I moved away.

Mowing the lawns of the Swedish manor, I thought of cutting grass as a conformist act. One either follows the set, manicured path of the last shaver, or creates a less practical pattern that will be conformed to next time. Since the fourteen-hundreds on that estate, there had been only one 'correct' grass-cutting pattern. My eyes and hands were devoted to lawn cutting, but my mind was unleashed elsewhere.

After a third revolution around the main orchard, I began to wonder why I was cutting the soft green grass carpet. Watching (and without option hearing) the mower-of-lawns doing its nasty business. I pondered the necessity of such a machine and its vile act.

Farmers had spent long winters yearning, through cold windows, for a plush green mat of grass. Many had died in anticipation of feeling fresh grass (instead of ice) underfoot. Thinking about winter, even on a hot summer's day, I couldn't help but appreciate all the more even the most picayune blades of grass.

I shifted the mower from rattling dirt and rocks quickly enough to retain my thoughts. Fresh lawns had endured, only to be cut down. What humans yearn for most are the very elements of life, which they most efficiently destroy. In his love of life, man has created the revolver and its precise bullets, the atom bomb and its hopeless potential. Politicians raise sons (proud blades of grass) only to shear them off with their wars. How rare the shavers of lawn are 'shaven' themselves.

Finding any depth of thought burdensome, and feeling my opinions fostering frustration and despair, I did as many of us do. I let my thoughts drain away from my attention. I focused again upon the menial task of mowing the lawn. Row after conformist row, severed blades of grass trailed behind me. My imagination disengaged itself.

Fog or *Diman*

In a fog
You hear everything.

You don't miss much
In a jail.
Life's   so short so....
Life's too short so…

Fuimos De Campamento (We Went Camping)

Fuimos de campamento;
fuimos en este Nord.
Fui, si, con mi hermano,
dormimos en la estacione.

Riots

(1)

It's Saturday night
The youth have garnered in the park.
Their homes are childless now,
And parents wait up in the dark.

Blond youths for weeks now
Converged upon the square.
They know too well the riot's strength
They've learned both how and where.

As we had hoped,
Police await, prepared.
Soon among our standing midst
The 'lawmen' ride their mares.

For those of us in sea of flesh,
The challenge has been made.
Against our throng the cops now push,
Yet few of us become afraid.

Juvenilia

A chant goes up of *"javla snut!"**
They take it as an insult.
The chant grows strong within our lungs
And anger soon results.

Fear is spawned, and fear breeds hate
Faster than the rabbits.
Police in fear are quick to hate;
It always was their habit.

With such a mob in lines defined,
The brutal don't take long
Soon enough, police in fear
Come thrashing through our throng.

We in crowd who drank enough
Begin to charge their horses.
The scene is fierce, the blood is real,
And screams are drowned by voices.

The youth; they charge, police use clubs
The youth, they charge again,
A whirlpool starts, and doesn't stop
Until we thirst its end,

(2)

Morning comes (though darkness still)
Adrenaline is dry.
In Stockholm park where riots were,
No one's asking why.

The scrubbers show
With mop and broom they hobble.
Across the park now empty,
They scrub the blood from cobble.

The day begins, the day goes on,
Reporters soon egress.

Eric Wiberg

The pigeons in the park flit
While the rioters take rest.

That night, of course, a cycle fresh
Of skirmishes begins.
Police prepare (as do me kids)
For riots no-one wins.

It's Sunday night again
The youth have gathered in the park.
Their homes are childless now,
And parents wait up in the dark.

*   *"Javla snut"* is mildly defined from Swedish into English as "policemen go to hell!"

I.L.U.

If only time we had today

Lazy dawn; please lie here, stay.
Only now and now alone.
Vexed by time we rest at home.
Every breath is sacred joy

Yearning, loving, be not coy.
Only you and I lie here
Under blankets of love's fear.

The Secular Ode

You are truly beauty ma'am;
The opiate I teal.
Were I the thirsty desert man,
You would me waters yield.
I bask within your milky eyes,
I shake your voice's peal;

I quiver with your gentle move
And marvel your appeal;
The slightest smile betwixt your lips
Filleth me with zeal.
If it were mine, I'd take the chance...
And truly make you squeal!

Flying Home

Flying over countryside,
And people that you leave behind,
And memories - now being waxed,
And moulded into altitudes.

The woman that you're longing for
Is living life just under you
In thriving town of Gladstone. You
Have seen the lights of Gladstone go
And now you're heading home yourself,
In airline with its assured wealth
Flying over countryside,
And into all the evening skies.

Table

There is still room at the round table of philosophy
For those thinkers of the late twentieth century
Free of the yoke of television.

To the Televangelists

If they wish to preach religion
To me, they'd better not try
For a human of the clergy
Is just a human - in my eye.

Eric Wiberg

Fill O'Sophie (Philosophy)

My philosophy of giving is a philosophy of living:
To these who live for hate - give pity,
And to those who live for pity - give hate.
(Basically, pity the hateful, hate the pitiful.

Thoughts

All thoughts are original.
Snowflakes are all snowflakes,
yet no two are identical.

On Writing

Writing is the mediator between the mind of the author
And the mind of the reader,
A book by an author is the ambassador to his or her thought.

Rainfall

To love a rainfall,
A smooth, soft rainfall
A blessing
Light shards of silver
Bring cooling warmth.

Drifting alone,
Kneeling head in hands
On the soft rubber floor
Grey waterbed bottom
Of an inflatable dinghy.

Drifting
On the open ocean
Nothing but ocean
Limitless,
Gently roiling ocean.

Rain-sounds
Upon the sea:
Pitter-patter, splash,
Plip, plash, splatter.
Rain blown across the ocean's surface:
Harmonious hiss
Hair across a drum.
Water-drops onto the water.
The mist hovers.

Oceans
Reveal so much life,
Yet so much life
Concealed
(From us)
Within the depths
That invite death.

Rain
On the swelling ocean
Inspires and nurtures an urge,
A gentle, suicidal urge
Bodily infectious;
Soothing the soul.
Tempting, cooing,
Bewitching…
The sirens
And nymphs of the sea
Dance their water-dance;
Lurers of spear fishermen.

They whisper:
"Slide into the gentle waters

Eric Wiberg

Calmed so by our gentle shade of rain
Coooooool transition
(Welcome)
Through the surface
Calmed by a spray,
Dimpled by the rainfall."

Out of the greyness,
Into the turquoise and dark blue depths
Floats the mind, sinks the soul.
Where so much exists
Drifts the heart.

Such a smooth transition;
Breathing life into the sea,
Inhaling the ocean
Becoming part of it.
Gentle merger;
Sinking, fish-like; filled with water.
Cool, warming, eternal.
Death lies beckoning.

Death enticing
Through the placid waters
Of the sea
Irresistible.

Fibres of your body pull
Toward an urge;
Away from the world
Into which you were shoved,
In which you now sit;
The world from which
You may soon sink
Forever.

Kneeling alone
In a small dinghy
Drifting in, on, and over

Juvenilia

The vast expanse
Alone,
Deserted.

Independent decision.
Such a tranquil transition,
This slide from gasoline down to grass!
All within your reach.
Without return.
Forever.

Watching the grass on the ocean floor
Wave;
Swaying from happiness to sadness
And back.
Luring you away from the
Pendulum mood swings of life
Away from her betraying emotions.

Aaaaah! Float downward
Forget it all...

...Brain caressed in the mineraled waters -
Body caressed by the seas.

Slipping slowly
Slowly slipping
Beyond your vision:
The bottom of a shrinking boat.
The boat a fading dream.

The bubbles of last breath escape,
Betray direction,
Expose the risk
Of detection.
They dribble upwardly
And out to sea.

Eric Wiberg

Drowning but a dream
A sweet, soft dream;
Short-lived bubble.
Bubble-burst
In a world of sharp corners
And roads of broken glass,
Bubble-burst!

Merely a distant, remorseful option
From this and that and this and
That and this and that and this and
That and this and that and this and that and…
…And fifteen blond years slowly draining.

PART II

Z. (For Zarathustra)

(St. George's, 1989)

Excerpt: Memory, Ambition

The old man remembers the lean-tos
And romping in the woods with his brothers
While his sister did - well, he never knew
What his sister did.

He desires to run around the Casuarina trees
Naked, yelling, cooking, burning, stealing, finding,
And swimming.

In his own strange way, he has to face that
Those celebrations in the forest are over.
Over.

Jungle birds end paths
(Which spread defers him like shotgun pellets)
Lead away from the past.
Dreams and decisions
Rule his present existence.
Visions and trails come together
Within him
The way he bends with women
Innocently.

Climbing Haiku

Roof or wall climbing;
Climbing of so many sorts
Don't understand climbs.

The Straw Market

Wandering through the market I feel the unending hustle and bustle of the growing crowds reach its prime with the day's peak. The stampeding crowds draw clouds of dust from underfoot. There is neither a breath of air nor droplets of rain to answer the prayers of those in the market. It is a scorching hot day. Things are coming to life. "Coming to life" is putting it mildly. Scores of jittery tourists stream into the market place. From the docking cruise ships, they flow steadily from the gangplanks, into ready-waiting cabs. They make a beeline for the inevitable eager for an exciting day of browsing and shopping in the straw market.

The market: it is comprised of rows of shanty; makeshift stalls heavily laden with exotic commerce extracted from the Family islands. In the misty blue waters of Nassau Harbour fishing smacks, full of talkative sailors, gently sway atop incoming swells. Each of these swells reveals afresh the heads of lads busy coin-diving for tourists. In a greedy cycle, the ocean envelops the divers' heads, replacing them with heads on the surface. Occasionally diving, they vanish into the murky depths. Their dark-skinned bodies fade gently into the indigo sea.

Restricting the water are massive concrete walls; granite piers. Their crusts are graphitised and dented. Atop these veteran clifflets rest ragged wooden stalls laden with turtles, colourful fish, fresh seafood, conch, and rainbowesque sea fans. Handmade straw hats and baskets boast their intricate and colourful designs to passers-by. Spicy conch and fresh-gutted fish fill the air with the aroma of a pier. Bead and shell necklaces are occasionally heard rattling above the noise.

Tourists more than locals waiting for jitneys are the populace of the market. They satisfy their eyes upon the scenery: unwavering palm trees, statues in all their grandeur, and sparkling fountains silhouetted grey against the azure sky.

Above the honking taxis, blaring music and bargaining tourists, one might hear one of many crate-ridden old vendors shouting about the quality of their work: he from the wharf, she from the stalls. They shout vain curses from toothless mouths at the backs of the less-vulnerable tourists, only, like everything else in the market, to be swallowed up in the rumble of loud noise and ever-flowing crowds. There seems never to be enough excitement wreaked in this marketplace.

Landing in Nassau

> I don't want to make the news.
> If it means our plane crashes
> While landing
> And they toll up deaths and injuries;
> If I become simply a number,
> Or (worse): one "American" dead
> (Which makes me "better" in the U.S.)
> Then I don't want to make the news.

Notes from a Stockholm Park

> On the steps
> Overlooking the park
> We nibble our peaches
> Gentle,
> Cool,
> Together.
> The fruit is unwashed,
> And the hands of a city
> Enter our mouths.

Don't Do Crack

> Don't do crack,
> (Whisk it in: "thud" into those lungs and hey
> In fifteen seconds "wowww; what a trip!"
> RingRingBingRingRing: a train enters a station
> [Which is right between your ears].
> Brakes screech and: "clang":

Eric Wiberg

It's a Coal Trane.

"Ohhhh…what a HiT…"
The sounds ease up,
Your body crumples to the soft concrete
Sneakers rubbing across chips of stone....
"Urrghhhh…"
Tired.
While coming down from it
Muscles un-tense
One   by   one
[Like floodgate grips of miniature dams giving way…]
"oochhhh, mAnnnn!")

Dazed and Running

Dared and running down paths of the mind;
Visions cantering away…
STOP!

Stop there…the film has run out
Streams of imagination have run dry.
CUT!

Scenes are mentally spliced, edited, censored;
(Blackened, or silenced, or worse;
unrestricted!)

Dream not! Skies and clouds are for Star Wars and
Reagan-omics;
Satellites and shuttles,
Stars are tor scientific analysis:
For answers and cures;
Explorations! (nothing more).

Yet the romantic persists:
Go, vou Hawkings, Copernicuses. Galileos
GO!

Yours are net the shooting stars of dreams,
But Orions, Zodiacs, and the infernal Seven Sisters.

I don't want your histories, your morals, and your analyses.
Take them!
Leave me to gaze,
To interpret -
To internalize.

Continue away, you cold western thinkers.

Hejdå Stor Båt (Goodbye, Big Boat)

We pulled the hair away from our faces and tangled it in knots behind our heads. While I tied down everything on the decks, Frank peered intently through the binoculars at the oncoming ship; I checked the harnesses holding my chest to both the bow and stern. We were ready.

The cruising yacht a religious white under the evening sun ploughed from the deep waters of the Ocean Tongue, it was heading for the cut through which waters raged. About half a mile from the passage, we paused like barracuda treading water before a kilt.

The ship became increasingly visible as she neared the passage. Sporting three aluminium masts, she was truly a modem breed of clipper, catering to wealthy Americans; a "windjammer" devoted to their every whim, as advertised in their *New York Times*. We could hear the sounds of *Amazing Grace* playing on board to satisfy the evening whim of her Caribbean captain.

I reinforced the bandanna around my forehead. Frank lowered the binoculars.

"Got it," he whispered tersely.

He gave the engine juice staying in neutral. It roared louder, then more quietly, much louder quiet. The ship approaches the cut at a good clip; it would take us at least thirty seconds at full horsepower to meet her be free sliding through the channel. Frank locked towards me. We were alone together strapped down. He flicked our search light on and off quickly (teasing), and I reached under the seat to feel a heavy, round object. We nodded at each other.

"O.K."

His hand caressed the throttle: a pause and then I jerked backwards as he gunned the boat ahead. My body hung in place as the harness in front of me tautened. Faster, faaasssteeeerrr …!!!

People basking on the white backs lazily looked towards the bothersome hum of cur engine, I gave a throat-chafing war cry. Our hair beat in the wind.

"Aaaargbhhh…!!!"

Our advance felt stimulating. Frank kept on a course heading directly for her without flinching. My face reddening, 1 clung onto the port rail. Frank saw an open porthole and aimed the speedboat for it. I stared at it intently, knowingly. I could have sworn that I saw someone's race peer out of it. People on the deck stood up and pointed. We hated them. Something stirred on the bridge; I glimpsed a white blur. The face filled the porthole for a moment more, and then was gone. I glanced to my right at Frank. He was bending over the wheel, throttle down, his back-harness straining.

Two seconds…One…We struck. Just forward of the porthole. Damn hard. Metal ripped where our bow slammed into their hull. We bounced off though, and the ship kept going; water gushing in, spray flying up, and women shrieking above us. I cradled my metal sphere for a moment. Then I pulled the pin. The momentum of the ship momentarily brought the open porthole within reach of my left hand. I dropped the grenade into the opening and heard it drop metallically to the deck.

Frank (a little blood streaking his temple where he'd hit the steering wheel) used the push of the ship to get away. As soon as we were parallel, he shoved the throttle forward again. Meanwhile I was pushing with my hands against the hull tearing my palms. There was a shuddering pause while the motor fought to hurtle us away. We had to get safely away in the three seconds granted us before the explosion.

Suddenly the boat slammed forward, towards the stern of the ship. We attained full speed in the opposite direction of the clipper, which ploughed onward at twelve knots. As we reached the stern props, heat seared the air. The explosion burst outward, ripping away from the vessel through the hull. We were far behind the ship when the shrapnel skipped, steaming. Along the ocean's surface.

We were out away from the clipper's side, skirting along the lee of Rose Island, full speed across the smooth surface. When we'd caught our breath, we could see behind us the flaming, torn vessel being sucked through the channel; she was crippled, beginning to list over on her side.

Frank and I would have been caught too because was hadn't expected the four-engine tender which the crew launched from the windjammer. I mean, we had feared a chase boat but not the monster we beheld while cruising away, smiling.

The idiots with their white uniforms and sailors' caps (which flew off one by one) managed to reach us twenty minutes after we collided with their mother vessel. They tried swerving and hitting us; sending up a wake before us they even fried to "rooster tail" us, (blind us with spray from behind their tilted engines). Their tricks, however, were nothing that Frank and I hadn't tried on each other before. We could have run them onto the reef we knew the waters well if it hadn't gotten dark so quickly. That was fun. We were protected by the thickening veil of night.

It was easy to peel off their course for Eleuthera Island and watch their searchlight going on and wandering over the sea. Ours stayed off. We knew the route back into the harbour under half the moon, so we turned back keeping to the deep water to avoid other vessels. We watched the flames from the windjammer petering out as it drifted by. By seven o'clock, searchlights were directed into the sea, and a flotilla of rescue craft circled her like hungry piglets around a sow. I clapped Frank on the back. He grinned.

Our return to shore went smoothly We floated the boat onto the waiting trailer and dragged off into Frank's obscure garage before staggering into his beach house for our evening rums. 1t had been a long day, but the wail until we could spearfish again would be enjoyable. We could always return our freshly wrecked clipper to dive up memorabilia perhaps jewels and valuables. We photographed our wounds: the caked blood on Frank's head and the deep, blue lacerations where the harnesses had bitten into our flesh.

Then we slept.

I Saw Men Running

>Running naked through the snow
>Trailing tails of long-born and dead devils
>Fleeing lost souls
>Fleeting moments of which? Despair?
>I saw men running
>And 1 ran with them
>Through the pillars of the Parthenon,
>Under the Callahan Tunnel,
>Twice around the Taj Mahal, and
>Into my own heart.
>(There, retracting emotions

Retreat - frail and fearful:
Hollow devotions
[Commitments unmade]
Fade…
…Cease

Down Fall the Bowman

Down fall the bowman
Into the waiting canyon:
Down went the bowman
He
Fell
    Fell
        Fell.

Life Versus Limits

Life is a limitless set of limitations:
Limitlessness with so many limits:
Life is contradiction.

On Gender

Women are bonded by womanhood - men separated by it.
Men are bonded by womanhood - women separated by it.

So Many Things

So many things going on
And not any motion.
So many things going on
And not enough.

So many things going on;
Too much emotion.
So many things going on
And not enough.

My Mind is on Guitar

My mind is on guitar;
On sailing: on scrapbooks
Keep away from my person,
My soul, and the mystery.

I'm thinking of music,
Of songs, and of dances.
I'm dreaming of dancers,
And lovers, and moons

Come with me, you dreamers
You artists, creators.
Come with to splash paintings,
And enter…to ponder.

Where will it lead me
This muting, this stifling?
Where shall I take thee,
My honour aspiring?

I welcome you wanderers
Into unknowing.
Welcome explorers
Into the unknown.

Grippsund

We first met on a train   he hadn't a seat, and while I was drinking vodka with some Siberian passengers, he left his bag on top of mine. When I returned shortly afterward, and not knowing who its owner was, tried to lift his bag from my seat, from somewhere in the back of the train, he came upon me and laughed as I was trying to unfasten the damn backpack from the seat he'd locked it to the armrest with a small padlock.

He didn't talk to me then sat at the window seat: I sat beside him on the aisle, across from two noisy women. Entering Siberia, I left him and trod down the hallway to the mail car, where I hung my head from the window for a long while, watching the flat, barren birch-treed landscape ripple past. All trees identical, all shrubberies were the same. The wind was refreshingly cool in my hair the late summer air, crisping with the advent of autumn, drove beads of sweat from my forehead and into the tangle behind my ears.

So, this was Siberia, miles or hours since the last collection of tiny huts. Like those huts, my travels scorn sudden and unpredictable.

'No stable home now for a few years no theme to thoughts(or writings): all a mix of smaller works epigrams, and unfinished, trailing words....'

I closed the window, thrusting it upwards towards its mechanical click. With my nose against it, the oils of nostrils and hair were outlined by steamy breath.

'Siberia and no plan. Siberia alone.'

I walked back through crowded aisles past Russian Soviets, Asians, and Ukrainians dark haired and alive. Their drinks jiggled with the train's movements. My companion on the wooden bench was the only other European aboard ironic. He was fussing with something in his lap when I stopped and stood over him. He looked up guiltily, still trying to stuff orange peels into the little trash box. He'd swiped one of my few oranges, and my water as well; I lingered between anger and laughter for a moment before shrugging and sitting myself. We rode on in silence.

'Another day and a half till Beijing then what?'

My supplies, which lay in a backpack above me, reassured me of my independence. The sharp whistle of the steam locomotive signified another pause in our journey East from Moscow along the Trans-Siberian Railway. More wood and coal had to be loaded; old ladies, men, and young labourers shifted on and off while girls sold liquor and sweets from outside the window. The village, clustered around the station on the vast plain, came alive during the weekly visits from the greater world.

The strange, orange thieving fellow beside me stood up. Ha was not tall. He wore his long dark hair pulled back behind a weathered forehead. His nose was distinct: straight, with nostrils symmetrically swelling around a thin bridge. His eyebrows shadowed brooding eyes. A thin mouth crossed the width of his face, spreading beneath an unshaven, brown-stubble lip. His face was almost triangular, his chin an angle. A purple bandanna hung casually around the taut skin of his neck. He seemed about my age (early-twenties), and was also travelling alone. I watched him amble down the aisle through the crowd.

Gazing from my window, I noticed him moving behind the crowd of preoccupied vendors and travellers who pressed against the train. Completely oblivious to the throng, he wandered through the few lanes of thinly spread houses and into an expanse of birches. Each step carried he and his shouldered pack deeper through the boughs. The train began slowly to pull away.

Transfixed I stared as he the excursion's only fellow European, vanished, silently abandoning civilized travel; daring the untamed. He was actually walking away from all towards which I was travelling the cities, stations, people, and restaurants. His departure screamed freedom, providing an inebriating sensation. Watching him sent me lusting alter adventure.

Juvenilia

'The infamous plains of northern Asia, and he's unafraid.'

I stood up, and as the train slowly gained momentum, slung my pack onto my sack, pulled my water bottle from the seat, and strode off me vehicle. Stepping from the train, I ground my boots into the gravel as though they belonged there. Then I set my eyes on the strip of purple on the back of his neck arc the green patch on his shoulders as he sank into the woods. Twitching the pack comfortably into alignment with my shoulder blades, I thrust the bottle into a deep pocket and made for my unknown companion.

I caught up with him as the train shrieked away behind us. He said nothing. The trees were so close enough together that I was constantly swerving around them. Ignoring animal mails, he followed a set direction. A compass dangled from his belt and slapped against his thigh. The murmur of the village soon fell mute behind us. I watched his face as best I could while keeping up with his pace, and felt rewarded when he looked towards me end smiled. Though ever so faint, his smile seemed to welcome my reckless, whimsical companionship.

We walked for a good two hours in a silence made less intense by the concentration it took to traverse the woods. As evening settled, he slowed, scanned the earth, and stopped. In German, he asked if I agreed with the campsite. Seeing my confusion, he repeated in guttural English. I nodded.

We both began collecting enough firewood to last a dinner, a warm sleep, and breakfast coffee I was reassured that he was also an experienced camper. The fire lit, and strips of bacon sizzling beside bread, we began to speak. My curiosity irritated me. Seven days lay between our first evening together and the next train. I knew that our supplies would last that long. Beyond that I knew nothing of our expedition.

He called himself Ulf, though his full name was apparently Wolfgang. Ulf spoke with a quiet intensity and carefully chosen words. His self-assurance and apparent pleasure in my company made me more comfortable with our strange lot. Our exchanges, though in broken English, were adequate. I told of my upbringing in Spain, speaking of the Pyrenes Mountains and my years of carefree travels. I felt compelled by an unnameable fascination with him and his intentions in so remote a terrain.

During the ensuing days of walking, I slowly conceived the purpose of our lunge into the wilds of Eastern Asia. That our journey was carefully mapped and calculated surprised me. It had its origins in the Second World War...

Ulf's grandfather, a man named *Grippsund* Klaussman, grew up in a Germany recovering from the defeat of 1918. He marched with Hitler's Operation Barbarossa during 1941 into the Soviet Union. For two years, *Grippsund* drove further into immense Russia, where he survived winters and partisans. He participated in the nine-hundred-day siege of St. Petersburg before moving East, towards Stalingrad. During 1943,*Grippsund* and a companion named Ullrich Broemell were captured and imprisoned by the Soviets. Their lives were spared for helping tend the other prisoners.

Ullrich and *Grippsund* spent the receding winter of 1943 and '44 travelling towards Siberia. They survived the marching and cattle cars, entering a prisoner of war camp near Lake Baikal. During his second year, *Grippsund*, overworked and starving died.

Grippsund's prison companion, Ullrich Broemell, returned to Germany after the war. His captors had freed him and taken him as far as Moscow. His was an arduous journey through devastated lands on foot, playing mute, deaf, and dumb so as to avoid detection, in Germany, he managed to trace *Grippsund*'s wife and Ulf, her young son. Ullrich (like Ulf later) maintained a veneration on for history; a nostalgia for humanity.

Assuming that he would die shortly after *Grippsund*, Ullrich had buried with his friend a small ammunitions case filled with diaries, trinkets, letters (from young men to wives still living), and worn photographs During his many months there, Ullrich had carefully charted the location of the camp in relation to the isolated station. The gravesite lay just outside of the fences, which the prisoners themselves had been forced to erect.

Ulf had been raised somewhat detached from the war, and it wasn't until the 1880's, that he met an aged Ullrich. The encounter was not accidental. An avid traveller in his early-twenties, Ulf seemed to Ullrich ideal for the task of recovering his and *Grippsund*'s memorabilia. When Ulf visited Ullrich in a 'Veteran Haus' outside Hamburg. West Germany, he received numerous instructions and maps. The order beseeched Ulf to venture into the Siberian wilderness for the capsule of time. Determined to unearth the enigmatic parcel, Ulf set cut alone to find a camp long since erased from public memory: a ghost in the closet of Soviet history.

The camp lay ahead of us crumbling and being slowly forgotten. Ulf was determined to familiarize himself with his grandfather's troubled death to confront the uncomfortable void in genealogical discussions, which *Grippsund*'s death had created. My understanding of our undertaking slowly solidified. Our quest was inspired not by the hopes for tremendous historical finds, but by the desire to open a sealed bubble, to glimpse into a horrific past; to force open a door (small as it may be) of history. Ulf's ferocity became infectious. By the third day, as we neared the supposed site of the prison, I found myself striding with purposeful ambition towards *Grippsund*'s grave.

By the evening of the third day, we were encountering the trash, which heralds human habitation. Scattered across the earth's floor was the litter and refuse of men which commonly scars nature: stumps of chopped trees among younger ones, rusted tin cans opened (their lids still attached, make-shift wooden shelters crumbling anxiously discussed our perspective search). Precision at plotting a course ruled travel in terrain, which was as an ocean. We slept restlessly. We could allow for no errors. We had food enough to last several more days. No more. We slept.

Dawn rose as we sipped coffee. Without saying much, we folded our tent and began again on our course away from the village. It wasn't until late afternoon that we encountered the crumbling perimeter fence. It was our first irrefutable evidence of a camp.

The prison consisted of the large perimeter fence (great wooden stakes strung with rusted fencing, and topped with barbed-wire) spread across a gentle knoll. Towers rose from each of the four corners so that the machine-gun fire could criss-cross the camp's centre. There was a guardhouse at the gate, and the remnants of barracks lined the fences.

Soon after the war, the prisoners had been freed and deported and the administrators had followed. After the initial ransacking during the late '40's, the camp had been deserted. Since then, it had been completely undisturbed save by occasional packs of wolves and roaming elk.

I felt uneasy walking through the ghost camp like the dazed correspondents who wandered through the concentration camps during *Grippsund*'s time. The mounds of earth ware the tombs of winter dead. When the ground froze, they were covered in stones and a thin layer of topsoil. My awkwardness did not abate.

I slowly recovered from these uneasy sensations and began to rake notice of Ulf's reaction. His face was rigid, stern. His eyes moved slowly as he concentrated on the scene. He brooded intently, as though internalizing images of the camp. His peck rung from stalwart shoulders the pots that dangled from its sides coming together with eerie clangs. His hands were clenched one of them around Ullrich's charts. The veins on the inside of his arms stood out. His jaw tensed, and his nostrils accentuated with long, deliberate breaths. In his eyes I read stories of hatred; sadness surfacing. Quietly, we lay our packs down and began to search for his grandfather's grave.

During the winter of 1944-45, Ullrich Broemell been forced to drag *Grippsund*'s corpse through the snow to the makeshift cemetery. The burying party plodded a few hundred yards into the woods and covered the body at the end of a long row of graves.

Using the meticulously drawn charts, Ulf and I were able to locate the gravesite on the uneven forest floor. Ulf fell contemplatively to his knees before the tomb into which Ullrich had longingly carved, "*Klaussman, mein Bekannte aus Hamburg*, 1944". We were surrounded by similar epitaphs dedicated to friends all over Germany. I searched among crosses and headstones for a suitable digging tool. When I returned with a few metal canisters, tears were following each other down the grandson's face.

I began to gently pull the dirt away from before the headstone, which had sunken into the earth and tilted. I was not interested so much in what remained of the man himself as what had been deposited in the box. I dug to relieve Ulf, who stared blankly at my hands in the hovering dusk. I lit a small fire and continued under the eerie glow of orange embers. Before long I wedged a tin container from between stones and the crumbling boards of a coffin. Despite my anticipation ever uncovering that vary box, I was surprised to finally retrieve the goal of our expedition. I brushed it across a denim-clad leg and slid I along the ground towards Ulf.

Weary, I left the case before him and wandered through our silent, private museum to our bags and food. We could examine and discuss the prize later. The box was his: a distant, remote objective. He had led us to it. The evening was Ulf's his victory. Over a cigarette, I sat back and watched the sun finally sink. It made silhouettes of the skeletal wooden structures and tangled wire. These stark reminders of imprisonment stood against the retreating light the way that crests do on a wax seal, I was asleep when Ulf returned.

Over a dawn meal, my sense of accomplishment lost its lustre beside Ulf's contemplative demeanour. At fireside, he read from s black-leather book a diary from the newfound package.

His face was grim and haggard   he hadn't slept. Eagerly, I fumbled through the contents of the box. Within it, I found several faded medals; iron confirmations of promotions made it relevant by death. Beside these were badges, unsent letters, and crumpled orders from Berlin.

Slowly, I stood up, straightened my knees, feeling the rush of circulation. I tucked the box into Ulf's gear before slinging my pack around the shoulders of my creased jacket. From my pocket I withdrew a rusted iron Cross which I had taken earlier from a wooden grave marker. The medal briefly chilled my chest when I slid it around my neck on a chain. Then I began to walk away. I strode towards where the train would carry us east to Beijing, away from each other.

Ulf followed silently.

Chameleon River Haiku

City's populace,
Chameleon river flow,
Surges before us.

Clang' Goes the Cross

"Clang" goes the cross: descending from the ceiling:
"Tick" goes reactionary:
One,   two,   three,
When was the turtle
Clucking and a-snarlin'?
Not since the rabbit lay with me.

I Fell Silent

I fell silent:
The bare minimum

Of social words -
Words of survival -
Escaped.
No more.
Nothing that
Made sense.
Except.
Silence.

My Boat and I

The boat and I
Travelled west at sunset; together.
Would I recall the gasps of engine,
The sounds of wave responding to hull,
And the splashing of gasoline in plastic tanks
When, further along the surface
Of my time sphere,
I remembered that moment?
Would I recollect the sight of an airplane
Suspended against the sun?

The sunset blinded me,
Yet onward we ploughed.
Over the shoals
Blinded.
My boat and me.

Looking back, I could see
The trail we left behind.
Our wake slithered away:
Our own frothy paint,
Smeared over a canvas of the sea
My boat suddenly became
The horse-hair and of a paint-brush.
Pastels of white spread;
Strokes applied by our forward motion.

Eric Wiberg

The thickening waves of paint formed small ridge
Hardening on the edges
Before finally cracking there.
Was our smear like the gossamer,
Semen-sticky trail of a slug across the glass,
Table-top-surface
Of the ocean?

Were we merely a water bug
Skittering across the filmy waters of a pond?
My boat and I; alone, together, painting.

Lean Back (Camping in Trondheim, Norway with John)

Lean back (as I did) in the sand of Monk Island
It is soft of hard stones ground small. Lean back.
The sun shines there, I imagine; cold water, cold,
During May of the year after (after when it really doesn't matter).
The woman (whose lover is now the dark, mystery
Of a summer gone) is not there
Boats slid back and forth around the barriers lean back.
From the harbour (lean back)   lean away from the mountain
(Which is above the fishery) and the forest, falling.
Lean back towards unknown mountains
And submerged stones that only tourist ships feel.

No Italians or Monk Island's beach today, no;
Not flexing with their girl who bounced along the shore
Using her beauty like a weapon.
Lean back, and break off a chunk of the bread.
For if is good, and tastes better than women. And easier.
Lean back; let sand stick to the skin between your shoulder blades.
The sky was grey then, and the kind woman-tour-guide

Has since given up guiding, and is alone now:
Real world's come.

Construction is going on still,
The black dog, though happy that the winter's ever, is
dying more.
The green paint of Nazi guns is chipping still
Rains push chips of paint into the rows of urinals
Where soldiers once slept underground, scared.
Army paint gathers in barracks where soldiers once
loved, alone.

Griffin, ancient prisoner of the island
(Which has been a monastery, prison, rod and museum)
Is gone now not to heaven or hell.
Gone Griffin gone and Cohn and I miss you.
We're not together either, and I don't lean back now,
The way I did then, after combing the shore;
After finding no memorabilia - not even bottles.
Now I'm gone. Never lean back now - gone.
Can't lean back now, Griffin, though I loved that I did
once.

I leant back as a boat pulled up: as new ones tame.
I leant at a pub too expensive for us
(Where the island's monks would have been ashamed,
But would smite at us).
We huddled under a menhir-stone
On Trondheim's mountain with the lichen and fern.
We were sniffed by a curious dog
Who was scared of John and me camping -
Scared by the honesty of our living.
His master was lured by it.

We leant back (and cried doing it) over our first meat in
days
And chunks of cheese frying in black oil, and water from
a stream (Which is some god's pee and not & stream), but
all we pot.

Eric Wiberg

We leant back while looking through the pines (which are evergreen)
And seeing Monk is and over the stink of the granary in the rain.
We leant back sadly, white watching an old man rowing;
His fishing lantern swinging
And Pollock not biting where subs once blew.
On that bay, no one leans back (or leant) during the last war

Or even the ones before it the ones at Castle Catharine
The castle still stands white:
Rimmed in barbed wire which students disregard;
Wire draped in the condoms of their destruction
And the butts of them existence.

Lean back and see, and grind your hair into that sand
See it all, god dammit! And feel it! Because I did.
I sat on the wharf white dead fish floated.
I sat while Americans (with beards and hair dangling) stared.

We left Trondheim with its camper's home,
Its store on the corner of the middle-class world
We left it with its hotel under renovation
And its 'Store One Thousand' (which is cheaper than the other).
Yet no hotels loved us (we without money),
And the books were in Norwegian, not in English.
We saw bicycles, and cannon (and maybe dreams of suicide)
Slide beneath the bridge over the Nideiva River.
Students' dreams flowed before the university.

We couldn't sleep in Tronoheim after a night in Demote;
After hitchhiking with hair that stung our eves;
After washing in bathrooms which were spied upon by concierges;

After the security who tried to sell us places in his university
(As if either of us could ever understand his culture).
We couldn't sleep.

There were no women in Trondheim that we met.
Except for a plump one who tried to sell herself emotionally
To another student who was too busy.
Perhaps she was in the wrong era anyway:
Eighteen-hundreds was the era when fat was beauty, history says.
Go back, then, fine-feathered one go back!
And when you do, also lean back in the sand,
Against cannon, which became anti-aircraft guns.
We'll be up on the mountain when, you do lean back.
We'll have trod through Scandinavian slums,
And forests falling, and fallout shelters (which are vulnerable to suburbia, not voices).

In Trondheim Iasi summer we missed our bus,
And lost our way to the campground,
And made the tough hike up the mountain
With packs, and meat, and oats.
At six in the *"anti-meridian"* we left our train from Dombås
Crossed a smaller bridge in Trondheim,
Rested at a bakery, and had cigarettes, coffee, and chocolate.
The previous day's pastries tasted divine on the curb.
We photographed a moon sinking over *Gamla Stan*
Over the Old Town. We saw the sun sinking behind Trondheim's Technical University.

We visited no museum there,
Though we saw the fish floating,
Visited a bank,
Gave tickets to a large first mate with a beard
Before boarding the ferry.

That was John and I
Before leaning back together
In the sand of Trondheim Norway last summer:
The sands of Monk Island.

Chapel Talk: Individuality

"Ziggy played guitar jamming good with Weird and Gilly and the Spiders from Mars."
- David Bowie; *Ziggy Stardust*

This lyric is original. It is laced with individuality. Unfortunately, there is a misconception that when songs (or people) stand out, they are strange, or even bad. Though it is often difficult, it is vital that we each nurture and defend that which makes us unique. Remember: it is through individuals like Christopher Columbus, Salvador Dali, Albert Einstein, (and, yes, even Sid Vicious) that our culture is able to advance. Like those before us, we that assert ourselves may do so at the cost of shallow popularity, but people who can honestly respect themselves often earn the respect of others.

In any worthy relationship, there are phases of conflict. A respected French film director, Trouffault, once declared that he would have never succeeded had his childhood not been full of strife. Often, the relationship of the individual with authority, religion, and peer pressure is tainted with conflict. Even at Saint George's, individuals can be made to feel restricted. Peter Rudy, a professor in Chicago, once observed that:

...Even if a man is born a rebel at heart, ...he can usually be effectively intimidated to the point where he will accept a rigidly controlled pattern of life for a long period of time.

Well, if you haven't noticed, we at Saint George's ARE accepting a "rigidly controlled pattern of life for a lone period of time". This is not necessarily bad, however, but then neither is rebellion; it is possible to retain your independence while feeling restricted. Thomas Jefferson once said, "a bit of rebellion every now and then is good". Characters who are able to weather conflict (even to provoke it when necessary!) can often contribute more to a community than those who never assert themselves.

An example of someone who has withstood tremendous opposition and has established himself, as a character and an artist, is Michael Moore. Mike has been a custodian in my dorm for many years. As a child, he was nearly blind, and his father always seemed to be against him. Even though his co-workers discourage his art, Mike persistently displays his paintings on campus and elsewhere.

Mike also told me that even those who care for us (like parents or teachers), can threaten our true desires by pushing us in contrary directions. Rudyard Kipling, in his poem *If*, warns us not to be controlled by either foe or friend. This brings us to the struggle for independence in the face of pressure to conform to social, religious, and peer standards.

I believe that religion and spirituality are most effective on a personal level; that it is important to be true to ourselves and to our convictions more than to the mechanical repetition of traditional rites. An enquirer once asked the Beatnik poet Allen Ginsberg if he was Jewish. "No" he replied, "I AM ME." Without this faith in yourself, confirmation becomes merely conformation, and conformity is dangerous.

Many objective scholars advocate freedom or religion, yet also stress the importance of freedom from religion. This is because people and institutions often want to influence, or control each of us. They use weapons like guilt and shame in order to contain us. They do not, for example, appreciate specific stars for their individual glamor, but, rather, they prefer to see human-named constellations like the Big Dipper, ZodiacL, and Orion's Belt.

It is important that you control yourself, and that you limit the control others have over you. This relates to experiences, which I have had here at school. For two years I sacrificed too much of my own independence for the sake of a relationship. I was made to feel trapped by groundless guilt. It is a mistake, which I hope never to make again.

Returning to the influences of shame, religion, and truth in our weekly lives; in the first *Book of John*, we are told that: "If we claim we have not sinned...the truth is not in us and we make (God) out to be a liar". In confessing sin, and in general, it is important to be truthful. However, several Christian scriptures do not leave room either for redeeming action or of individual, personal truths. Often, we recite the *Confession of Sin* from *The Book of Common Prayer*. As a mass, many of us declare that; "we have sinned...we have not loved our neighbours as ourselves".

I feel that if we, as individuals, DO make an effort to "love our neighbours", then it is unfair that we be expected to confess to having not done so. Thus, I implore you simply to speak your own singular truths to claim guilt only when you think that you should otherwise to rebel against collective shame, and remain silent.

I have mentioned many of the negative elements of individuality: the responsibility, the isolation, and the struggle against powerful establishments. Many great thinkers; men like Friedrich Nietzsche and Jack Kerouac, went too far, and isolated themselves from their peers. Donovan, a folk singer, implores us to "dare to be different", and "learn to be lonely". Loneliness, however, is a heavy price to pay for individuality.

Several past students here, like Ollie Brooks, Chuck Kirsten, and Xander Paumgarten, were nonconformists who provided a relieving break from prep-school regimen. James Devlin even *celebrated* his independence last autumn by packing up his room in Diman and setting off for Bermuda! It is unfortunate that Saint George's and these students were not compatible.

More important, however, is that each of us, almost in order to have been accepted, is in some way unique. We can learn to establish ourselves, and then channel our powers towards helping each other and the school. People who are unassertive does not run clubs and nations. Yes, there is opposition to be overcome, but, armed with your own independence and convictions, you should persevere. Though few had faith in them Michael Moore kept painting, Columbus kept sailing, Galileo kept computing, and, yes, Mr. Babbitt went on with the Parents' Concert after totaling one of the school's pianos. Essentially, we must first become individuals, whatever the cost, and then utilize our particular skills to help others as well, if we so desire. Goethe, Germany's renowned poet, summed up my ten pages in ten words. He said: "Whatever you can do, or dream you can, BEGIN IT!"

At Night, While Cycling

At night, while cycling, I can tell if there is s car behind me by looking at the light reflected off signs ahead of me, or by the shining blur bouncing off the wheel spokes. I jam the Grateful Dead on my Walkman as I sprint from the coast to home.

Sophie

Lying or white beach,
Your back in the sand,
Her boat whizzes by,
There's a beer in your hand.
Her hair's pulled by the wind
It tugs every strand.
That was yesterday.

Visions can frustrate
The day after love,

Eric Wiberg

When beauty must leave you;
Must soar as a dove.
Each image makes worse;
You stare up above.
Frustrating departure.

Slithering as two snakes
Through smooth, silky water;
This image of Sophie
Makes blood boil hotter.
Bodies entwined (snakes thrashing wildly):
Echoes of laughter
And memories of lust.

Image of nightclubs
Talking together;
Soft-shining neon;
Sunshine or weather.
Memories of Sophie
Embitter forever.
Turn to the wall.

Cycling, forgetting
Her airplane reminds;
She flees from your sight,
But into your mind.
You watch the machine; s
He's no longer thine.
She's gone.

Standing there lonely
And watching the plane
whisk away lover
(Alone in the rain)
From you sadly standing;
Anger contained.
Your own farewell.

Sophie is going,
And (cycle at side)

Juvenilia

You kneel on the tarmac.
Despair storms a-rise.
Memory; it struggles her to revive.
To no avail.

PART III

Shorts

(Boston College, 1990)

Skull and I

Stirring over-sweetened coffee aboard *Bahama Daybreak*on a January morning, death could not have been farther from our minds. My brother, Lance, sister, Carol, her friend Gerard, and I, set off by mail boat, from Nassau, Bahamas, for a peaceful weekend vacation in Dunmore Town, on Harbour Island. The boat-ride lasted between dawn, at six, and noon. We happily went through a case or more of Kalik beer, a few packs of Dunhills, and a roll or so of film. After exchanging cargo and passengers at The Bluff settlement and Spanish walls in Eleuthera, we disembarked onto Dunmore Town's crowded out-island deck. We settled our baggage into a Whale Villa on a cosy street overlooking the harbour. Returning by foot to the bustling quay for lunch, we passed several women muttering among themselves and looking pensively in the direction of the dock. From the shade of a large tree, they returned our greetings cursorily.

We were eating our fish 'n chips on a bench outside when the ferry from mainland North Eleuthera pulled up and caused an unusual commotion. Atypical of the happy enthusiasm with which Bahamians were greeting the mail boat, a group of matronly women were wailing and crying around the little ferry. Several men were jostling and handing cumbersome objects from the boat into the hands of other men, who waited on the pier. All that we could see were dozens of bright yellow and white flowers, until they hoisted the box into the back of a pickup truck.

It was a coffin. The women who had waited under the tree were, by now, tearfully moaning arid screaming around it, hitting their feet onto the concrete and leaning faintly on one another under the afternoon sun. A dozen or so men stood in a semi-circle around them: arms akimbo, they watched silently.

We'd stopped eating. Our beers warmed in the sunshine, and cigarettes burned forgotten between our fingers. As the coffin-laden truck nudged its way past us, down the wharf, one elderly Bahamian sitting nearby tore our attention away (and our voices back into cur throats).

"Dat's Captain Johnston", he said, "roun" hero day call him Cap'n J. Lived here for mos' seven'y years, 'E was in Nassau when's dis a couple days ago. Day jus' fly I'm from dar 'aday. Plenny people liked 'im. He mussy been nin'y yeas ol'."

Quietly, we reflected on what he had said. The man must have been around ninety himself, and no doubt was wondering how his own funeral would go in comparison to Cap'n J's. Much of Dunmore Town's small island community was quieter, especially the elders, We returned to our villa, subdued for only half an hour or so before setting off on foot for a swim on Harbour Island's famous Pink Sands Beach.

It was a Saturday afternoon. Captain Johnston had died during the week, and was to be buried on Sunday. We were to return to Nassau on Monday. We strolled through the quiet lanes of town towards the beach. There seemed to be a church cm every lone. On our last visit, we'd sat atop new paws being brought over on the mail boat. By now they were wall broken in.

Moving away from the settlement and toward the beach, we passed the island's graveyard, an expansive sandy lot backed by slow escarpment. We heard men talking and looked over, across while-washed tombstones and wooden crosses. Four men were standing casually over a grove, leaning on their picks and shovels and having a smoke. Beneath thorn, a fifth man was digging a grave. We could only see his head and brown sand flying from a hole. Unnoticed, we paused to look. The digger stopped and climbed from the small pit. He handed some objects to another digger, who lay them on the ground before climbing into the hole himself. The original shoveller lit a cigarette and worked his way into the elderly overseer's conversation. We continued along to the beach.

After a lengthy swim, we set off for the villa in the late afternoon, with early dusk settling in, we came upon the graveyard again, its little wooden gate hanging ajar. The gravediggers had left. It was quiet. Sharing a morbid curiosity, we nimbly stooped through the gate end, headed post dozens of sites for the freshly dug grave. Standing at Its foot, we gazed into the mesmerizing, human-size hole, which was about six feet deep.

"My God," my sister whispered.

Then silence. I was the first to look up. My eyes followed the side of the grave, passing over a mound of sand and settling on a curdling sight.

"Holy shit." I said, "Ho-ly shit!" My companions shared in vocalizing startled bewilderment. There, where ahead stone or cross had once rested, lay a pile of bones, tapped by an empty-eyed and jawless human skull.

I hadn't seen a skull like it since Lance and I had accidentally dug one up from the bottom of a muddy pond, thinking that it was a turtle. Before that, we'd, discovered one at the bottom of a well, in the bush near what we called 'Jack the Ripper's Coves'.

After showers, smokes, and rum-and-cokes on the balcony, we sat for dinner. The evening progressed into swigs of rum, guzzling of beer, and drunken card games between the four of us. Eventually, we made our way back towards the beach, in order to sample the island's nightlife. It often began at the Pink Sands Hotel. Towards midnight, we'd had enough smokes, games of pool, and drinks from our handy jug of rum and-coke. Quite drunk, we were ready for the return trek back to the villa. Inevitably, we passed the graveyard. Again, we paused before the gate.

Lance was the first to speak up."Let's go take a look, come on, we'll only be a minute."

Coral replied. "No way. Let's go to Willy's Tavern. You've already seen the grave."

Lance became more eager. "What do ya' mean? We're in no rush. I just want to check out the skull. It would look great in my room. He turned to me.

"C'mon Carl, you gonna wimp out? It's just a skull. Nobody'll notice."

Lance had a mysterious loft to himself, filled with moose and deer skulls, posters, tapestries, and dim lights. The last skull we'd found had been confiscated from the Bahamian Criminal Investigation Department. An interfering neighbour had called two detectives to investigate it and they had speculated that its owner bed been murdered.

I consented to go into the graveyard with Lance and check it out.

Corel protested."You guys are sick. Gerard and I are going to Willy's."

They left. Drinks and smokes in hand, Lance and I made our way towards the gravesite, which stood out white against the green-brown of dead grass under a luminescent moon. Lance poked around in the bones. Placing the small skull near his drink, he searched for the detached jawbone. Finding it, he held the two together, giving the skull on almost comical, near toothless grin, into which we placed a lit cigarette. Holding it up to the moonlight, we noticed a small, bullet-size hole in its base, near where the cerebrum had once been.

Lance wanted badly to take the skull, stash it in our bags, and return borne to Nassau with it. I was afraid that if we did, someone would notice its absence before the following day's funeral, remember spotting us in the graveyard, search everyone leaving the island, and catch us stealing their historical and personal culture. All hell would break loose, I thought. What a faux pas it would be. The newspapers would surely run the story; it would be full of evil, death, crime, and mob justice. I felt pretty uncomfortable, especially after Lance tossed a coin in the moonlight to see who might carry the skull back to the villa. I lost.

Knowing practically that the theft would have to be then or never (the funeral was to happen the next day), I needed some time and a place to think of Lance's proposal over. While he rustled among the aged and worn bones, I crawled my drunken self down into the grave and lay on my back there for little while.

The full moon hovered directly before my eyes. Terrified, I realized that within seventy or so years (at most!), I'd be in the same position lying at the bottom of a grave. Only then it would be for keeps. Sealed coffin, no air, and some ceremonial bullshit going on above me. I'd be unable to do a damned thing. What would I have to show for the remaining fifty years? What did I have to show for the first twenty? A few short stories. A few adventures. Great. The initial sandy discomfort quickly wore off. I balanced my drink or my chest. A butt hung between my fingers. What was I going to do?

I worried that I was having difficulty excusing the theft of the skull on the basis of religious reservations. Had going to parochial schools whipped from me my spontaneity? Had ancient, guilt-rated religious dictums gained the final say in my actions? I began to justify the theft. Wasn't the skull merely an ownerless and useless conglomeration of morrow? What ever happened to my seize-the-day battle-cry? Wouldn't grave-robber look badass on my personal resume? Couldn't this be the beginning of the utilization of the next fifty years? Dammit, hadn't I better start fighting death somewhere? Hell, 1 could *conquer* death. That skull could be *mine*! I emerged from the grave determined to steal the skull.

As I clambered out of the abyss, Lance told me to shut up, I hadn't said anything. A drunken couple was staggering along the lane. They passed us, heading towards town. Nervously, I stuffed the skull into my shorts. We had no bag, and to hold it might have been suicidal. A dog barked. I told Lance that the townspeople might blame our theft on bone-hungry canine. He agreed. Silently, we left the graveyard and heeded for Whale Villa. Halfway there, we passed the funeral service for Captain Johnston. Much afro-spiritual singing. Music permeated the air, punctuated by mournful wails. These made me very nervous. The sacrilege!

We continued. The skull started slipping out of my shorts, sliding down the inside of my thigh. I kept violently shifting it, trying not to hurt myself, thinking I'd deserved the discomfort. We passed a villager. I looked at the ground, scared that the skull would roll onto his feet. Ha strolled by, unsuspecting. We finally madeit to the villa. Worried that the maid might uncover it in the morning, (or that vigilantes would find it) if we kept the skull in the house, we at first placed it in an old clay oven in the garden. Afraid again that a gardener or the maid might use the oven the next tier, we eventually stashed it in a compost heap.

Lance and I washed our hands and went out to Willy's Tavern and George's Place, drinking end dancing into the morning. We'd almost forgotten about it when, early on hungover Monday morning, we packed for the return voyage home, I made sure that Lance carried the skull, wrapped in a sleepingbag, aboard the boat.

Though we had told Coral and Gerard that we left it at the grave, they discovered our skull among the baggage. The two of them had stopped in to pay respects at an open-casket viewing of Captain Johnston early Saturday morning. The Captain of *Bahama Daybreak* barely missed finding it.

Later, Lance used the family bleach to cleanse the skull. He gained full possession of it. To this day, it hangs from a nail in his secretive loft. Illuminated by a small, pale lamp. I let him take it. Drunk, I had tried to face the death, which it represented. Sober, I wanted it away; I tried to put it out of sight and mind. As for the theft: Lance's skull, his fault, right? Yet I couldn't get off saying that I'd just been following orders. I thought I'd conquered mortality, or at least faced it. Little had I known. Conquer death. Humph! Ever, faced it, I should try telling that one to a veteran.

Now, whenever I see it, I think of our weekend vacation, and whenever I think of our excursion to Harbour Island, I think of that small, brutal skull.

Station

Momentum and speed. A train through a tunnel. Burst into summer, the infectious gaudiness of nature. Sleeping on your seat (second class), you feel momentum ebb as tired brake pods clutch spinning wheels. Screeches (as sharp as lightning must be) peek out and fade. Those seconds between forward movement, baiting, and end lurching backwards ensue.

You can hear tires rolling up to the train across a multitude of smooth pebbles. They stop. Your ears are more awake than your mind, which shimmers between sleep and sobriety. The train is stationery long enough for you to feel the almost audible throb of sunbeams baking the Swedish country earth; to hear the insects rustling flowers with their pollen-laden limbs (and the silence) with their noise. The doors of automobiles swing open slowly and shut quickly. Many of them the soft murmur of a woman's voice weaves its way between cylindrical shafts of sunshine into your ears. Curiosity brings you to your feet.

A village station, which juts from a rugged forest clearing, has been edged into your window frame by the train, located between the rocky fishing settlements sod the roiling monotony of farm land, its appearance is startling, bringing you to conscious curiosity.

You pull yourself out of the bunk and lean against a window. The air is too warm to make your breath cloud the glass.

Your nose makes a sweaty smear. Your perception and sensuality focus on the still setting. The small groups of people on the wooden platform pay you no heed. The villagers; though not poor, are weathered. The station house, which is really a waiting room, has sprung from thorn. Baggage leans against its stone walk. An elderly men rests against the conductor's booth, smoking. A snow shovel leans patiently against this structure's skin, waiting in the sun for winter. An unpaved reed pushes itself from matronly weeds into the clearing from around a bend. A simple harbour of pebbles, torso-deep in dust, provides berth for cars oil of which have seen good use.

The people are spread comfortably across the waiting area. You mosey down to the caboose, where the conductor's call for the engineer to open the doors intrudes the peace, is echoed, and dissipates.

Those who disembark do not whisk themselves away. They linger. Two boys race from the train to greet their father's mother, and her dog. Their mother strolls behind them, smiling. A big lad on aluminium crutches jerks his way off the train. A cheer ripples from a cluster of his boyhood friends. His travelling companion trots proudly ahead of him. Soon the injured youth is within the warm congregation. He is bathing in their engulfing hugs and the murmur of concern.

Longing eyes gaze outward from within the train from behind straggly curtains and half-open windows. Pollen, in misty clouds, pushes its way from buds, seeds, and branches; it weaves among the parents, lovers, and friends.

The train's whistle blows, making the conductor's eyes bulge momentarily. His coat hangs draped across his forearm, and his hat dangles from his pinkie. His tie swings from a sweaty pink neck. That very tie, undone in the village, will constrict as the train nears the city.

When the separated platformers fall silent, the train doors slide closed. Slowly, the wheels make their practiced revolutions. Their energy comes not steamed and sweated from within, but from along the 'danger' wires, which are strung, taught overhead.

The dust that had settled on the tacks stirs to movement. The caboose is pulled well around the band. The travellers shift their attention from the village to a name-on-a-schedule destination, ignoring the train's motion. The villagers slowly turn from the station towards their cars and the woods.

The Man in the Uniform

Myrdal, Norway, with its six or seven inhabitants, was the last place that one would expect to see a uniform. As evening sat upon my brother and I, like a swan cloaking her offspring with a wing, the station-master was stuffing an empty thermos into a pouch on his backpack and preparing to close his humble station. He slid the pack onto his shoulders, stuck a filter-less cigarette between his lips, lit it, and closed the station door quietly. Leaving it unlocked, he strolled down a winding pebble trail toward us.

I watched him from our tent halfway down the thin valley, surrounded by tremendous snow-peaked mountains. Only after he had crossed the wooden bridge (which hovers over a waterfall) could I hear, over the hollow flapping of our tent in the wind, the sound of his leather boots grinding into the natural gravel. His tie was undone, and the gold tinted "Scan-Rail" buttons of his coat flashed with every footstep in the subsiding glare of day. He was heading home. Further down the valley, right near the base of the fjord, his hut crouched among evergreens, its grey wood hardly stood out against the backdrop of granite cliffs across the fjord. Legging on my belly before the firs, with my chin nestled in my palms, I couldn't help thinking how damned out of place his uniform seemed.

Myrdal is tucked quietly into the Flamsdal Valley, an extension of Aurlands Fjord, where the snow never melts. The station master's evening walks without a necktie and a summer blessing, far from the norm. No more than two families live in Myrdal, tending the station, its kiosk, and various sheep. The groove-in-the-mud paths connect no more than six wooden huts. Yet, for all its isolationist beauty, Myrdal is an accessible village. Tunnels are carved into the innards of, or skirt the hips of, its mountains. It straddles the Osio-Bergen rail route, and serves as an exchange centre for tourists bound to nearby Flam, whose fjord brings in cruise ships from all over the globe.

The point is, that the station master, if he really wanted to, could easily escape. I am sure fast, in his uniform; he could take off for Oslo or Bergen at leisure, free of charge. Someone else could run the tiny station. This man, robustly healthy in his forties, must have at some point chosen to live in Myrdal. One doesn't live there just for the pay or the station. The struggle and beauty of life in those mountains makes the railway seem a mere diversion. The splendour of that rugged charm is all encompassing. Something in the station master's character must have yearned for the solitude, the peace the honesty of Myrdal.

Despite the ruggedness of Myrdal, the station master hardly seemed cut off. His life was a wonderful juxtaposition of the privets and the cosmopolitan. When the social urge hit, he had not only the Scandinavian travellers and the Norwegian neighbours within conversation's range, but that little station of his was a miniature painting, particularly of Western culture. 'Earthy' backpackers and their travel tales permeated the place, as did the more wealthy, ocean-traversing cruise ship passengers, who daily came in droves to Myrdal from Flam along s renown scenic rail stretch: twenty miles of hairpin turns, tunnels, fjords, and waterfalls, making their trek to Myrdal a worthwhile expedition. Arabs, Americans, Europeans, Australians, Japanese, and numerous other visitors huddled under his station during the summer's light rains, providing the station master with a cross-section of the world at his own doorstep!

As the station master, oblivious to my brother and I, nimbly weaver; between familiar boulders and fir trees, I began to feel that he had in a way disproved my prejudices. A finger of smoke coughed itself away from his chimney, and I found myself in a curious muddle. The station master had decided to live in solitary authority (end almost solitary inhabitant!) of a miniscule community, commander of a train station in a world of transcontinental railways: holder of a grain of sand in a beach of a world.

As in freedom *from* religion, the station master was never obligated to put anyone up. He never had to deal with their antics after the evening's last departing train. The world was at his disposal no strings attached. With the recession of the sun, he trod home into a hearth-warmed hut, filled, if he wanted, with books, liquor, a lover, or his wife and children. I imagined him leaving his shoes and socks under the steps, stretching his wool-socked feet out on a log before the fire, and savouring a coffee, a book, or companionship. Freedom to him was intertwined with routine. I envied him. An urbanite might be uncomfortable with his simplicity I've known young Americans who relate untamed nature to fears of 'Jason' of the movie *Friday the Thirteenth* fame. But would this station master have chosen Myrdal if he longed only for the exciting confusion of cities? Had he been forced to take the assignment (in which case he and his uniform would seem repulsively inconsistent with the setting), couldn't he have transferred? Escaped? Gone down to Flamsdal nightly for beers, music, and one-night-stands'? Myrdal is not a prison. Except, perhaps, for a few restless tourists those who are there because they want to be there. They savour it, knowing the ease or inevitability of departure.

The more time I spent there, the more I realised that Myrdal's station master quietly demonstrates a life that went rewardingly deeper than his appearance alone, which was so enigmatic and captivating. Seeing him in the addictively beautiful setting of Myrdal, I at first hunted sceptically for flaws. Then it occurred to me that he and Myrdal had faced casual visitors like myself. Only a fool would see Myrdal as representing merely confinement or simplicity. The wise visitors yearn to experience its raw, expressive nature, secretly wishing that they could live like he. The station master wasn't a lonely man stuck in the Kathmandu of Norway. He'd obviously made the decision to live there, or at least not to escape. Myrdal is not a rural dead-end street. It is far from it. It is the prototype of every hamlet, village, tribe, or nation. The roots of Norwegian communities and culture lie in a Myrdal that once was.

The station master simply played host. Host of a village, yet more:he was the unsung host of a nation: Saint Peter of Aurlands Fjord. Visitors entered and exited, taking with them their criticisms, praises, diary entries, or raspberries. Myrdal and its station master remained. He allowed or refused himself interaction. Myrdal's loyal station master celebrated contentment with nature within the context of responsibility. He had proved me wrong. He was a human in uniform, not the uniform in human, which I had first imagined him to be.

The Uniform in the Man

I recall an afternoon, the previous summer in Arlington national cemetery, Washington D.C. A young soldier, his uniform pristine, shoes spit-shined, shaven head motionless, and back erect, was silently guarding the tomb of the unknown soldier(s). For hours this contemporary of mine didn't twitch, waiting for his commanding officer to initiate the 'changing of the guard' for a cluster of spectators. Rated in an asphyxiating uniform and bedecked with a small arsenal under the oppressive humidity, the youth was protecting the 'eternal flame', memorial to the unknown soldiers of the United States' colonial wars (World War One [the 'war to end all wars'], the Second World and Korean wars, and the Vietnam 'advisory intervention', or whatever you call an undeclared war).

Ploughing through my Marlboros, occasioning twirling my earing, and sweating like a pig, I was enraptured by this youth and the uniform which he seemed to have assimilated through osmosis. I thought only actors stood perfectly still for hours! Was this guy *born* with a rod up his ass, or did the army insert it?

What does someone think when they have to stand in one spot for so long, hardly blinking? Can someone see himself as an individual or a character when they emulate to the "T" the motions and steps of every memorial guard since their conception? When his commander finally came on the scene, booming orders in synchronized fury, and replaced the soldier with a clone, I felt that none of my questions had been answered only transferred onto another coast's hairless scalp.

What kind of lives do these kids live? How do they get from the cemetery to home for back to base camp) without revealing their humanity; that they (isn't goose-step to get milk from the fridge); that they too (heaven forbid) pick their noses? Of one thing I was convinced; they couldn't possibly think spontaneously and independently while condemned to stand stock-still for so long. That would so dangerous. Better off counting sheep or trying to ignore bates of sweat making their gravitational way to the tips of their noses before dropping and soiling their uniforms. No thoughts of travel, freedom, or independence. For most, the urge would be too compelling towards action. Perhaps they simply repeat, over and over and over a phrase like 'I'm a good ol' boy.'

In a way, I admired the guy. His role protected him from potential freedom. His role was simple: do nothing except concentrate on nothing, and you will get your cookie. What was the cookie that the army gave? Barracks? Food? Perhaps alittle beer; certainly not women. He was to become void of thought or expression for a certain amount of time. This takes practice at the equivalent of a coat rack. Practice at being deaf, dumb, and mute. Yet, in those trim uniforms, with stainless swords and rifles, with their gold trim, white gloves, and shaven chins, they *looked* good, those guards. Essentially they had *become* uniforms.

Memory of the soldier-robots had fostered in me the conviction that uniforms are ultimately all consuming; that character and conformity cannot coexist dually within one. Typically, indeed puritanically, I was disregarding the Ying-

Yang incorporation of good and evil in favour of extremism: you're either in the uniform or you're not.

I suppose that their uniforms provided those soldiers with a sense of function, reward, and pride at being tied in with an overall 'system'. They choose to do as all 'guards of the eternal flame' had done, ally themselves with a tremendous, all-providing bureaucratic family: a national brotherhood: The United States Army. They weren't supposed to show personality. Expression of character might have led to Independence! Even the flat marble setting of Arlington national cemetery seemed void of humanity and sentiment void of life. Like the identical gravestones, which they guarded, the soldiers had become uniforms inhuman.

Two Bedraggled Men

Two bedraggled men Roy and Ben, both young vagabonds huddle at night over a small fire beside railway tracks:

Ben: "I've been thinking."

Roy: "About what?"

Ben: "About hating life."

Roy: "Oh. Why?"

Ben: "I don't know."

Roy: "Put your finger to it."

Ben: "Go to hell."

Roy: "o.k…"

(A pause)

Ben: "When did you die?"

Roy. "What?"

Ben: "Never mind."

Roy: "No, what did you say?"

Ben: "Never mind!"

Roy: "Why do you hate life?"

Ben: "Because it's so damned real."

Roy: "It is."

Ben: "I know."

(A pause)

Roy: "Look, why don't you just go to sleep?"

Ben: "Why?"

Roy: "Better than mooing."

Ben: "Hummph."

Roy: "I think about flowers. About chocolate."

Ben: "I hate my life because it's a long road, and it's grey, and the road is pavement and the roadside is gravel and dust. Because luxury is a lie and you know it when you're on the road, because you see everything through reality and through time and you can't avoid seeing it. Off of the road there are nettles and fences to be torn down and flies. Sod the flies! (Shaking) They're diabolic! Luxury is an illusion that you can live; an oasis you can swim in...an oasis you can drown in..."

(Ben trails off, and then falls silent).

Roy: "Goodnight, Ben."

What?

"Well, well...Sleep again, well, maybe just one more brew, just one more, then I'll go to sleep..."Denny thinks to himself.

"Same thing, drink myself stupid..." he thinks. "Alone," he thinks...

s
l
e
e
p

Dawn

Denny awakes again,

Some thing, he awakes.

But no, some urge festers between the hung-over tissues of his brain. has Denny had enough of Los Angeles?

Will he kill himself?

"No, I won't kill myself," thinks Denny, "But 1 will leave, yeah, that's it, I'll leave! I don't have to put up with this Blimpie Burger bullshit any more," thinks Denny. "I'll go to Tijuana yeah!"

Denny swings his feet onto the floor, crushing an empty beer can with one foot, gets up, and puts on his high-tops and a sweatshirt (inside out), he holds his breath when its armpits go aver his nose.

Juvenilia

"Urghh," he groans.

"And it costs fifty cents for laundry," he thinks. Denny doesn't have any detergent even, he sees on TV that each detergent is the best quality and the best buy, and since he can't buy all of them, he can't decide which one to get, so he just pours rum, vodka, or rubbing alcohol on his laundry to disinfect and clean it. He never washes his polyester. Blimpie Burger blouse in his room, he's not ashamed to even take it out of the joint, Denny just slides his dirty clothes in with the Blimpie Burger bowls and dishes, just slides them in with the dishes.

Anyway, this morning Denny isn't thinking about dishes. Denny is thinking about leaving i.e. he's thinking about travel.

"Someone in my family must have travelled in order for me to have gotten here to California," he thinks.

"Yeah, plenty of people travel," he thinks. Denny doesn't have a lot of money, he wants to head south, he looks downstairs at the map his landlord has hanging over the drying machine, which also costs fifty cents to run.

"Tijuana. Isn't that for south?" He thinks.

"They have Blimpie Burger booths down in San Diego," thinks Denny. "I'll head south. I've got a dad in Tijuana I can crash at his place." His dad is trying to get back into the statessohe can knock around Denny's mother, who's up in Hollywood as alive-in maid. She's seeping with her boss's son, who, at eighteen, is younger than Denny.

Denny doesn't think about his mother getting banged by a kid, though. He doesn't think about, his older brother, who keeps begging to bring weed to him up in the San Bernadino state penitentiary. Denny thinks about his smokes, he finds them under last week's "people magazine", with its cover-story on how kids want to be adults'. He grabs his smokes, his last two bud tail-boys, a torn pair of jeans, a few tube socks (whose coloured

71

rings don't match), a leather ball with a big metal star on it (he stole it from a taxon Blimpie Burger bus-boy), and his landlord's map (from above the dryer), he throws these into a sack he used to fill with peaches when he was younger; when he was helping his dad with migrant labour. Denny attaches the wire clip, ordinarily used to hook the sack to a wire (which lead into the peach cannery), to a rope handle at its base, he flings it over his shoulder the way pancho villa wore abandolier. Denny leaves the fifties-style diva he lives in and heads out towards the highway.

"It is hot as a devil's tent." Denny isn't too happy at first; the bear fumes get sucked out of his body by the sun. He gets over it after a few blocks.

"The goons dashing for cusses or edging down the street in their hernias are no better off than me," he thinks. "In fact, I'm better off than them!"

"I'm going south, they're just going to the Blimpie Burger break-your-back-until-you-get-paid work joints, yeah, I'm better off than them." A few hours later Dennyis walking south along interstate five, wishing he was in an air-conditioned car with a radio, and maybe a cold plastic litre bottle of water. A few hours later Denny is wishing had just called in sick, turned the fan in his room on high, had a smoke, cranked up Led Zepllin, and maybe called Maria to see if she would call in sick too.

But a few hours later is too late for Denny, he's crossing the expressway (to head bock into L.A., grab himself some water somewhere, and show up late for a Blimpie Burger bowling), when a dusty maroon thunderbird slows town a few yards from where he stands.

Rock-n'-roll by Midnight Oil wafts backwards with the exhaust as Denny sprints down the gravel shoulder after his salvation wheels. The cloth handle of his sock tears free with his running, and one of his shoelaces drags. In the dust, hindering him every second step, by the time Denny slides into the passenger seat, the thunderbird being revving begins to roll forward, with a peel of Goodyear radials, the car negotiates itself into the mainstream, south-bound flow of traffic.

Denny looks nervously over at his courier.

Dark shades, strips of greasy hair swing against the lenses, smearing them like upside-down windshield wipers.

"How far south?"

"Just past San Diego."

It's a dry reply, hoarse. The driver takes a drag from a Lucky Strike before letting it continue to dangle from thin lips.

"Where to?"

"San Ysidro."

"Oh."

Denny stares to his right after passing the Capistrano mission on his left.

"They're just a bunch of square white chapels on a clay hill," he thinks; "Soon, if I really crane my neck, I'll see the ocean."

Over telephone poles and the orange, Spanish-tile roofs of houses he distinguishes the thin strip of dark blue held down by the lighter blues of the sky. Then he remembers where he's going.

South.

Down by Mexico way.

He turns to his left again, the driver is cleaning the fingernails of his left hand with a stiletto and trying to steer with his right, Denny doesn't let that distract him. No. Not Denny Ramirez. He has some place to go. A farther to see. Whores to screw. Tequila to gulp.

"You goin' to Tijuana?" He asks.

"Yeah."

"Can I go?"

"No."

Silence.

"But I'm goin' there too." Denny sputters before he can catch himself, it comes out sounding almost like a squeal.

"Shit," he thinks.

"Mistake. I'm fucking whining to a driver who's cleaning his nails with a stiletto."

The driver is slow with his reply, but quick in giving it.

"I got business in Mexico. I don't need you there." He pronounces the 'x' in Mexico with a 'h', the way some Mexicans do. Silence again.

Denny tries to cover up the weakness he'd revealed. He stutters out a question any question.

"What you doin' down in Mexico?"

He tries real hard to get the 'h' in Mexico right.

The driver is quiet, Denny relaxes a little.

"He didn't pick up my whine," he thinks.

"So what about the ride, just as long as this hombre don't give me a hard time about bein' a kid."

They drive a few more miles down interstate five, past an embalmer, then a slow grin smears itself across the driver's face.

"What?" Thinks Denny. "What's this guy thinking?"

"Yeah, kid," the Chicano begins, "Sure, yo soy un embalmer I got corpses to pick up in Tijuana, ha!"

"Oh shit," thinks Denny; "this asshole's going for the throat."

More smiles from the host.

"Yeah ha little is my hearse, chicoyou don't wanna' be goin' into Mexico with dis hearse here... I got bodies to pick up there he..."

The laugh pierces the music, pierces everything; Denny's sense of security... everything...

The Chicano smiles and laughs more, then he begins hitting the dashboard to the beat of the Metallica drums and jerking his legs at the knees.

Denny stares out to the sea.

Through Oceanside, post Dal Mar, past La Jolla, and through San Diego. They don't say anything for some two hours, just outside of San Ysidro, Denny staggers into the dust, humiliated.

He walks across the late afternoon bitumen to the Mexican border. There, an American in uniform tells him to get lost.

"You ain't got a passport, green card, or nothing," he tells Denny. "Can't lot you in, cause then you won't come back."

"That's bullshit," thinks Denny as he's walking back to San Ysidra.

"That tight-ass yankee is playin' with my mind. He don't give a shit if I come back or not. He's just being a fucking prick!"Late afternoon nudges its way around Denny. He's hot as hell and angry. Real angry. Disappointed. Lonely. Lost.

"Won't get to Tijuana…" He thinks. "…Mom's with the riches. Maria hasn't called in days."

"Maria! That's right! If get back to L.A. tonight, I can act as if I never left and crash at her place tonight!" He walks faster for San Ysidro. After a glass of water and a piss at a Burger King, Denny hitches a ride with two surfers coming up from Baja in a family camper; they take him to the Pacific Highway on the San Diego bay.

Around ten that night, after hours of waiting for a ride, a tired old man in a banged-up Chevy station-wagon picks him up. The man is Mexican. In broken English, he talks and talks about now rough it was a kid in Chihuaha in the thirties.

Denny falls asleep in the car until he's jolted awake on the Los Angeles freeway.

"L.A. again…Urghhh…"

a
l
l
t
h
a
t

NOISE!

L.A. again.

The old man drops him off within walking distance of Maria's.

Scribbles from St. George's

DATE: 7:33 a.m., December 11, 1987

PLACE: Room 111, Arden Dorm, Saint George's School, Newport/ Middle- town, Rhode Island

ENTRY: Good morning. I'm in my bed. In 22 minutes I will be taking s Spanish test. For breakfast I am eating Kool-Aid powder (grape flavoured) by the spoonful and drinking another coffee. This morning allowed me some two hours of sleep from 5:30 to 6:45 a.m. Less the night before. A.P. Music History term papers are due today. Mine is far from completion.

I want to go home.

DATE: October 1988

PLACE: Room 2, Blue Dorm, Old School building, St. George's

ENTRY: An opera drifts from my transistor radio a lotus in the mud of my mind. A flower amongst friendlessness. Empty coffee mug. Broken spoon. Useless money. Vain memories. An attitude, which won't pull me through hundreds of miles of chlorinated pools this winter. Outside, beyond my revolving-stool lament, relationships abound.

DATE: 11:00 a.m., Sunday, October, 1988

PLACE: Blue Dorm, St. George's

WEATHER: cool and sunny despite mist/fog on Second Beach

Eric Wiberg

ENTRY: Outside of my window birds (crows? gulls?) caw, and the wind is causing autumn dry loaves to sigh and whisper to breathe. Across the fields some of the faculty dogs bark to one another. Below on Main Steps a door slams, an ignition starts a car engine, a steering shaft grinds, and a large car accelerates its way down the tree-domed tone towards the gates.

The room. An unusually large single. It was originally occupied by three students, then two seniors, and presently the residing prefect. Nestled among four other senior male rooms, it looms three stories above Main Hallway, and provides views through four windows on two exterior walls of both Rhode Island's Second Beach and the school's Main Drive.

The Interior mine for eight months. To the right of my desk lies a copy of *Sisterhood is Powerful* and various magazines. Out-dated copies of *Newsweek, National Geographic, New York Times Magazine, Soviet Life*, and *Selling World* litter a Formica patio table. A towel hangs drying from the upper bunk bed. A mop of the world, one of the Caribbean, and a Bahamian flag dangle from the walls in the corner. Beside them are hung an oil canvas depicting a jungle scene in colourful Haitian style, a small en-framed example of Native Australian bark art and a roe deer trophy from Ripsa, Sweden.

Meanwhile, "curtains dangle, pull the wind beckon minds, seduce and win..." My attention is drawn outside by the flutter of curtains. A woman's footsteps resounding below. A print of Dali's *The Broken Bridge and the Dream* brings me back into the room. Beside it are posted a Soviet propaganda image of Yuri Gagarin dated "12-4-1951" and a poster advertising Reggae Sun splash. Beneath them a sign addressing "*Svensk i Varlden*" (which beseeches "Swedes of the World" to unite) bestrides atattered couch, which I pilfered from storage a month ago.

Records, boxes of cassettes, and photo albums stretch between this couch and a wooden bookshelf. My stereo and its only, fading speaker rest upon this wood-shop masterpiece in the day of compact discs, when 6-track cassettes long ago withered out of production, my 8-track stereo seems strangely antique.

A director's choir stands before the window while the adjacent heater clangs in its sporadic efforts to neat audibly bubbling water. The floor is covered in little circles of paper, as I have been punching holes in various writings and filing them in binders. Each page provides my abode with three more papyrus rings.

The cardboard garbage box, which lies beside the desk, is full of faded sketches or worthless scraps of writing all of which are sprinkled in drained coffee grounds. Intermingled between these are empty envelopes (from *Amnesty International* or college admission offices), pencil shavings, soda cans, and 'Premium Cracker' wrappers. One poem in the trash is an attempt to describe the riots in *Kungstragarden*, Stockholm the previous summer. An empty box which once held no-longer-fresh, half-price apple muffins reminds me of evenings in Le Patisserie, Newport's French cafe and conversations over coffee and copies of Nietzsche about mono, Wheeler School, the Marinas Leningrad, and Italian.

Outside, young faculty emigrate in their Saabs and Blazers. Where to? Sunday brunch in Newport? The beach? Silently, I wish them pleasantly. My typewriter lies on the floor, in a few days it will be replaced by a Macintosh computer costing a hundred times what I'd paid for this manual typewriter. (I am spoilt). On my desk a'Camp Rockmont' laundry bag holds several hours of schoolwork, which shall keep me in the library till late this evening. A note to myself reads "10:00 a.m. breakfast with Natasha in Freshmen in my art class who just moved from Zimbabwe to Malawi, Africa." The note continues... "Letters a must college applications / homework first / library / sleep early." I've missed Natasha at breakfast, procrastinated on the letters, and will have to stay up late to get homework and college app's done.

Above me, a window bids entry to rays of sunlight. They illuminate a poster reading "Club Med Antidote for

Civilisation", which depicts the buck of a topless women holding an umbrella and facing towards the ocean and the sun. Taped to this is a smaller parody, which reads: "Club Ded Antidote for a Doomed Civilization" atop a photo of a clad woman, also on a beach, gawking at the red mushroom blaze of an atomic bomb exploding.

Which holds my most favourite or most valuable possessions. My passport and ticket home are tucked away, along with a few packs of illegal Marlboro cigarettes, in a small box holding my Rhode Island Hospital Trust cheque-books, fly earners, address book and wallet shift among the drawer's contents. Sometimes I also hide small bottles of vodka in pairs of socks (maybe with a joint or two), but the locked drawer is always the first place that the authorities look. All of my original writings, drawings, or published manuscripts are kept in there, including five or so diaries.

Outside, a girl is shrieking a sound often heard here, yet so difficult for me to understand. Perhaps it is a typical indication of spoilt brats who still yell and whine when in want of attention. Perhaps merely childish expressions of surprise? The open window slams my door finally closed. I used the janitor's "Windex" this morning to loosen the hinges and decrease the squeal of opening or closing it. Vaseline, Noxima, and Windex have all been proven inadequate for the task.

Before me hangs a framed copy of Rudyard Kipling's poem *If*, as does a poster of the flags of the world. On the windowsills are a reading lamp, an alarm clock, and several bedside books, including Commander Cameron's *Across Africa*. My piggy bank commemorating the wedding of Prince Charles and Lady Diana holds up a framed photo of my Eagle brook School dorm parents. A desktop S.G.S. "Classof 1982" plastic mug holds my pens the school's "Nathanial P. Hill Library" book marks. Dorm prefect, sports, and class schedules, a calendar, and a *Time Magazine* colour photo of a Dutchman pitchforking yellow tulips in the wind also grace the wall space immediately before my desk.

Juvenilia

A separate section of the wall one which slants inward where the window doesn't jut out houses a photo of Wickes. She kneels next to a 'Wilderbeeste' on the spot where she shot it in the Luangwa Valley, Zambia. Adjacent to this is a photo of me camping above a fjord in Myrdal, Norway. They were both taken, at about the same time. These two photographs hold their own above a collection of gift colognes Dakar, Paco Robanne; the works.

The week's clothes are either done and spread across the sparse furniture or stiffen in one of three drawers. My only other clothes the required coat and tie hang on no more than ten hangars in the closet. I have two closets; the one holds my Vietnam-veteran combat boots, sneakers, 'Beanies', boxes of scrapbook material, and a concealed chair for silent contemplation. The other closet holds my books. These I could go on about extensively, but it should suffice to say that there are some fifty sections to the collection, ranging from 1700's volumes and first editions, to 3 language section which can educate me in some 25 tongues. Most of the books are inherited from the school library or bought second-hand at the Corner Book Store on Spring Street in Newport.

I complete a circular spanning of my room the best accommodation that I have been able to call mine for more than a few hours by resting my wearying eyes upon a pocket size Germen chess set with magnetic pieces, which Hon Kolff of Rotterdam and I piddle over late-nights. Outside I hear an eccentric teacher coaxing her dog Ilex into a van filled with picnickers. I stand and stretch. Noon has swung by. On the beach surfers surf. People stroll and chat. Even from half a mile away, they seem greatly more relaxed than the beach-goers I've seen in 1920's photos. A bicycle struggles up the hill. An empty public school bus wheezes by. Crows nag at refuse in the gross. A mist rises over the sun and wefts landward.

DATE: February 5, 1989

PLACE: Senior Porch, Main Building, St. George's

ENTRV: It is winter. I am out on Senior Porch. It is raining like spring relatively warmand I hear the surf following itself to shore like a cog chasing its toll. There is fog it makes me feel almost private, but my life here is far from private. I hear an aeroplane. It sounds like a dull knife being sharpened. I hear the halyards of an American and a St. George's flag being hit against the pole by the wind.

I am alone. Despite my girlfriend, alone again. A vast, unpredictable future stretches before me like a patch quilt of all the relationships I've had or will have. There is a person on the beach and a bird's nest in the bush. I wear a feather in my lapel; am laughed at. Someone hammers on the headmaster's new house. My first day here, 1 walked to the centre of the field, looked at my watch, saw my shadow, and figure out rows to point in the direction home. The ocean is more free than I will ever be. That same day I watched a dancer on the beach, thinking that I was in love with her. I thought that was real.

I live in an environment of unfair warmth, comfort, and security: extravagance. It's too bloody easy I don't intend to spend a life here. I intend to get out. I'm reading about Moshe Dayan, cooking, and Buddhism. I dream I avoid starting families and marrying. I see fences aid Bohemian flags in my mind. I hear pianos and wish to conquer. I think that biographies reveal what was intentionally hidden. Writing is an escape. Dance is a form of seduction. I am a sitting whim; I don't like religious teachers who wear pink and white. The World is a microcosm. My memory organizes it challenges the chaos.

I remember, which defies what I foresee.

John Coltrane: 1926 1967

Born a rural Afro-American in 1926, John William Coltrane blew his tenor saxophone from obscurity to international renown as a master of a predominantly black-American musical style known as jazz. Coltrane revived the tenor saxophone a European instrument and, through determination, powerful self-confidence, and religions conviction, he and his instrument jammed to the forefront of the fifties and sixties jazz scene. Though Coltrane made a point of incorporating various international end ethnic musical styles into his own, it is of an American genre. Jazz evolved from early Afro-American work songs, call-and response styles, and primitive blues. Coltrane, also known as Trane managed always to progress and innovate. He was a driving force, along with Thelonious Monk, McCoy Tyner, and Elvin Jones, behind the Bebop and Hard Bop movements, which controversially aired between the late 1940's and '60's.

Coltrane was born in Hamlet, North Carolina on September 23, 1926. In 1944 he was stationed with the U.S. Navy Band in Hawaii, where he grew to love the saxophone, which was invented by a Belgian named Adolph Sax but popularized by the likes of the American, Sydney Bechet. Through constant practice, he mastered the tenor saxophone; at times 'blowing' an astronomical 32 beats per measure songs like *My Favourite Things* at least to his versatility. His life long goal was to communicate with the world through his music, demonstrating what he believed was a superior musical gift. He drew support from faith in Middle-Eastern and African religions, an influence that he incorporated into several of his songs. Though Trane enjoyed remarkable respect, and was both successful and internationally adored, his life was marred with self-obsession and self-abuse.

During his tour of Japan in 1966, Trane was seen, regularly clutching his right abdomen, where his liver pained him. The heavy drinking and bodily abuses, which characterized his flamboyant life, were beginning to harm him. He was some 120 pounds over-weight by the spring of 1967. After a charity concert at Olatunji'scentre in New York, he near collapsed, but refused to admit himself into a hospital until too late. At that point, with adoration by almost religious followers peaking, he had begun to see himself as saintly even immortal, someone naturally gifted to "be a force for real good" and to communicate religious messages through the tenor saxophone. John Coltrane died on Monday, July 17 1967, in Huntington, Long Island. His Harlem funeral attracted more renowned contemporary musicians and music critics than had come together for many years.

Impressive for evolving from rural North Caroline to global jazz acclaim, John Coltrane man, musician, and messiah became idolized for his religious insights, respected for his mastery and revival of the tenor saxophone, and (though later egotistically over-extended), admirable for his personal self-control. In short, Coltrane triumphed.

Thus Spoke Nietzsche

Friedrich Nietzsche, as a philosopher and a man, was vast and complex; so much that William Barret, halfway through the twentieth century, claimed that man was still catching up to him. His discussions of Dionysus, Nihilism, Super-humanity, Atheism, and Zarathustra are less easy to understand, as they are to misinterpret. Nietzsche himself described his work as "not easy to penetrate...profoundly wounding and at the same time profoundly delighting." (*Nietzsche's Preface, Genealogy of Morals*). He denies the blame that his work "is incomprehensible to anyone or jars on his ears" (Ibid.).Many of his catalytic predictions of what might transpire is proposed in his 'Will to Power' (man's basic drive, as he supposedly deducted while watching his regiment march to death in the Franco Prussian War of 1870-1871) have been realized in the century after his writings.

Nietzsche's depiction of a Godless world manipulated by a few who gain ultimate power ('Supermen,' Dionysian heroes, or Masters) in which the majority are ignorant slaves trapped in a vicious cycle of guilt and death-worship (pie-in-the-sky concept) was understandably met with disdain. People generally fear and ignore truth, especially when it reveals their weaknesses even Nietzsche detested his own weaknesses: sickness, homelessness, a burdened conscience, and lack of religious faith, eventual insanity, apparent sexual failure, and unfathomable loneliness. Yet Nietzsche's predictions; those of a negative and despairing human of the superman who looked down from his lofty Zarathustrian genius have generally been proven true, though often they and the prophet were ignored.

One need only look as far as the American Civil War, and the First and Second World Wars for catastrophic events. For supposedly 'Leviathan' or 'Superhuman' political/military leaders, there are the painfully evident aftermaths of Idi Amin, Pol Pot, Mussolini, Franco, Stalin, Hitler, and Truman, and for masters of the religious cults, to the likes of Charles Bronson, Ku Klux Klansman, the Ayatollah Khomeini, and the Pope. Ironically, Nietzsche has been blamed for the fulfilments of his predictions, though industrialization, technology, propaganda, science, and fascism all added to the thirst of power which only needed someone with a keen eye and religiously unpolluted minds to perceive.

As he had done in his twenties with Classical philology, Nietzsche merely foresaw the evil to which the increasingly homogenous populations were failing victim in the unleashed, atheistic quest for power, which is still rampant in the podiums, the playing fields, stock exchanges, and bedrooms of the modern world that Nietzsche beheld. Nietzsche warned. Nietzsche died trying to convince. He "came down," and told the masses, for this he has been condemned by many as a forefather of Nazism, a madman, and propagator of atheism; as though the public needed either Nietzsche or Hitler to enact what it had obviously been yearning to wreak upon itself.

Psychologically it is the equivalent of an aggressor identifying an external force and blaming it, as the Versailles victors did to Germany in 1918, when they were just as much at fault. As Barnett explains, Nietzsche:

…Was the philosopher of this present age in history…But when a thinker comes along who seeks to explore what lies hidden behind all this dynamism, we cry out that we do not recognize ourselves on the image he draws and seek refuge from it by pointing an accusing finger at his derangement...Nowonder that the age should have branded him as a wicked and malevolent spirit (*Irrational Man*, p. 201.)

Nietzsche held little faith except in his own ability, as Tennyson might say, to step "over the bodies of his dead selves, onto new, more rewording lives". His unapologetically bellowed nihilism and atheism has been reverberating through Europe and beyond since his tormented life, which stretched between October 14, 1844 and August 25, 1900. As a radical philosopher, he has been both defended and ignored for his endorsement of the superhuman, the agnostic, and a godless world. Of his many writings (spanning 1867-1889), several are particularly relevant: *Thus Spoke Zarathustra, Beyond Good and Evil,* and *Use and Abuse in History*(also known as *On the Advantage and Disadvantages of History for Life*).

Among the many philosophers, historians, and artists who had either been in contact with him, debated his polemics, or whose ideologies fell in with variations of Nietzsche's, are Dionysus and Zarathustra as references; Schopenhauer and Wagner as contemporaries; Machiavelli, Pascal, Hobbes, Marx, Hegel, Descartes, Darwin, Rosseau, Dostoevsky, Scathe, and Kierkegaard as predecessors or fellow-atheists; Existentialist followers Sartre and Jack London; and William Barrett, Haideger, Andre Side (whose *The Immoralist* of the 1920's was based on Nietzsche), Hitler's Nazis, and Carl Jung as his commenters or defendants. His philosophy opposed the absolutism of Plato and the religion of Luther, Paul the Apostle, John, Matthew, Saints Augustine, and Thomas Aquinas. As the man who despised that "God is dead!"in his *Boy Science* (#125), Nietzsche has raised many on eyebrow and turned the cheeks and backs of many man academician and theologian against him.

Nietzsche was beyond all else a thinker, a questioner, an individual. He was relentlessly led through a wild and lonely life in search of himself, a home, and the solution of man's dilemma in a world without God, which teetered upon eminent courage. History "which merely instructs" seemed useless to him if, in the words of the Romantic Goethe (whose *Faust* is reminiscent of Nietzsche's *Zarathustra*): it "instructs...without quickening activity." Here Nietzsche finds a sympathizer in Karl Marx, who declared, "up until now philosophers have only interpreted history. My job is to change it." Nietzsche said professorships and chairmanships in philology, Greek, and philosophy at Basel University in Switzerland beginning in 1869 at the age of 24. However, he only taught for ten years before resigning over poor health. He then set out to balance his academic and physical lives and "organize the chaos" (*Use and Abuse in History*). In response to the ancient philosophical quest for happiness, Nietzsche responds: "Do I then strive after *happiness?* I strive after my *work*." (*Thus Spoke Zarathustra*.)

Especially in his work *Use and Abuse in History*, Nietzsche lamented the ignorance, which many people (slave-types) had of history. He compared these types to dumb animals that graze without communicating. Like Rousseau before him, Nietzsche resented the acquisition of historical knowledge for superficial, solely academic, or "decorative" social goals, and not for a fuller and truer comprehension of the past, which would help to confront the future.

Nietzsche is a lover of the despisers those who despise lovers of death (as clergy are referred to), and the waste of historical knowledge. Nietzsche despises those who, in cattle-like ignorance, live only for the moment. Just as the creatures do; without questioning or challenging the past. He writes: "again and again a page loosens in the scroll of time, drops out, flutters away..." (*Use and Abuse in History*, p.8). He lamented Philistinism, especially that of which the Christian Church and proven itself capable, of its occasional destruction of history.

Luther and Colvin's followers rampantly destroyed church organs, stained-glass windows, paintings, tapestries, and other religious ornaments during their Reformations. (Ironically, they would have been justified in destroying Crucifixes by their own book, *The Bible*, whose God supposedly commanded: "Thou shall not make unto thee any graven image, or any likeness or *any thing* that *is* heaven above, or is in the earth beneath, or that *is* in the water under the earth." (*Exodus*, 201)

Since Nietzsche would probably ignore the existence of God and his 'word' altogether, an historical example demonstrating Christian destruction of art (or which the erudite Nietzsche must have known) came in A D. 591, when the Christian Emperor Theodosius was responsible for the destruction of the Alexandria Library, which housed mostly irreplaceable documents based not only on Mediterranean and Afro-Arabic primitive cultures, but also works by Greek Classicists.

Later, there evolved destruction of true culture through secular disasters which have erased public history, such as the fire-bombing of Dresden, which not only levelled the city, but took with it Courbet's painting. *The Stone-Breakers*, among others. Nietzsche could not have missed the abuse and mistreatment of historical culture; the Turks and Austrians carelessly allowed a power magazine to ignite within the very centre of the Parthenon during the 15th century, mutilating a "world wonder," which had survived since Periclean Athens. Later Hiroshima and Nagasaki, Japan, as well as a timeless library outside Leningrad, recently burned, have suffered similar fates.

Milan Kundera treats the theme of erasure of history in his novel *The Book of Laughter and Forgetting*. Kundera's insight is particularly poignant to (and ambiguous with) Nietzsche's work, as it asserts the ability of 'Superhuman' leaders or (in Kundera's case, Czechoslovakian) autocratic dictators to gain control of 'slave' people by erasing their personal and cultural history. Kundera also depicts insane laughter as a symptom of historyless-ness, which is ironic because not only must Nietzsche, who grew more psychotically mod after 1889, and went mute till his death in 1900, have laughed thus, but also it ties in with one of Nietzsche's many references to

Juvenilia

Zarathustrianism. When Zarathustra was born in Zariaspo (probably not 'Pied Cow', as Nietzsche named it), Persia, in c 660 B.C., he is said to have laughed. Like Nietzsche, the pre-Christian prophet went on a mid-life sabbatical as a hermit or anchorite.

Zarathustra's description of man as "a rope stretched between the animal and the Superman a rope over on abyss" in Nietzsche's *Thus Spoke Zarathustra (Prologue, Modern Library* ed., p.8) is most likely referring to Zarathurstrianist *Chinvit* rope bridge, over which the souls of dead cross towards *Yama*, God of Death, and, after 'Towers of Silence' treatment, achieve on afterworld on the moon. There are numerous references to gold, discs, and sunshine in the work: the prophet tells the people: "to you throw in the golden ball" (Ibid. p.78), and Nietzsche ends with "Thus spoke Zarathustra and left his cave, glowing and strong, like a morning sun coming out of gloomy mountains" (ibid., p .368). These are doubtlessly references to the fact that Zarathustra, or "*Zer-tasht*" in the Avestan tongue means 'Golden Disc', and he the Zarathustrian symbol of ultimate good (Superhuman?), the God '*Ahura Mazda*,' is a winged creature straddling a golden disc.

At least seven of the cities to Nietzsche's chapters are drown from the writings of Zarathustra himself, including *Redemption, Manly Prudence*, and *Old and New Low Tables*. Nietzsche's work is historically monumental: Herodotus, Plato, Plutarch, and Aristotle had revered Zarathustra's teachings, but the prophet's works did not resurface in Europe until Anquetil Duperron, a student of the Oriental School of Paris, translated Zarathustra's *Zend-Avestan* to French In 1735.

Nietzsche viewed everyone as facing a tremendous and terrifying task; a divorce from shame and religion, and a confrontation of the weaknesses of mediocrity and slave-hood. Faced with these himself, Nietzsche led an extremely unhappy life. Rather than being irredeemably pessimistic, however, he embraced life in the face of an adversity fierce enough to compare with the hardships of Job or Abraham, only without their faith in God. Despite this, Nietzsche believed in the scientific concept of 'Eternal Return', maintaining that if energy is not dispersed, it remains in the atmosphere, only in different forms of matter or living particles (the Hindus also tend to believe in this reincarnation). This is a particularly courageous view, as Barrett says; requiring "the greatest affirmation and love of life..."(*Irrational Man*, p.195).

Nietzsche straggled with his vision of man as superman; one who could, overcame the burdensome 'camel' stage of manhood, evolving into a god-like 'lion', and triumphing as a historyless 'child', akin to Blake's '*nous*', or Locke's '*Tabulare Roso*'. Superhuman life is depicted in *Thus Spoke Zarathustra* as the ascent of a mountain in order that the few supermen, or masters, may lock down become down-going as children who have triumphed over the devilish elf which plagues the seeker of virtue in his or her quest of super humanity.

In a strange way, Nietzsche seems to have striven to replace the God, which he so vehemently claimed was dead. He certainly exhausted himself in an effort to supersede man and eventually, as a sun-reincarnate, descending to his level to aid him. As a nurse during the France-Prussian war, he apparently stayed awake tending the wounded for four or more clays and never recovered, eventually resigning from his University post and looking in France, Italy, and Switzerland for a home away from his own Germany, where his Pastor-lineage family was mostly deed. That Zarathustra was warned on penalty of death to leave the village in the *Prefaca*, is undoubtedly parallel to the way Nietzsche was rebuffed. Zarathustra was actually killed by a *Magi* priest in 583 B.C., and Nietzsche was condemned to live in utter loneliness.

When he was finally stricken with 'progressive paralysis' in 1559, and became in mind 'like a child', he described himself in his least legible letters as a Dionysian character, one who had been 'Crucified'. This is a dramatic and revealing shift: die he did, and with him the dream of creating a global race of supermen; the dream that everyone in egalitarian fashion (not necessarily in accordance with Darwin's or Hitler's 'dominant race' theories), would overcome guilt, shameand a preoccupation with a God whom people had begun to despair of. In a past-war European setting which T. S. Eliot referred to as *The Wasteland*. Actually, the silencing of Nietzsche, the Classicist, in 1989, paved the way for a dramatic rejection of Classicism end imperialism in the arts, which was put into offset by lovers of primitivism and non-conventionalism like Gaugin, Picasso, Matisse, Stravinsky, and Debussy soon after the silencing of Nietzsche.

Had Friedrich Nietzsche, the titles of whose works include *Behold the Man(Ecce Homo),How Does One Becomes What One Is, Human, All Too Human*, and *Daybreak*, actually tried to become a saviour of man, and to his dying breath bean scoffed at? Had he in truth been aChrist-like, Zarathustrian-esque martyr, dying a Dionysian death in Weimar, Germany, for the sake of mankind? Had Nietzsche secretly espoused, behind a protective, all too human veneer of cynicism, the universal concern of the once Reverend John Denne, who, in 1623, thinking himself to be dying, wrote that: "…any man's death diminishes me, because I am involved in mankind." (*Devotions Upon Emergent Occasions*)

I've been meaning to write a relatively comprehensive summary of Zarathustrianism for some years now. The closest I came to conquering this entangling topic was giving a brief class lecture on it. I began at St. George's to amass articles, encyclopaedia entries, and eventually books featuring information on Zarathustrianism. For weeks and months I alternately relied on a growing manila folder of photocopies and dozens of books about Zarathustrianism. I desperately wanted to prove to my fellow students and teachers that I could find something elusive to them, yet religiously respected. I would go to the very root of their own religion bum them at their own game!

I learned that Zarathustra was an actual man; that Alexander the Great's expedition came across his ancestral devotees. I learned that he rejected guilt and shame, that his followers incorporated both good and evil, celebrated sunshine, and relied almost on bridge-crossing athleticism to enter an after-world. Though modem Zarathustrianists (Parsees) speak Persian tongues, have adifferent ethnic heritage than I, and are extremely exclusive, I found that I could be an objective advocate.

I transferred select titbits and historical facts from my sources into notebooks, I dug up all kinds of vague or specific references in the religion; some overly speculative, others concise, and factual; spent afternoons and weekend nights smoking and drinking coffee in Viewport cafes, researching Zarathustrianism. The ensuing essay has been accused of reading like an encyclopaediaentry. Also, a Zarathustrian expert has not proofread it. So, please excuse any specific discrepancies it is essentially a detailed outline. In many ways, it is a footnote to my reflections on religion and on Nietzsche. Also, my last such, collection was entitled "Z. (for Zarathustra)", which Î should substantiate. I hope that you find it more informative than soporific.

Zarathustrianism

Zarathustrianism is one of the oldest existing religions. Its influence on later religions is noteworthy, as is its history. Zarathustrianism, which is also known by its Greek pronunciation Zoroastrianism, has also been called Madaism, Magism, Fire-Worship, Perstism, and Dualism. The religion began when Persian rulers and their subjects (in what is now Iran) began practicing the teachings of a man named Zarathustra, who lived around 600 B.C. Though John Hinnells claims that, "most scholars accent 1500 B.C.", many would mere realistically place his life between 650and 583 B.C. Such broad speculation as to when he lived places him in a category similar to that of Homer. Joseph Campell went either farther, comparing the Zarathustrian God,*Ahura Mazda*, to *Yehweh* (God), Allah, and the Trinity.

Juvenilia

Zarathustra's views of humans incorporating both good and evil (dualism) and having to combat evil in order to pass safely across a hellish chasm into afterlife have had obvious ramifications on global religions, including Judaism, Gnosticism, Mithraism, and Manichasism. Zarathustrianists, calling themselves Parsees, Persians, still practice their religion today, especially around Mumbai, India. Zarathustrianism can be seen from four major perspectives: its history, its religious rites and ideologies, in relation to other religions, and in the modem world.

Zarathustra was probably born to the Spitemes clan in Zariaspa, then the capital of Bestria, between the Hindu Kush Mountain Range and the Oxus River. This region lies southeast of the Caspian Sea, in what is now Russia. When he was born (around the middle of the 7th century B.C), he was said to have laughed, and also to have survived burnings. His name, in the Avesian tongue, is supposed to mean 'Golden Disc' (*ter-toshi*), which helps explain why the symbol of his god, *Ahura Mazda*, is depicted straddling a sun-like disc an object of Zarathustrian worship with its wings. At the age of thirty-three, Zarathustra experienced his first visions of a god. He was chastised, and left his home and family. Supposedly, a priest killed Zarathustra at the age of 77, around 583 B.C. During his travels as a prophet, he is accredited with having transformed the Persian religion from nomadic to pastoral, made heaven universally attainable (democratic), and created a system of afterlife judgement.

There are four basic chronological periods of Zarathustrianism, centered around one 1400-year period (c.700 B.C. to c.700 A.D.) during which, with a few exceptions (Hellenistic rule 330-256 8.C. and influence 750 B.C.-225 A.D.), Zarathustrianism ruled Persia. The first stage in the establishment of Zarathustrianism most likely began around 600 B.C. and lasted until 330 B.C. During this stage, Zarathustra lived and wrote his focal *Zend-Aviato* as well as seven or so other works, and he converted the Persian King Vishtaspo (*Hystespas* in Greek) to his new religion. Cyrus the Great and the Acnoemanid dynasty defeated the Babylonians and Medions around 540 B.C. Under Darius the Great (522-486 8.C.), Zarathustrianism was the official religion of the Persian Empire.

However, this first phase ended suddenlywith the invasion and conquer of Persia by the young Greek, Alexander the Great of Macedonia around 330 B.C. Not only did Alexander, under the pretext of shaping a 'Hellenistic' world, destroy the Persian forces of Darius III, but he also sacked Persepolis and burned many Zarathustrian manuscripts, of which mostly only chants and rituals are remembered. Between his death in 323 B.C., and 250 B.C. Alexander's Persian satraps and Greek allies ruled Persia. This Seleucid Kingdom was unfavourable to Zarathustrianism.

The Zarathustrian religion found its political renewal slowly (through determined priests) under the Arsacid dynasty (250 B.C.-226 A.D.) and securely under the reign of the Sussenion dynasty, which lasted between 226 and 641 A.D. This third phase; a halcyon period during which Zarathustrianism flourished, ended with the brutal invasion of Persia by Islamic Moslems from Arabia to the West in 641 A.D. These followers of Allah and Mohammad (570-632 A.D.) swept through Zarathustrian territories, intimidating or decimating the population. Many of the Zarsthustrians who survived the invasion, escaped East into India, and settled in the region around Mumbai. They began their calendar (AV) in 632 A.D., which, is the year that King Yezoegird III, the last of the Zarathustrian Sussanian dynasty, died.

The fourth phase of Zarathustrian history has lasted from the 640's into the 1990's, A.D. Known as Parsees, for their Persian extraction, on exclusive community of about 100,000 Zarathustrianists has grown in India. These modem Zarathustrians mostly reside in and around Mumbai, on the Northwest coast of India, near where their boats landed some 1400 years ago. There are only about 7,000 true Zarathustrianists left in Iran/ Persia, though there are similar communities conglomerating In New York City, London, Sydney, Hong Kong, and Washington D.C.

Juvenilia

There are certain principles and traditions, which have distinguished Zarathustrianism in past and present. Avestan is the official language of the religion, though the Sanskrit, Vedic, and Pahlavi tongues have also been used. Only about ten percent of today's followers actually speak Avestan. The two dominating forces are good and evil, (light and dark), which are represented by *Ahura Mazda* (for whom there are 54 names), god of all which is good and true, and his evil counterpart, *Angra Mishnu*, God of darkness and hatred. All humans have both forces within. Life is an eternal struggle between good and evil, climaxed by the crossing of a bridge of trial (*Chinvit*). Good people make it safely across the bridge to eternal life and safety (apparently on the moon). The evil fall from the *Chinvit* into a fatal river chasm.

This chance at redemption is available to ail, although. In what was considered a liberal move, women were granted the status of only half-person (two women equalled one man) for several hundred years. The basic goal is virtue over evil. *The Vendided*, an ancient Zarathustrian scripture, relates, "anyone can win purity with good thought, word, and deed". Translated, "good thought, good word, and good deed" is "*Humata, Hokata, Hvarshte*" a revered code in Zarathustrianism.

Among the rituals and rites of Zarathustrianism, fire plays a focal role, despite Zarathustra's attempts to downplay its importance and that of sacrifice. Known as *Agni*, fire must be pure, and not even the *Magi*, or high priests are allowed to breath on it. They cover their mouths when in the presence of sacred fire. Priests, who train for years for the privilege of handling the fire, must approach it barefoot, and walk away from it backwards. The *Agni* must also be constant (in Mumbai, they maintain a flame which is said to have been lit since 936 A.D.). One particular ritual requires that the sixteen fires be employed, and that some of them be relit 91 times. This emphasis on purity carries over into their treatment of the dead, who are placed on 'Towers of Silence', where vultures can get to them and pick their bones to a Melville-esque, clean white purity. In modern times, Zarathustrians often settle for cremation. Yama, supposedly the first to die, is the King of Death.

There are numerous scriptures used by Zarathustrians, some of which were composed by Zarathustra himself. Others were written many centuries later, perhaps contradicting what the prophet expounded. The overall name of the collection is *Zend-Avesta* (or simply *Avesta*); the religion's basic writings, songs, and treatises. Specifically, the *Rigveda* is the book of low-end commentaries, 17 *Gathas* are songs (possibly by Zarathustra), the *Yasna* are liturgical maxims, the *Vandidad* contains analysis and description of rites and traditions (especially these based on fire), and the *Yoshis* are more songs to Gods. Many of these writings were written in the Pahlavi tongue, popular towards the end of the *Sassinian* period, when Zarathustrian leaders became more polytheistic. Zarathustra himself is accredited with having written *Old and New Law Tables, Of Manly Prudence, The Homecoming, Of Redemption,* and *On Blissful Islands.*

Among other convictions, Zarathustrians tend to place no value in suffering, a contrast to the puritanical or stoic religions later to grow in Europe. The practice of rewarding the devout with fertility was particularly alluring to laymen and agrarians. The ox was chosen as the universal representative of the animal kingdom. One ceremonial ritual entails drinking *Hoame* a potent liquor or strong herb. Chronologically, Zarathustra proposed that four cycles would occur, each three thousand years apart. Each cycle would shift, beginning with the reign of evil (*Angra Mainu*), and ending with the domination of the world by good (*Ahura Mazda*, or 'Wise Lord'). By rough estimate (c.600 B.C. to 2,000 A.D.), we are nearing the end of the first evil cycle. Preparing for the triumph of good.

Because it is one of the oldest surviving of the world's established religions, Zarathustrianism has been closely tied to others, which followed it. Assuming that Zarathustra and his religion began in 660 B.C. (not 1500 B.C.), the founding of Hinduism (1500 B.C.) predates it by about 800 years, one Judaism (1200 B.C.), by about 500. Zarathustrianism would be as old as Shinto, and older than Taoism (604 S C.), Jainism (599 B.C.), Buddhism (560 B.C.), and Confucianism (551 B.C.);

Juvenilia

though virtually contemporaries of all. Christianity (4 B.C.), Islam (570 A.D.), Sikhism (1469 A.D.), and Mormonism (c. 1840 A.D) followed considerably later (based on Robert Hume's *The World's Living Religions*).

Some elements of Buddhism can be attributed to Zarathustrianism. It is possible that the concept of crossing the *Chinvit* over a raging river is related to the Buddhist use of Mahayana Theravada religious trial imagery. Others have proposed that the life of Siddhartha Gautama (the Buddha himself) was based on that of his near contemporary Zarathustra, though this claim might befiercely contested in Tibet, Japan, and South-East Asia. Zarathustrianism had a profound impact on the religions of Northeast Africa (the Nile basin), as evidenced by innumerable references to the Zarathustrian symbol of a winged *Ahura Mazda* straddling a golden disc in early Egyptian art. Zarathustrian symbols etched onto the mummy and pyramid exhibits, as well as the Temple of Dendur in the Metropolitan Museum of Art in New York City attest to this.

Both historically and religiously, Zarathustrianisrn is said to have had a profound influence on Christianity and Judaism, especially as it was the major religion directly to the East of Palestine during the time of Christ (Peter the Apostle roamed in Persian territory for several years); Cyrus of Media liberated the Jews from exile in Babylon around 545 B.C. His and Darius the Great's adoption of the Zarathustrianist struggle to overcome evil appealed to the Jews, and many returned to Jerusalem. Between 520 and 516 B.C., the Jews were allowed to construct a new Temple in Jerusalem and reconstruct the city walls. Cyrus' Archemenid Successors, including Darius, ruled Palestine for a time before the Greeks conquered Persia in 330 B.C. and established the Seluacid Kingdom, which lasted until the Romans invaded during the first century B.C.

After Julius Caesar was assassinated in 44 B.C., the Moccabean Antigonua called upon Zarathustrian Parthians, who captured Judas (Palestine) from the Romans in 40 B.C. However, the Roman King, Heron, recaptured it In 38 B.C., and

Romans held onto Palestine for some four hundred years afterward. Thus Jesus Christ was raised under the Romans. Had the Parthians retained Jerusalem, Jesus may have lived under a Zarasthustrian or more openly Jewish Palestine.

Spiritual and traditional influence of Zarathustrianism on Christianity can be easily drawn, and just as easily debated. *Angra Mishnu* might have been a prototype of Satan, (Christianity's Devil). Hell might be an imitation, of the fall from the *Chinvit*, heaven the crossing of the bridge, and Purgatory the chasm below. The apocalypse (or Jehovah's Witness' predictions) may have found their basis in Zarathustra's foreseeing the prevalence of evil during 8,000 out of 12,000 years. Zarathustrianism contradicts Christianity in some ways, in their view of resting and celibacy as sins, God as either all loving or all-powerful (not both), and the violent conflict of the soul, which is a battleground of good and evil. References to Zarthustrianism can be found in Christian scriptures to the *Magi*, or *High Priests* in *Matthew*, as well as to Zarathustrian kings in the *Hebraic Old Testament*(*Chronicles, Ezra, Nehemiah, Esther, Isiah, Daniel, Haggai*, and *Zachariah*)

The influences of Zarathustrianism on Western thought, both ancient and modern, have been far-reaching. According to the scholar Joseph Gaer:

Herodotus and Plutarch among Greek historians, and Aristotle and Plato among the Greek philosophers, showed an interest in any teachings that bore the name "Zarathustra", which came to be used as an equivalent of wisdom. At one time Zarathustra and Plato were treated as belonging to the same school of philosophy (Joseph Gaer's *What the Great Religions Believe* c. 216)

Western interest in or knowledge of Zarathustrianism between Plato's era (4th century B.C.) and 18th century A.D. seems to have waned and become minimal. Then, in 1735, a young French student named Anquetil Duperron of the Oriental School in Paris learned to translate the Avestar/ Pahlavi tongues, and travelled in Persia and India, particularly focussing on Zarathustrianism. From his studies, he produced a French version of the *Zend-Avesta*, the first known modern European translation.

Duperron thrust Zarathustrianism into an increasingly literate Western culture, where scholars, theologians, historians, and writers have been poring over, interpreting, and becoming inspired by it since. During the 1880's, the renowned atheistic German philosopher Friedrich Nietzsche wrote a four-part treatise entitled *Thus Spoke Zarathustra*. Another philosopher, Carl Jung, analysed this work extensively in his work *Nietzsche's Zarathustra*. For almost three thousand years, the works, biography, and teachings of the Persian prophet Zarathustra have been reverberating through the cultures, religions, and philosophies of the world. They continue to do so.

The Stars

...And I stood there alone, leaning against a corroded iron bannister (which had endured a hell of a lot more winters than I ever would), and the party ground on into the morning, oblivious to me... and after the drinking games, the rugby songs, the ecstasy of being surrounded by, spat on, end poured upon by a team of temporarily woman-freed men... after all this: the boat-races of beer-chuggers and initiation into a strange new male subculture..., after it had all faded, and the empty kegs bounced down the stairs, the buildings began to spin, and I began to gaze at the ground at my shoes...

And then I realized; the male bonding, the brotherhood, the bear. It had all swept past me and diasporized, and left me clinging to the banks as like a patient grasping a doctor...reality and consciousness were my last salvation, yet they too neglected me...so that I finally realized my aloneness; the closing of rugby night; the ride over a chestnut-speckled hill to an alien room which constituted home.

So the buildings spur and swung, and the lights careened in frenzied blurs until I feared people walking by, and then suddenly the fears, the paranoid; the *conscience!*, my shoes: those detestable beanie loafers which scream 'prep-school: wearer extremely sheltered' began staring at ME, blaming ME for countless, repetitive abuses; for the two-hundred pounds with which they constantly dealt; for my hating them in a panicked effort to put these vengeful shoes out of my conscience, I disembarked from the wrought-iron railing and staggered toward Commonwealth Ave.

I ran.

Courtney at Fourteen

The party, which my parents took us to, was on a ship, which was of Norwegian wood and we slept at twelve. My friend Chris came along; I was repaying for many sleep overs, which I often took at age fourteen. There were Heinekens on board, and for once my Dad told me to grab a beer (not acoke!), and I felt free, and I felt good, and I remember there was a girl aboard who wouldn't stop staring at Chris and me and I leaned off the barricaded bow while she, with lassies of blondness, gazed towards us. Leaning softly against the mast; its spars, halyards, and rigging, she was making me edgy with a nervous, sexual high.

Then Chris wanted to leave the ship, and the 'rents ware deep with other fossils (as we called adults), so Chris and I walked around the floating docks as if we knew about 'life at sea' (such a cliché); as if, as Bahamians, we should have. We passed two young women chatting and smoking in the cockpit of a sailboat, which swung vertically; up and down gently (as though breathing), and came down with a quiet splash. The boat and the young women were another sea-and-sex shock very new to us.

We sat on a piling at the end of the pier and felt like two lonely kids, realizing how little we knew about the women, alcohol, and ocean life which confronted us. We were nervous and dissatisfied. Chris sent me to burn two cigarettes off of the young women in the sailboat. Anxious to face our new challenge, I set off down the dock, dressed in snappy duds and impractical penny loafers. I almost felt seasick. The scant of crisp salty air encouraged me, but made smokes seem repulsive at the sametime.

The sailboat was named *Against the Wind,* which seemed a depressing name. I approached it warily. Finally, I stood facing the pair, who looked up with curious interest.

"D-d-do you mind landing me a cigarette?" I stammered. I'd never asked for a cigarette before.

"What did you say?" The older of the young women asked.

"I think he wants to have a smoke," the younger one quietly told her. I looked at the younger woman - a girl, actually for the first time. She was beautiful; very tan.

"Can I have a cigarette for me and my friend?" I addressed the older one now. Though, she had thrown me off balance, I thought that I was finding my ground.

"How many do you want?"

"Two would be great," I replied, feeling as though my communication was slipping. Was there a dialect used to bum smokes, which I didn't know?

"Well, I only have a few left, so I can give you one," the older one replied. I was looking at the younger, as though for support. It took me a few seconds to hammer out a cursory thanks and reach for a cigarette.

Then, I stood there, cigarette in hand, looking at them both.

It was quiet. I could hear the waves hitting the hull and see Chris at the end of the pier looking at me. They were looking at me too.

"You want a light as well?" Finally, the older one spoke up. I was looking at Chris, who by now had his arms raised questioningly. Would he help me?

The woman's voice brought ma back.

"Oh… Yes. A light."

"You want one?" she queried.

"Yes please. I was struggling to regain my sensibility, to figure out how to bring the cigarette to Chris. She handed me a lighter. I started to walk away, towards Chris.

"Hey!" She called. "What are you doing?"

"Oh, I was going to bring the lighter to my friend, so he can smoke the cigarette."

I thought you had to light it right away; that it burned real fast. l was feeling frazzled and confused; out of my element. She took the lighter from my hand in an assertive, motherly manner, and held it up, burning, in front of my face. I put the cigarette to my lips and allowed her to hold the flame to it until I inhaled smoke and it was lit. Holding the finished product in my hand, 1 thanked them. The girl was smiling faintly at me; I was afraid that she was mocking me. Then I walked quickly towards Chris.

We puffed away at our only cigarette. Then we strolled to the marina's security shed. I looked at my feet, when we passed *Against the Wind*. We were sitting in the shed when, 'Oh!',the younger girl from the boat came over; without the older one. She stood silhouetted at the entrance of the shed. I expected her to ask for the security guard, who wasn't there, and then leave. But she lingered. Chris and I gawked at her. Then she spoke.

Juvenilia

"How you doin'?" She spoke American.

"Alright," I replied. She was looking at me.

"You guys live here?" She asked. She was chipping away at the awkwardness.

"Yeah, we do," Chris replied, with a Bahamian tinge.

"Oh. Do you guys know of anything to do around here? I'm pretty much by myself, and 1 haven't really gone anywhere except the straw-market." What an exciting surprise! Shocking! She was asking as what to do in Nassau! Rather than being acondescending adult, she became a girl alone in a bizarrely free nation, which pleased me even then. She had broken the dam of uneasiness that had plagued us until then. She wasn't the belittling adult that the older women had beer. I was relieved and happy. Imitating my older peers, I tried to explain the nightlife in the city as though I knew it first-hand, aggressively taking on the role of someone very familiar with the city as though to make up for my previous hesitancy with the cigarettes.

With that one sincere question, the girl, whose name, she soon told us, was Courtney, released a deluge of eager conversation, allowing Chris and I to eagerly catch make up for our fear of women, beer, and the ocean. We snuck a few Heinekens from the ship and got some cigarettes from the older woman, who turned out to be the girlfriend of Courtney's father's. She was sailing on her father's boat for a few weeks visiting the city for several days. Though her brother was with her, they did almost nothing together. She was fifteen years old. I lied to her, telling her that I was sixteen. We realized that none of us were old enough for the nightlife, and that her question had been an ice-breaking guise in order for her to talk to some of the only young people in the marina.

Eventually, my parents rounded Chris and I up to head home, I told Courtney that I would get in touch with her. The next day I bicycled ten miles to the marina after leaving unanswered telephone messages with the marina secretory. I didn't see Courtney that day, and hiked home, crestfallen. The day after that, I went out to her boat and woke her up. We talked for hours. For some reason, I told Courtney that I had a girlfriend in the city, which was only half true. Later, a sailor walking by asked us how we knew each other. Courtney replied that we were just friends. This disappointed me. Though she still had a few more days in the city, I decided it was a good time to leave return to my life at home.

It started to rain. Late in the afternoon, as the bitumen steamed what was left of the summer shower, I climbed on my bicycle prepared to say goodbye to Courtney. I was saddened by her platonic view of our relationship, which seemed to leave no ream for adventure, I told her that I hoped her sailing want well, and that she had a good time in Baltimore, Maryland, where she lived. I started to pedal away. A matronly Bahamian woman was standing nearby. Just as I was getting onto the main road, with my wheels leaving a smudge on the slick road, Courtney called out to me.

"Eric!" I slowed down, without stopping, and looked over my shoulder at her.

"Come back," she said. I smiled to myself. The old women smiled too. I slowly hiked back to where Courtney stood on the curb. Puzzled, she looked me in the eye. Eagerly, I waited for her to speak.

"I'll be here for two more days, you know. I'd like you to stop by again." I was elated! Happily, indeed singing, I bicycled sway. I called my mother and asked her for permission to spend the night at a friend's house near the marina, That night we talked more, with the beat of the marina's discotheque in the background inebriating us. The next day her last full one, we set talking for hours in the carpeted hallway of the marine apartments while outside it rained gently. In the morning, I told her that I'd never had sex. I lived at an all-boy boarding school at the turns, and eighth-graders generally never made it to the dances. Then I asked her a question that I had poured over at school for months. It was composed of all of the adult sayings I had encountered in paperback books and movies.

"Will you make wild passionate love to me tonight at the beach?" I asked. She laughed. She didn't reply. Later that day she told me that it was her 'policy' not to sleep with virgins. She had slept with two guys before, I was disappointed; I fait childish and vulnerable. We spent the afternoon in the hallway and lounging on the balcony overlooking the road when the rain stopped. At one point a friend drove by and waved, calling me my name. Then, in the hallway as it got dark, she broke and excited silence.

"What time do you want to meet tonight?" I was startled, especially at the simplicity of the question.

"I dunno...1 suppose after your family dinner or something..." I stammered. Actually, I had made no plans at all, having rejected the remote possibility of her saying yes. I still thought she was beautiful, and many days at sea in the Bahamas had made her skin a bronze tan. My mother had never allowed two sleep overs in a row, and the previous night's host could no longer put me up. We agreed to meet at the base of the bridge that led from the city to an island of many beaches. Then I raced off on my bicycle in search of somewhere to stay for the night. Somewhere within riding distance of the bridge and where 1 would not have a curfew. Another friend the guy who had passed in the car, agreed to put me up, and I convinced my mother that my bike had broken down, and I would have to stay in the city. I borrowed a condom from my friend, ate dinner at his place, and bicycled to our rendezvous spot half an hour before she arrived. She had to pay my share of the pedestrian toll, as I was broke.

We sat on the beach under the lights of a hotel, smoking cigarettes, for an hour or so until finally she suggested we go down the beach to where it was darker. An hour later we returned. Until then, I had never so much as held a girl's hand. Never kissed, never done anything else. Covered in sand, we virtually staggered into a hotel discotheque where I ran into my host and several friends. They were mostly older guys to whom 1 looked up. One of them had taken brotherly care of me during my gang-like fights at our old school, and had promised to get me 'laid' sometime. I think that my ear-to-ear grin and sandy face answered any of his questions about whether I had or not!

My time at the disco that night took on the effect of a grand initiation into the adult world with Courtney as a glaring testimony. She felt understandably uneasy and angry, refusing to dance, and threatening to leave if I did. Eventually, a friend offered to drive us home in his pick-up truck. Courtesy sat in front while I held onto my bicycle at the back. We rode over the bridge, viewing Nassau harbour and its cruise ships at night. The highest point in that bridge was the peak in Courtney's and my relationship. The marine was locked, and I had to hoist her over a tail fence so that she could get to *Against the Wind*, a truckload of my friends looked on knowingly. It must have been horrible for her. We bid goodbye. We may have even kissed through the fence. I watched her check in with the security guard; walk through the gate, and head behind the marine towards her boat in the darkness. I never saw her again.

The next morning at seven o' clock she, her brother, father and his girlfriend sat off for the Berry Islands. Then she flew home to Baltimore. I went off to camp in Maine, where I talked, thought, and wrote constantly of her, inscribing my blue jeans with the words "Courtney, June 25, 1985". In my scrapbook I have her address, which she wrote for me that night on hotel stationary. I wrote and called her often, sending her photos and my 'virginity anklet', which I had worn until June 25, 1985. She never wrote or called me back. The next year I told her that I had been fourteen, and not sixteen. She laughed in disbelief and then I think she cried. It must have been harsh on her.

From simply not returning my letters and birthday cords, Courtney went further. She told me to stop getting in touch with her, telling me that she wasn't worth it. I still thought she was. Except for birthday cards, I stopped writing to her. Then even those were returned. Updates on her slackened until friends of mine at Garrison Forrest, the school she attended, told me that she'd been in a nasty car accident in which she'd been thrown through the sunroof and was convalescing with a broker, hip or something. I sent her get-well cards. No reply. I think she changed her address. I know that she changed her phone number.

The last thing Courtney told me was that her boyfriend was throwing darts at a family photograph, which I'd sent her. At age fourteen, I'd learned something about sex and heterosexual love.

I was Killed in Mesquite, Nevada

I was killed in Mesquite, Nevada,
Crossing the road from Michael's Pizza
Where I'd eaten over-priced green pepper slices and learned that
"Michael reserved the right not to serve certain customers."
I was carrying a copy of the *Desert Chronicle*
And striding thirstily towards a 7-11 across the road
When I was hit.

I was killed in Mesquite, Nevada:
Run over by a Texas-Mexican migrant labourer
In a battered pick-up truck and the caravan that followed
(I think his kids enjoyed the bump I caused),
I was almost to the gas pumps, too;
Almost to a seventy-nine cent 'Big Gulp' of Dr. Pepper
They found me staring at a blazing neon sign, which read.
"American Automobile Association Senior Citizens Jacuzzi Special."

I was killed in Mesquite, Nevada,
With its palm trees, pools, and golf courses in the desert...
Killed before the windows of a 7-11

Through which I'd seen docile gamblers (glaringly human)   ,
With their leather-clad, bejewelled lovers glancing nervously through mascara eyes
At someone's savings sliding into a slot machine receptacle
Initiates were laughing
Terse gambling vets were drawing towards themselves
Legs of iron and gazing silently at the spinning colours.
They glanced up at my screams.

I was killed in Mesquite, Nevada,
And the Sheriffs peon hosed my blood from the bitumen,
And the "Chronicle" feasted on the tragedy
(Will they sell the rights to the networks?),
And my parents weren't called till next Tuesday
And my smiting corpse was shipped home
With a digital watch, an empty '*Grolsh*' beer bottle,
A back-pock, and a sleeping bag. No will.
Thirty-nine dollars, sixteen cents.
A fellow hitch-hiker stopped in to pay respects on his way to Vegas
After 1 was killed In Mesquite, Nevada.

The Jameson Raid in South Africa: 1895-1896

The Jameson Raid, a failed British cavalry invasion of Transvaal, Southern Africa, and a hopeless attempt to secure a revolution, is seen more as a touchstone of imperialist policy than as any fantastic military feat. The raid alone, which took place between December 29, 1895, and January 2, 1855, only furthered a rivalry between the conflicting British-African and Dutch-African governments. As a complex invasion by a British-backed force (under imperialist Cecil Rhodes} into an established Afrikaner state (under Paul Kruger), it attracted international debate. The conflict indirectly spurred European powers towards a closer revision of international policies. Disagreements over the raid helped to determine foreign allies end political stances in conflicts for decades to follow.

The irony surrounding such an influential occurrence is that the Jameson Raid was militarily little more than a skirmish in the long struggle between *Uitlanders* (foreigners or British colonists) living order the supposedly oppressive rule of Boers ('farmers'). The victorious Boers were Dutch 'Afrikaner' colonists in nineteenth century Dutch-South-Africa. Indeed, the raid did more to bring about the reserved contemplation of military action than it rushes on inevitable military conflict: the Boer War. However viewed, the Jameson Raid was both an interesting military conflict and notable for providing insight into often bureaucratic colonial strategy.

The roots of the conflict lay in an imperialistic rivalry, which, having gathered momentum since the first Europeans explored Africa's Cape of Good Hope in the fifteenth century, reached an ugly ferocity with the fight for South African gold and diamonds. Colonizing more than the Portuguese, British settlers had established themselves along the coast, of the Cape of Good Hope. With superior numbers, higher levels of productivity, and intentions more toward agrarian independence and religious freedoms, Dutch settlers began pouring into what is now South Africa. Resentment between the two groups grew, and with the Great Trek of the 1870s, the travelling 'Boers' (as Dutch farmers were called); went inland in order to escape British imperial rule. When, inevitably, British settlers also 'trekked' inland, they were seen as *Uitlanders*, or 'foreigners,' and resentment grew.

Sir Leander Starr Jameson, the eventual lender of the Jameson Raid, was born in Edinburgh, Scotland, in February 9, 1953. He studied medicine at the University College, London, and showed great potential to become a doctor. As fate would have it, poor health intervened, his health and his adventurous spirit found Jameson in South Africa by 1878. In the years following, the ambitious Jameson became involved in many imperialistic activities. After trying his luck in diamonds at

Kimberly, Jameson befriended Cecil Rhodes, a diamond magnate, and shared imperialistic furore with the powerful British-supported leader Jameson and soon found himself trying to negotiate for the undermine Chief Lebengula of the Matabele or Ndebele tribes, on behalf of Rhodes British South Africa Company.

By 1891, Jameson was being given powers in Masonaland, what is now Mozambique, and in the budding Rhodesia Colony. As Administrator of Rhodesia under Rhodes after 1891, Jameson shared these radical imperialistic views of his 'baas' (boss), which would later lead to conflict and Jameson to infamy. By the early 1890's it became evident that "the Boer government of the Transvaal Republic was the chief obstacle to Rhode's plans for the federation of all South Africa under the British. He plotted with Jameson..."

By late 1895, the *Uitlanders* were weary of peaceful and vain petitions for their better living conditions and minority rights within Kruger's Transvaal. They began to "turn to that flag (Britain's Union Jack) which waved to the north the west, and the south of them.... constitutional agitation was aid aside, arms were smuggled in, and everything was prepared for an organized rising." Since November first of that year persons in support of such on uprising like the British Colonial Secret Grey in London. Joseph Chamberlain, Sir Hercules Robinson, the Governor and High Commissioner in Cape Town, and Cecil Rhodes, Premier of the Cape, had pushed for the establishment of an *Uitlander* reform committee (notional reform union) assigned to rise against the Transvaal government. Arrangements for a rebellion and subsequent support were made.

It had been arranged that the town was to rise upon a certain night; that Pretoria should be attacked, the fort seized, and the rifles and ammunition used to arm the *Uitlanders*. (Rhodes) allowed his lieutenant. Dr Jameson, to assemble the mounted police of the Chartered Company, of which Rhodes was founder and director, to the purpose of cooperating with the rebels at Johannesburg. Meanwhile, 'Oom,' or 'Uncle' Paul

Kruger, President of the Transvaal Republic, awaited the outcome of growing tensions. An easily defeated force from the Cape would help to cover a true source of unrest.

The tension by 1895 was extreme, and many *Uitlanders* discussed rebellion. Attempts at peaceful co-existing were tried; "in 1893 a petition of thirteen thousand *Uitlanders*...A formidable list of grievances...Submitted to the Read (Boar Council), was met with contemptuous neglect. Rebellious uprising grew in appeal as tension mounted; ultimately involving the adventurous British imperialist Sir Leander Starr Jameson who, so instructed by Cecil Rhodes of Cape Colony, began to make his way towards the border of the Republic of Transvaal in late 1895.

Kruger's disputable treatment of the *Uitlanders* in 1894 rose when he temporarily imposed compulsory wartime military duty upon *Uitlanders*, prompting "a heated reaction; the *Uitlanders* in Pretoria draped his carriage with a union Jack." The set was never forgiven, and tension had grown. Petitions by *Uitlanders* for better equality had been scoffed at, and some Boers went as far as to "challenge the *Uitlanders* to come out and fight." In Johannesburg, discontented mine-owners were often threatening to rebel, and British news agencies anticipated that "disfranchised and abused miners were in spontaneous revolt against the corrupt, tyrannical Kruger regime." However, "the rising had to come first to justify the raid," and leaders on both sides knew it.

As the moments of real conflict drew near, Rhodes sent Jameson and the British South Africa Police Force to the Transvaal border, a move not un-observed by well-informed Boers. On the twenty-seventh of December 1895, a reporter wrote, "the situation is grave...At any moment an insurrection may take place, but I think they (the *Uitlanders*) underestimate the Boer strength. Moreover, the *Uitlanders* are divided amongst themselves." Urged to take military action, the calm, deliberate Kruger was not unlike Raleigh before the Armada when he said, "Before one can kills tortoise, he (the tortoise, or *Uitlanders)* must put his head out."

After weeks of impatiently patrolling the borders of the Transvaal, Jameson grew very restless. He believed that there were anxious, united Outlander rebels about to overthrow the Transvaal government and that his dream of an Africa under British imperialism from Cape Town to Cairo was perhaps about to be realised. With on undated letter a desperate appeal from Outlander women and children hoping to be liberated, Jameson prepared for the New Year and for orders from Rhodes or Chamberlain to charge into Transvaal and victory. The orders never came. The weathered Uitlanders within the Transvaal remembered their defeat in 1861 at Majuba Hill by me hands of Boer sharpshooters, a British loss where "most of the dead wars shot above the chest (and) some had as many as six bullets through their hoods."

Before confirmed reports that the uprising had been postponed could reach him, or perhaps even after receiving orders not to invade, Jameson began to move his "column left Mafeking on Sunday evening, 28^{th}December, (and) was reinforced at Pitsani the following day." By eleven o'clock on 29^{th}December, Rhodes was assured that Jameson was going ahead as planned, apparently ignorant of the impending and inevitable disaster. Before the New Year had begun, Chamberlain had sent orders, through Rhodes, to call off the raid.

There is debate as to how much Jameson knew or was told at the time of the raid; some say he acted independently, others that Rhodes misinformed and manipulated him. It is known, however, that Jameson charged into Transvaal late on29^{th}December 1895, with some five to six hundred mounted raiders. Essentially Jameson had, "with or without orders front Rhodes invaded the country with a company absurdly inadequate to the work he had in hand."

The raid, led by "Dr, Jim", was an utter failure which ended up leaving Kruger in an excellent standing; militarily and otherwise. The horsemen, negligent in cutting ail of Kruger's telegraph lines, were anticipated and ambushed by a Boer force under commando Piet Cronje. By the 2nd January 1896, the Raid had gone only as far as Krugersdorp and Oomkop on its intended 290-kilometre journey to Johannesburg. After thirty-six hours of fighting, Jameson surrendered. All surviving raiders were imprisoned. Seventeen of his men had been killed and forty-nine wounded compared to the six dead Boers. The Jameson Raid had failed.

The raid had accomplished none of what the British had roped for; it only stalled rising opinion against Kruger, brought to the Transvaal Republic the military aid of Britain's enemy Germany, and left Britain an imperial super-power, with weakened moral authority. Jameson, utterly humiliated and essentially disowned by Britain after the mishap, was released by Kruger and sentenced to a mere fifteen months imprisonment in England he only served sight on account of week health. He later returned from reclusiveness as a politician in South Africa, succeeded by J. K. Merriman as Prime Minister of the Cape. He died a single Baronet in 1917. Cecil Rhodes suffered quite a blow from the raid as the mar who sent the dog (Jameson)' Into the Transvaal.

Enough people in British imperial offices of South Africa lost positions as a result of the fiasco that the 'British State' there became known as 'lying in state'. Rhodes resigned and was eventually replaced by Alfred Milner. He later resurfaced as a political lender in the region. The prisoners captured interestingly enough represented twelve western nations; six of were Americans. Kruger was not brutal to his prisoners; the four sentenced to death (including a brother of Rhodes) were eventually freed, and die brief hardships suffered by the common prisoners under Werden Du Plessis pales in comparison to the hardships British concentration camps in Boer history. One man cut his own throat during the imprisonment, and two were held for two years. Humiliatingly ridiculous financial compensations, were demanded of the British by Kruger, and several demands reaching 25,000 pounds each for certain officers must have given the captors a degree of satisfaction.

To the Jameson Raid several long-term effects can be attributed. The global outcry was mostly directed against an 'imperialistically greedy' Britain, and away from Kruger's mistreatment of the Uitlanders. Through such occurrences, South Africa gained a place upon the European political map as an area in which European super-powers could flex muscle with removed consequences. It is amazing how much significance too little or too much has been attached by history upon this wild, brief event.

Fall Football

"…!", "…!". Your name is hurtled across a cold field; it's shriller than those of the catches. You pull yourself upward from a stance-dug wall into mother earth. A football game is raging around you. A replacement pats your helmet. You back out of the hole you'd occupied in the offensive line. The scrub fills it in bodily.

Your lags pull your upper body towards the bench and the coaches. Shouts, roars, and the sound of contact burst behind you. You sprint off the field. The coaches' eyes pass around you and into the fray. Victory is in their veins. It glistens evidently in their eyes.

The side-lines are a place for breath. Wincing, you bend forward at the hips and inhale deeply, Sweat Is allowed to trickle through your hair. It rolls down the ridge of your nose, where it chills and falls. Breath is a visible mist on the side-lines, it is a cold November afternoon.

Tired eyes slide open and focus. You can see your two knees.

"Wait, focus in on the right knee. What is it?"

A stain spreads on the moist white cloth of your uniform.

"Blood." You straighten your back quickly.

"Got to find the injury. Have to find the source, is it someone else's blood?" Glance at your calves.

"No blood." Glimpses over your forearms.

"None." Reach your left hand inside your facemask to your face and rubs it across the skin. Withdraw it.

"Blood. Plenty of blood." Yet your face is painless. You hold both hands in your eyes. The right hand has been lacerated badly. In the cold drizzle, the cut has curled on itself, turning on eerie bloodless pink.

The blood has gotten onto your fate by rubbing your nose during the game. The incision runs from the bottom of your right thumb down, to your palm, near where your watch normally is strapped, it begins to bleed again, basis of the blood dropping irregularly.

A sense of bewilderment nibbles at you. You wonder if that's why the coaches pulled you out.

"It's really alright. No lie."

The game continues. You look from your outstretched head towards the players. Then back to your hand in amazement. The cheering is feverous. The teams thrash against each one another. Your injury, as minor a flesh wound as it might be, has put the football game into a new perspective. You wipe the palm against your pants; slowly, so as to ease the pain. You set your low in a subtle grimace. The game is suddenly vastly mere significant.

Wind whistles through the ear-holes of your helmet. It tears across a crop of brown grass. The players dig their cleats into the soil like roots without flowers. They face each other. The replacement obeys a command to lean himself forward until his nose is almost muzzling the grass.

A whistle blows. Contact. Synchronised brutality. Excitement. A player limps, wincing, from the field. He'd been injured in the knee before. The medic climbs under the rope between you and the spectators. While the injured student is still out of hearing distance, the medic leans over to a parent and says:

"This is the kind of kid that makes used salesman out of doctors." The parent laughs uneasily.

The front linemen are getting tired. Its cold out there, even the benchwarmers are breathing mist. A dog lies between a man's legs. The coach eyes the side liners, mentally selecting replacements. You put on your helmet.

"The draft is coming soon," you think to yourself.

There may be a war.

A Happening Hitch

Cold, fucking cold, and I wait on the highway and nobody stops...Nobody stops.

Nobody stops...

...For a long while in the cold, and finally -yes, finally, someone a tow-truck driver stops! ...And he takes me out to where the highway leads south to Rhode Island, and I thank him (without giving him any weed) and then I catch a ride with an airplane conductor/controller dude who says he used to drive Ferraris in California but who's now whipped, with kids and a wife.

So I get dropped off at the southbound highway after leaving Boston some three hours previous, and while waiting in some goddamn three-degree weather, I get sirened down by some state trooper, but Rhode Island is the smallest state, and they are just clicking around, asking me for identification and whatnot when a drunk driver trying to show off his skylark to his ex-girlfriend hits the northbound curl and flips three times before taking out a light post all before by eyes.

As I get my ID back (but only one of them), run across the highway, and help some chick out of the wrack her shoulder is fucked up and she faints, but all is eventually cool, and I walk away...

But then the troopers call me back to give evidence, and one of 'em gives me back my selective service card, and after yelling at me for crossing the highway when they told me not to, they give me a ride to Providence.

In the car; the older cop:

"You got a home?"

Me (I'm damned tired):

"Yeah."

"Where you guys from?" Asks the five-year 'smokey'

"Boston"

"That your home?" same one.

"No." I don't care very much.

"Where's it at?"

"Bahamas." I tell him the truth

(Silence)

I start trying to figure out why the cops are suddenly silent they're probably thinking:

"Enough questions; this guy is obviously full of shit, trying to be important, trying to pull our legs and be more powerful than us."

(Silence)

They keep on thinking:

"We are state troopers! We are the next thing closest to God (the only reason we don't call ourselves God is because our mothers believe in it, and know we can't be equal with him they'd know we're full of shit.

Pensée

I - Notes from a Summer in Stockholm: Alone on the Roofs and in Cafes

A man races across the street to his car just before the policewomen can ticket him for illegal parking. Score one for humans vs. bureaucrats!

Overheard while at the 'Yo-Yo Café', Stockholm: "You must speak the language of the country. Otherwise living there is useless." Said in English

Same person (a Scotsman? from the accent): "You know, I never *really* lived here never had a *girlfriend* here." Interesting concept.

On fellow cafe-goers in Kungstrayerden: They came, they ate, they left.

Haiku:

City's populace

Chameleon river flow

Surges before me

With a friend: on the stops overlooking the park we nibble our peaches. Gentle, cool together. The fruit is unwashed, and the hands of a city enter cur mouths.

People come and go. Am I a hotel?

I just saw myself (a clone?) walk before me. Scary.

On joining the riots, cops on horses broke up a car show, youths restless from constant rains drank, throwing bottles and firecrackers in the heat ...Rainy Stockholm night on *Sveavagen* near where the Prime Minister, Olaf Palme was killed.

In U.SA and Sweden, apartments generally occupy one floor: they arc 'horizontal', yet in London there are many 'vertical'(multi-story) flats.

In Europe most towns emanate around a place, square, or centre, but in the United States, especially out West, they string out along a railway or road.

There is such a fine line between Europeans dressing to look American and Americans to lock European. Or woman to look male, males female.

Crowds pass before me with blinders around their eyes. It seems: women whose defeat you can read in their faces and men whose penises seem lodged permanently among the weeds of their brains. With smirks, they meander among each other.

I saw a man on the street curb. He was black in a predominantly white culture. He was trying to cross the road. He watched the cars speed by; following them with his head from left to right the way tennis audiences follow tennis balls. It seemed to me as though he was shaking his head at the whole scene.

II - Observations and Quirks

Advertisers are innovators. Seducers.

Ingenuity is borne of determination.

Lieutenant Colonel Kilgore, in the film 'Apocalypse Now', sat in Vietnam, declares: "I love the small of napalm in the morning." Living on Canter Street, in the wealthy Boston suburb of Newton, Mass. I note the sound of yuppies driving by in the morning.

Imagination and travel: Lands of a thousand dreams and then.

Everyplace is a memory.

Hate the pitiful. Pity the hopeful.

Questions of the future are soar, questions of the past. Do they differ?

Time nullifies the past.

Life is the defence against death. Religion a reinforcement. Or do both pursue death?

Life is the accumulation of nostalgia, against which memory can be either a defence or its antagonist.

Conformity kills. Convention chokes.

A joy and torment of life: There is always more to be done. Hence, death as completion. Death as freedom.

The bath: Body-encompassing warmth, relocation, peacefulness, and stillness. Opportunity to read or smoke. No rush. Reassurances; a sense of belonging. The shower, (cold feet} sputtering, pelting, loud, violent, rapid: American.

Juvenilia

Many despair, crying: "I'm only human." Well, you ARE human! A race thought more avoided (for better or worse?) than others. Employ your humanity.

Happiness is the balance between enjoyment and accomplishment. Yet what is one without the other?

Do pregnant women *really* go barefoot?

To the Pentagon: I would rather live a man than die a hero.

There is a human beauty in error.

Vincent sought an ideal.

Always, he sought, sought, sought.

"Is there an ideal?" he cried.

Now, read the first letter of each line to know Vincent.

Fact fails before faith, Fact without believers? A bridge without supports.

The only thing I don't procrastinate is procrastination itself.

Surmount sensationalism.

Life is full of fine lines: Fall off of them.

It is hard not to be a cynic. Very hard.

We are little bubbles waiting to be burst.

Marble theory: Each person's and animal's life is a marble rolling down a sheet of ice. Death comes when the marbles fall into little circular holes in the ice. Cities and fertile areas are merely areas of high marble concentration. There is nothing to stop any of the marbles from rolling. Some roll faster than others. None can prevent their reaching their hole in the sheet, and none know what lies beyond the hole.

An illustrative example might be a lampshade. Imagine all living things popping from the inside of a lampshade at birth and rolling down the smooth sides of the cylindrical shade towards an abyss (for humans not more than about 150 years down, for tortoise more, dragonflies less). The rim of this lampshade is like the equator of the Earth. Thus, most South Americans roll from one starting point, most Australians from another, most fish from yet another.

The holes are unpredictable and could be dug at any lime. Another image might be the bubbly foam, of a beer head or froth. The carbonated contents of the glass spill over the rim and descend downwards like marbles over ice. This concept requires imagination. It also has vastly more facets and detailed substantiations than touched on here.

It's almost enough to drive one mad this loneliness. Everything claims meaning and its interpretations/interpreters, yet it all adds up to nothing.

Life without laughter: Is that life?

Love is flatulence: Unpredictable, unpreventable, unenforceable. To love may bring regret, fear, vulnerability, and humility, yet also personal icy, self-pride, relief... They differ in that people rarely enjoy another's flatulence.

III - On the Mundane

Smile on insignificance: are humans more like ants or mice?

A look at systems of living: Is not the weekend merely a carrot on a stick before workers' eyes? Is it not just a small reward to further entrench a long-term enslavement to a life-draining work ethic? To employee and employer silks, the weekend has become like a bone thrown to a dog.

On habitation: Do not dormitories condominiums, office spaces, and parking lots represent a system of habitation and industry inextricably parallel to the system which ants and bees have devised; tiny cubicles of residence, general mass labour, frenzied industry?

On 'sitcoms' and 'soap operas' Why is it that the settings, plots and characters are so exaggerated in their gore and repugnance? Why are many of these shows sat in hospitals, fields of battle, or police stations? What is this spreading American fascination with sickness, evil, warped justice, and manipulation? Why the mind deadening commitments of audience to the flaws in immunity? It is baffling.

On chronology: The exactitude of the wristwatch and the dependent, omnipresent emphasis on time which it brings with it, are derogatory to man's independence and his respect for nature. Life for many has become a timed race; slavery under the yoke of deadliness. The worship of the wristwatch (as not many of us watch-carriers bend down to refer to them several times a day?) has limited man's basic appreciation of the Sun. We forget that there is joy and fulfilment without having to pay homage to a machine; that the sun can replace the throttle of strictly regulated time.

The Earth shall continue in her own cycle of life end teeth, of seasons and ecological systems, as it has since long before the evolution of man. Whether or not it is tracked and graphed, nature's own cycle of time shall persist. The cycles of the Earth and the Solar System are independent of man's interpretations. Man is not independent of natural cycles. By looking at his wrist rather than at the indispensable Sun for the time, man diminishes his respect for and communication with Nature.

IV Images

Imagine building an airstrip, landing planes, on the side of a hill. Imagine.

Towards Manhattan: I'm so this train and snow is piling up all over the aisle. Ploughing through cracks and my feet are freezing despite the gin and tonics, despite the Buds. Despite the lemons and waking up with two women. All these despites are making me spiteful after the Thanksgiving. Prices for this Amtrak 'Narragansett' for New York ...All this so I car crash in a youth hostel on West 24th and 7th.

I imagine William, a prep-school student during the 1800's. William becomes ill. There are few around to truly cars far or cure him. William Oise. His death is announced in assembly.

Boarding school held on to me the way a freighter might kidnap a rat.

If sharks could fly? The ultimate predators.

I was told that somewhere in Asia, women's sandals have a loop not only for the biggest toe, but for the smallest as well. What cultural ingenuity!

The beaches of Tierra del Fuego are composed of stones so smooth they resemble eggs. Imagine all that crush able fragility inviting cur feet!

On wall-written history: 'In 1616...Dirck Hartog, an. Amsterdam captain, reached the West Australian coast in his ship *Endracht* and nailed up an engraved pewter dish as proof of his visit." (Robert Hughes, *Fatal Shore*, "Chapter 3"). Fodder for imagination. Who will be the prospector to unearth this treasure, which must still be embedded in a tree on what is now Dirk Hartog Island, Western Australia?

Juvenilia

Poetry in Japanese falls vertically from the top of the page; dropping like beads of inspirational sweet; dangling like shredded curtains.

Pick up a bottle or cologne or perfume sometime. Apply some to your palm. Patter some on your face. Than fill the 'perfumed' hand with water and drink, it makes for quite an exotic taste!

The swimming start (and life?): Jump high, dive low, kick.

Genius: Mechanical stoves.

My life is less than a cell in the body of time; my generation a penny the global economy. To acknowledge this is not necessarily to submit.

Where is my point of stability? My centre of gravity?

I could roll up and down, defying gravity but I would rather live.

White straws with red stripes down their sides look pink when at a bar.

Dance is a form of seduction.

Do I dare became a thermometer? I could land your tears a number.

On circumcision (or clitoridectomy): Both of which are violent first sexual experiences still in practice. First words from doctors are explanations of sex; soon new-borns with phalluses have penises without necks.

There once was some Who? God that lived in a cloud; He told all the humans: 'No foreskins allowed!'

I wonder what in deep recess of mind the babies think; when first they're born and then they see their foreskins float in sinks.

Killing fishes. Fishing kills.

Fish: A superior race indeed; for not drinking alcohol; for not bleeding.

Whales sing. But do they write books?

Do turtles yell?

Stress imagery: Stress what is your name? Brotherhood why are you void? Shaven head on an island why are you a mere phantasm? And pain; that too. Where to, Moses? Stop. Phone call. Stop. Telegram from Africa.

On the power of words: Have you ever thought of a long, thin razor? Think about putting your thumb forcefully upon the blade until it slices through the skin end digs into the bane. It would sound like a thick, deflated balloon being punctured by a nail. Try and imagine keeping your thumb up to the bone and slowly pulling bank toward you. Think about the flesh smearing sharpened metal, hugging the blade the way monorail trains embrace the tracks at Disney world the way a lover's legs tighten around a torso.

V- On Writing

I was driven to poetry. It was not meant that I should be a poet.

A day without having written is a day misspent.

So many great thoughts have been wasted by the inability to gain the right median, adequately express them, or to gain an audience patient enough. Or simply by wars killing the thinkers. Hemingway almost got it many times.

Juvenilia

From a Setter to Shelley Evans, March 1990: Writing is no longer my life, as it has been during various productive intervals. I could create various and imaginative accuses for my feeble trickle of creative writing, my dry streambed of poetry, and my lazy replacement of reading for film watching, spontaneity, and unrecorded insights

However, as always, what counts is what is before the reader, typed out. I may load a life as worthy of chronicle as those of Gogol, Hemingway, or Ginsberg. I could travel immeasurably farther than they did, but no one would care unless I could present them with accounts or insights, which they could read and possibly respect. The fundamental goal of a writer (which makes her or his emotional and biographical quirks accessory), is to share 'it' in an original or enrapturing manner.

Ibid: Fingers loosen up around the keys of the word-processor and perhaps some honesty might transpire. Perhaps not.

VI - On Pederasty

Rolling, tossing, trying not to remember crying not to remember for remembrance's sake. Words tumble forth from writhing, bony fingers. Indians watch from the beach.

The pederast from the students' perspective: Wandering campus, just wanting to talk to someone. Anyone. To let it out. To scream. The pain always just scraps from the surface, the hurt always ready to explode…

The molester smiles on: Laughs and giggles; "Giggle giggle giggle, tee hee heee…Slap slap."

Guilt-trips, planned and heavy, are carefully laid upon the victims dispenses like loads of stone. Children going mad as a result. The pederast moves on. Children banging heads or desks, tearing from scalps, burning themselves, crying, whimpering, writing.... violently thrashing against anything;

gifts, friends, flowers, shirts, bedrooms, speakers...Whole souls driven from children by the hands of apederast, who atop them probed and found. Who stop them penetrated their souls their imaginary souls...And they were not resurrected.

VII Getting Slightly Political

Organized religion has become an often-politicalmammoth syndicate that everyone in some way 'sins' nullifies the concept of heaven and hell.

On chaos: Friedrich Nietzsche beseeched man to "organize the chaos within himself" (end, Untimely Meditations II, 1874). Mayor Richard Daley of Chicago supposedly once said that the role of police is not to prevent, but to preserve chaos. Here is the internal contrast with the external. Personal organization of chaos is most important. Daisy's view is a realistic assessment of what happens when this fails. Mr Bensinger, once a leader of the U.S. Federal Drug Administration, explained c.1989 that the best way to slacken drug trade is for more individuals to make a personal decision not to use drugs. Thus, I would attempt Nietzsche's proposal to avoid falling back on the chaotic preservation, which police provide.

The more one moves, the more one 'normalizes' counteracts change. The more one struggles for abnormality, the more she or he in truth reaffirms a sense of continuance. The Mamas and the Papas: "Nothing's quite as sure as change." ...Janis Joplin: "Freedom's just another word for nothing left to lose." Hemingway gave away many of his possessions so as not to become too attached to than (Hotchner). Hence, less left lo lose. Sounds Buddhist.

Soren Kierkegaard begins his *Eulogy on Abraham* with, "...If underlying everything there were only a will, fermenting power that writhing in dark passions produced everything, be it significant or insignificant, if a vast, never-appeased emptiness hid beneath everything, what would life be then but despair?" (*Fear and Trembling*, 1643).

Juvenilia

Well, truly; what is life but despair? Does not society create great lies employed merely to cover the void with a superficial veneer? Is that not the purpose of religion? Is that not the purpose of capitalism to make consumers believe that they cannot live without essentially useless products from acne cream to lawn mowers? Are machines not designed to need repair soon enough so as to make their purchasers depend on the producer? (They even have a name for it: manufactured obsolescence). Is not love merely a supposedly safe conviction overly advertised that matrimony will disguise the fact that we were born alone and die alone? We are told that aspirin will cure all "minor aches and pains", we believe that alcohol and drugs, that prayer and marriage, that war or peace, will cure out problems, but what do they really do but perpetuate superficial dependencies in an attempt to conceal true despair?

And, if this is the case, then is there net some value in chess has? Do we not all desire something, no matter how false or illusionary, no matter how abstract or ideal, no matter how realistic it may seem which will convince us that life is not despair? Are these lies truly not all that keep us from committing suicide?

We seek some form of divinity. We seek on answer for life, a defence against death. We seek pleasure, happiness, and fulfilment. Yet have we found it? Not even *Jesus* proved, beyond reasonable doubt, his resurrection. But does not that hope that desperate desire for something great, does that not hide the vanity of it all for us, if only for a brief time? Religious figureheads propose eternal life. They choose sin for an enemy blame sin for despair. Hitler and Pol Pot proposed genocide as a solution. Agamemnon persisted with the Trojan War, Cleon and Alkiebiedes endorsed the Pelopponesian War, and Lyndon 6. Johnson refused to give up the Vietnam conflict in order to avoid the despair of defeat. It seems universal not to acknowledge the despair, but to find constructive ways to fight or ignore it.

An analogy: The Regan Administration's supposed dealings in the Iran-Contra affair are analogous to those of 3 football captain selling off his team's jerseys to the arch-rivals so as to buy himself a car.

The U.S. government during the late 1980's focussed on a publicity campaign entitled the 'war against drugs', concerned not so much with the internal chore of educating end informing drug-addicted youths, but on cessation of the international drug trade, citing foreign importers as the problem, Television and the mess media rod a field day against this new enemy. Hence Noriega fell to an invasion force of soma 30,000 troops (after more than a week). Carlos Lehder and many others are behind bars.

Meanwhile, on the 'home front', crack became more pervasive. The drug 'ice' made its appearance (another mow to already Beleaguered impoverished communities). As Spike Lee noted, racism seemed to have increased. An ex-Klansmen was elected to office in Louisiana. Efforts to help the impoverished seem rarely to have gone beyond garish, moralistic slogans like "Just Say No". As in AIDS research and Endowment of the Fine Arts, little in the way of financial support seemed to have appeared The message which the government seemed to be sanding was this: "We don't care about the peer, but we *do* care about what they smoke!"

On accountability: Since the days of Socrates and Plato in 5th century B.C. Greece, all have been responsible for personal or moral attitudes. They still are today; ask Salman Rushdie, Malcolm X, John Read, Lea Harvey Oswald, or John Brown. Indeed, for several millenniums, persons like Antigone, Creon, Socrates, Copernicus, and Caius Marcius Coriolanus have been prosecuted or put to death for holding unpopular polemics.

Essentially, and with few exceptions the general public will hole parsers accountable for the philosophies, which they expound - be they popular or punishable. People seem to feel cheated that J. C. Salinger avoids public life and defence of his works Catcher in the Rue and Fanny and Zoe. Neither for that matter, has Alexander Solstzhenitzyn been thanked for retreating after producing such notables, biting works as Gulag Archipelago, August 1914 and his Harvard Address. The essential message is this: if a member of western culture dares to present a moral or personal attitude to an audience, she or he runs the risk of being frowned upon by democracy's fashionable majority. Retribution for this has ranged from bad press to being ostracized or even killed.

The 'polls,' or members of an open society, defend the right to hold their members accountable for their opinions. The modem media is constantly concerned with presenting to the public analyses of the attitudes of others. Hence film and literature criticisms., hence political analyses and private or public investigations, hence televisions in the U.S. Senate. While public figures like Mother Teresa (for her Altruism) and Bob Geldorff (for his live Aid donations) are commended, Nixon (for his under-handedness) and James Watt (for racist remarks) were condemned. These parties found their words and actions scrutinized, and were held responsible for them.

Modern examples are prevalent and various far accrediting black athleticism to slave-era breeding, sportscaster Jimmy 'The Greek' was banished from televised sports. T.V. Showman Geraldo Rivera, either for angering specific group or airing a sensationalist and press-starved show, supposedly suffered physical assault. Columbian judges who confront the Medelin Cartel and United States officiate who fight racism are harassed and killed (letter-bombings). These examples remind us all too constantly of the risk in modem society of stating or defending opinions.

The most important polemicists ware the pioneers, some of who lived 2400 years ago. Among these were Aristophanes, Plato, and Sophocles, and Shakespeare; each famous either for defending his own moral outlook publicly or for portraying characters forced to answer up to controversial opinions end deeds. Aristophanes, in his comedy The Clouds, depicts the Greek philosopher Socrates as a corruptor 5th century B.C.

Athenian youths. In the play Philosophy confronts Socrates Sophistry and triumphs. Socrates is brutally killed, and his school is razed by Philosophists. Within a few years, the citizens enacted Aristophanes'drama, pressuring Socrates into suicide by hemlock poison in 399 B.C. This vivid demonstration of philosophical accountability has since reverberated throughout western culture.

Other accounts of this relentless analysis (especially of unpopular thought) within western culture are numerous. William Shakespeare wrote the tragedy *Coriolanus* to snout Rome's pre-Christian ruler Casuis Marcius Coriolanus, who held a harsh opinion of common people. After betraying them, despite numerous victories on their behalf, he is killed. Sophocles, in his work *Antigone*, depicts the brutal punishment of the heroine for brooking the laws of Athenian leader Creon.

Examples of such public or personal backlash for holding and enacting one's opinions have littered western cultural, religious, and political history, Martin Luther King, Olaf Palme, Joseph Smith (Mormonism founder), Abraham Lincoln, and innumerable others have had to pay with their lives for their controversial views. Their deaths remind us that in our society all are responsible for their personal moral attitudes.

This Sea

This sea:
Oceans.
Waves.
Wrecks here too
(And bones).
Coral structured
On membranes
Of polyp dead.

This surf:
Gales, reefs,
Wind.
Victims float (then sink).
Communities
Thrive beneath
Their deepest sky.

This life:
Dolphins,
Crab.
Men drown there
(Stone)
Whales, turbot, grunts,
Crustaceans
Indifferent.

Gulf stream,
Doldrums,
Squails.
Ships drifting
(Calm).
Plankton, manta,
Man o' war
And seaweed reign.

Mollusc,
Reptile,
Squid.
Your milieu
(Not men's).
Seahorse, turtle,
Eel, why can't
I live with you?

PART IV

Travel Writing 1987 2003

(Newport, RI, 2003)

John and My Travels in Scandinavia

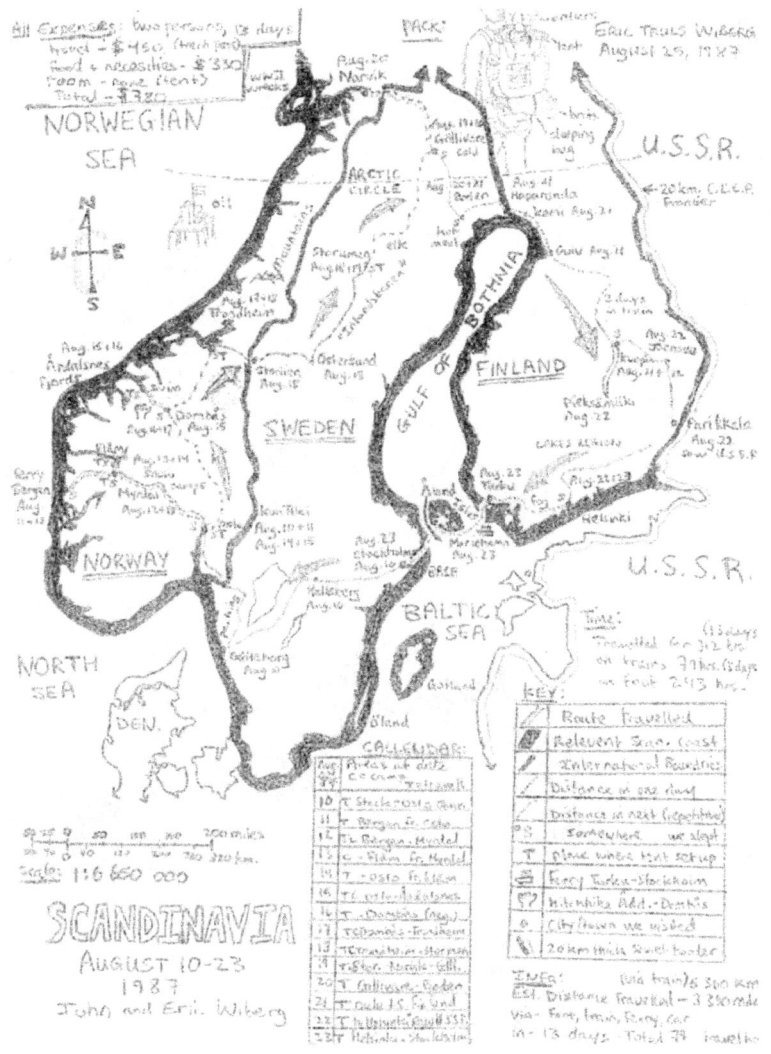

Eric Wiberg
EuroRailing Itinerary and Map

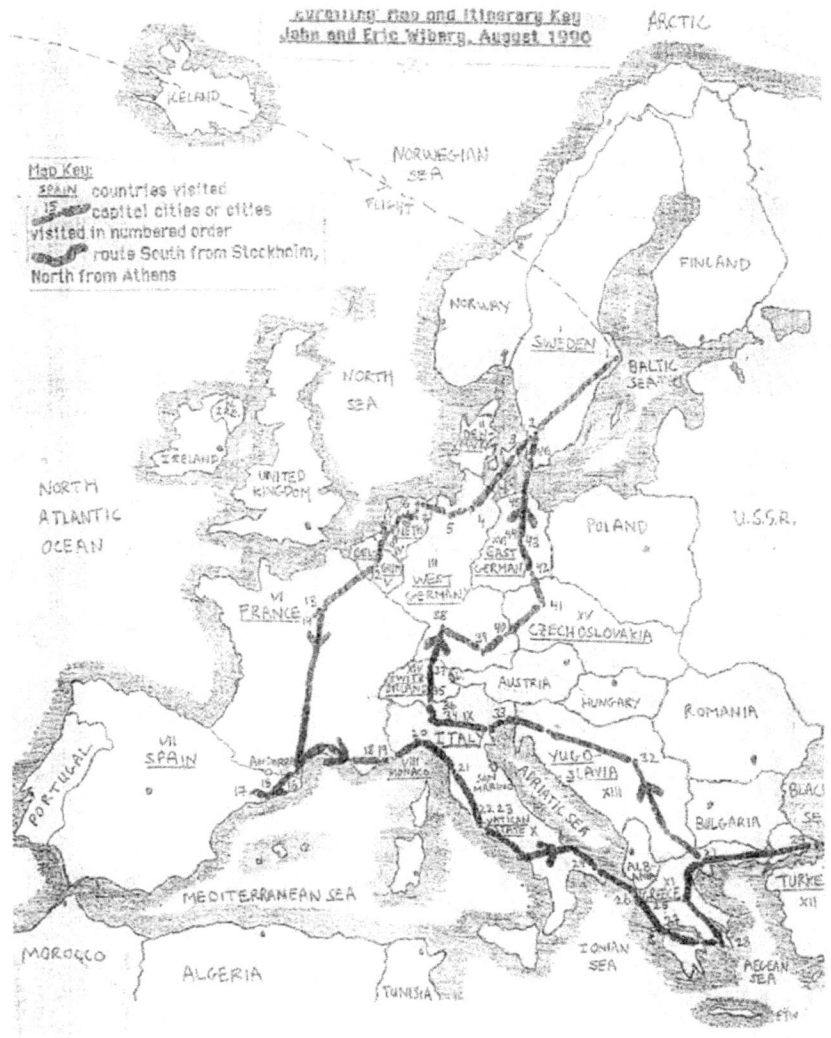

Juvenilia

A Report to our Parents on EuroRail 1990

Notes:

Days: 30

Countries: 16

Cities/destinations/stopovers: 46 (12 capital cities)

Continents: 2 (Europe and Asia)

Time zones: 3

Distance travelled: c. 8,000 miles (c.12.500 kilometres)

Backpackers:

> John (age 21) and Eric (19) August 2 to 26, Eric August 23 to 31 Tony Strano (an Australian/Italian friend) August 13 to 31

Average daily expenditure: $30 U.S. Dollars (John: $750, Eric: $900 total)

John and Eric's expenses (each) while together:

> Travel (not including $380 'Eu-rail Pass'): c.$200
>
> Food: c.$200
>
> Room/lodging (total 6 nights in bedrooms, 6 on roofs): c.$150
>
> Beer: c.$100
>
> Gifts/souvenirs: c.$50
>
> Museums, boat rides, entertainment, etc.: c.$50
>
> Itinerary Key:

IV: Roman Numerals indicate countries on map

4: numbers indicate cities on map (* signifies capital city)
Country (notes) (English name)

City visited (time/day/date arrived/departed)sites, adventures, lodging, food, notes on world events, spending, etc.

John came up with the idea for our EuroRail adventures, doing most of the research and organization (procuring American Youth Hostel Membership, for example). As well as taking dozens of fantastic photographs, he and Tony managed to put up with the sometimes-stressful Eric for the duration of our trip! Mom made extensive address lists of who to see and where, Dad somehow managed to get us both on our way from Nassau not a moment too soon, Without the invaluable trust and support of our parents (especially in Athens), our travels would have never been possible. This itinerary is a small tribute to them, the Kolffs and Grassis who hosted us, and the people John and I met during our whirlwind introductory tour of Southern and Eastern Europe.

EuroRail 1990

I - Konungariket Sverige (Sweden)

1 Stockholm* (Nassau-Miami-New York-Stockholm, Tuesday, August 1)

Stayed with our Farmer (Father's Mother) on Karlavagen in Ostermalm, visited Nordiske Museet or, Djursholm: Lappland artefacts Kungstradgarden (King's Garden): giant chess set, music.

Gamla Stan (Old Town): cobble lanes, canals, mounted cavalry. Kungenslott ('King's Home' Royal Castle) changing of the guard didn't qualify to receive interail Pass ($250 loss, 7 more countries). Met Edgar at station he works In Nassau, was visiting Swedish girl first, all-event World Equestrian Games held during our stay.

Juvenilia

2 Helsinborg (Skane, S.W. Sweden, P.M. Weds. Aug 1 to a.m. Thurs. Aug. 2)

Had our 'Eurrail Passes' unofficially validated

Met Magnus, a Swedish 'interailer' on his way to Greece

Caught ferry across Dresund Strait onto European 'continent'

Slept through a train switch had to jump off moving train at station

II Kongeriget Danmark (Denmark)

3 Kabenhavn (Copenhagen)* (pass through to Kiel, on German coast) (Aug. 2)

III Bundesreoublik Deutschland (West Germany)

4 Hamburg (p.m. Thurs. Aug. 2)

Ferry to Puttgarden from Denmark, train to Hamburg Atlanta station strolled through old town to a park along the River Elbe brewery-hopping to taste local Jever Pilsner, Dortmundar beers.

5 Bremen (p.m. Thurs. Aug. 2)

Passed through this Beck's Beer capital, Oldenburg, and we heard that President Saddam Hussein of Iraq repossessed Kuwait on this day news of the U.S./U.N. military reaction followed us all month

IV Koninkrijk der Nederlanden (The Netherlands)

6 Groningen (Thurs. Aug. 2 to Sat. Aug 4 12 nights)

Stayed with good friend Han Kolff a student of Groningen University Han's apartment is on Niewstad the legal 'Red Light' district many lively cafes, bars, and discotheques enjoyed Dutch beers suck as Oranjeboom, Grolsh, and Brand

139

spent an afternoon sailing off infamous 'Horny Place' beach 1990 is Groningen's 950th anniversary a beautiful cathedral. Han described his 3,000-strong student 'fraternity', of which his club,'Tout en Chaos' ('Everything is Chaos') is a splinter faction.

7 Olden Gaerde (p.m. Sat. Aug. 4 to Sun. Aug. 5)

In Han's car to beautiful family estate South of Groningen tennis, swims, wooden clogs, windmills general relaxation 'treasure hunters'.

8 Sneek (pronounced 'Snake') (p.m. Sat Aug. 4)

Beautiful old sailing town site then of a 1,000-sailboat race! Delightful group dinner, compliments of Mr. and Mrs. Kolff. Han's friends, brother Lukes and sailing crew joined us.

9 Amsterdam (in province of Holland)* (official capital) (p.m. Sun. Aug. 5)

Drove in from *Olden Gaerde* for restaurant dinner and cafes. Buildog Cafe, smoke-shop, and street-side fire-eaters (crowded). Missed famous Rijksmuseum and others, as it was late Sunday. At a dam on the Amstel River, Amsterdam boasts. Amstel Beer canal/harbour tour at dusk, fascinating and beautiful saw: thinnest apartment in Amsterdam (c.1.5 meters).

Tall Ship *Amsterdam* built by convicts for 'Sail Amsterdam 1990' quaint youth hostel, barges with marijuana plants, cats, and punts saw Anne Frank house, where the diarist and family hid from Nazis.

10 Rotterdam (drove through Utrecht Sun. Aug. 5 to Tues. Aug. 7)

Hosted by Han at the Kolff's lovely horns on Haflan Platz Tuesday: took a guided boat tour of the harbour the world's busiest port, at the mouth of Germany's Rhein River there are 9,090 actual ports or harbours (c. 5-10 ships each)! c. 25 kilometres of active docking: ships from all over the world.

11 Gravenhace/Die Hague (The Hague) (de facto capital) (p.m. Mon. Aug. 6)

Sadly missed Mauritshuis and museums, as they are closed Mondays picturesque old town and government/U.N. buildings we excursioned up the coast to a beach on the rough North Sea satisfying dinner at Han's and snooker at local 'Gulpener' brewery/pub grateful for the Kolffs, John and I left Rotterdam a.m. Tues. Aug. 7.

V Royaume de Belgious-Koninkrijk Belgie (Belgium)

12 Bruxelles (Brussels)* (a.m. Tues. Aug. 7)

Passed through after Antwerpen, on way through Quevy to Paris train took us through Franco-Prussian, WWI, and WWII battle sites failed to get in touch with Ceebs Hartman or Gina Arahna of Brussels.

VI Republique Francaise (France)

13 Paris* (Gare du Nord station, p.m., Tues. Aug. 7)

St. Michel Notre Dame on the River Siene cafe and baguettes our first 'roughing it' night (though we'd backpacked Scandinavia before): attempts to call Parisian friends failed Lauren was in Australia! Supergas da la jeunesse (youth hostels) filled up were left homeless wandered to the Tour Eiffel (Eiffel Tower) at dusk with backpacks we ended up sleeping on the Champ d' Mars listening to guitar music gazing up at spectacularly lit Eiffel Tower, and drinking Bohemian rum.

14 Versailles (a.m. Weds Aug 8)

Toured the Palace of Versailles, fantastic Baroque estate designed for King Luis XIV by Louis Le Vau and Jules Hardouin-Mansart (1669-1685).

Hall of Mirrors, Garden Front, Andre Le Notre's extensive Gardens. Paris again for the Luxembourg Gardens,

Arc de Triomphe. Avenue des Champs-Elysees, and view from the top of the Eiffel Tower (1887-1889).Visited the timeless Louvre Museum: 'Nike of Semothrace' (3rd century B.C.), and foundations of original Louvre fortress and palace.

Were able to see the works of Delacroix, Jean Antoine Gros (*Napoleon at Arcole*), Jan Van Huysum, and Gericault (*Raft of the Medusa*).The works of Impressionists are displayed at the Muses d'Orsay. Saw Leonardo Da Vinci's Renaissance painting *Mona Lisa*from c.1505.We relaxed at the Piramides, rinsing our feet and sharing a smoke. Bought a bottle of French wine, several baguettes (three francs each) boarded the night train for Barcelona from Gore d'Austerlitz passed Orleans, Toulouse (Henri Lautro's home), and Perpignan.

VII Espana (Spain)

15 Barcelona (were in vicinity a.m. Thurs Aug. 9 to p.m. Sat. Aug. 11)

Drank with several Austrian mountaineers on the southbound train. Skirted Andorra, crossed the Pyrennes Mountains into Catalunya. Were delayed while switching railway tracks in Port-Bou, on border met Swedish backpackers, Erik and Ulrich, in station on Thurs. p.m. Sought vacancies in youth hostels (Alberg da Juventad) none the four of us headed North along Costa Brava to find place to stay.

16 Calelia (stopped there on John's advice) (p.m. Aug. 9 to a.m. Fri. Aug. 10)

First to rent a pension apartment with beds, patio, kitchen, and bath. We enjoyed a case of San Miguel beer, a hot meal, and discos all night. Met up with a group of Spaniards who knew families in the Bahamas Friday morning relaxed on the beach; very lenient dress codes there. Metro into Barcelona's station where our sister had been robbed the four of us secured beds at Alberg Mare de Montserrat. Shared a six-man room with Khalim of Morocco and Miko of Japan. Socialised over a hostel dinner with other backpackers. Saw an over-a-cliff car accident while walking to a bar in town. Eventually c.15 backpackers representing every continent but Antarctica (New Zealanders, Africans, Americans) assembled in our room on Saturday made a walking tour of Barcelona with Miko, Erik, Ulrich.

El Quadrat d'Or (Golden Square); a centre of Modernist architecture, especially the works of Cataluniyan Antoni Gaudl.

La Pedrera and *Le Familia Sagrada* original 'melting' wall texture enjoyed a delicious and inexpensive lunch of squid, beef and wine.

17 Les Planes (P M. Sat. Aug 11)

Took a train West, over mountains to the village of Les Planes.

We enjoyed drinks in a quaint cafe and inspiring hiking in the hills. Took gondola and hiked to a monastery on a peak above Barcelona. Bid "adios" to our new friends before night train to Nice, France. Overtaken by the high-speed luxury train "Tango'" in Port-Bou.

France (our second visit)

18 Nice (a.m., Sun. Aug. 12)

Took train through Aries (Van Gogh setting), Marseille (site of a huge forest fire a few days later), past Avignon, Cannes, and St. Tropez.

Woke in Nice very early, bought a baguette, walked to the Blue Beach on the Mediterranean's beautiful Cote d'Azur, and swam.

Aired out our clothes and relaxed, watching the Sunday rooming rustle to life of backpackers on the beach, sailboats, and elderly citizens. Met English backpackers Yvonne, Miriam,

Sera, and Claire Robbery while on our way to the station from the beach. Sara, Claire, John, and I were suddenly surrounded by half a dozen noisy children who shoved newspapers in our faces. Confused, we pushed them away. A few yards down the road, several French couples started yelling at us. We spread the word "thieves!" My (Eric's) wallet had been heisted, and John's camera bag had been gone through. I chased after and confronted the children, but couldn't field my wallet. To my embarrassment, they (ages 6-10) were stripping to prove they didn't have it.

While searching for the thief who got away, I came across the same group in the process of robbing some German backpackers. To my relief, John was able to find the actual culprit and grab the wallet from her while I was gone it held my license, but all of our traveller's cheques, passports, and tickets were safely around our waists and inside shirts. Later, in Athens, I was able to return John's favour when I found his camera in its bag on the steps of the Lozanni Hostel.

A little shaken, we boarded a night train and secured a cabin.

VIII Monaco* (second smallest sovereign state besides the Vatican)

19 Monte-Carlo (p.m. Sun. Aug. 12)

During a relaxing sunset we passed through the cliff-nestled city, home of yachts, tax-free estates, black-tie casinos, and expatriates.

IX Repubblica Italiana (Italy)

20 Genova (Genoa) (p.m. Sun. Aug 12)

Passed through Columbus's homeport.

21 Pisa (a.m. Mon. Aug. 13)

Juvenilia

Too dark to see Leaning Tower on Italian Riviera.

22 Roma (Rome)- (early a.m. to late p.m. Mon., Aug 13)

Shamefully we only allotted ourselves one day in 'La Roma', though we made an extraordinary dawn-to-dusk walk throughout Rome.

Rome terminal to the Colosseum we toured the battleground of Gladiators and killing ground of Christians was the home of 4,000+ cats! Through the Arch of Constantine (4th century S.C.) to the forum ruins.

X State della Citto del Vaticano (Vatican State)

23 Vatican City (a.m., Mon. Aug 13)

Bascilica San Pistro (St. Peter's Cathedral), designed by Carlo Maderno and Gian Berniniin 1657. Represents Italian Renaissance statue of Michelangelo hand damaged encased within. Had to rent a German backpacker's long pants in order to get in!

Sistine Chapel, with Michealangelo's *The Creation of Adam, The Fall of Adam*, and *The Last Judgement* calling frescoes (1608 to1512) from the Vatican Museum, we walked back into Tome along the Tiber River passing a tremendous mausoleum and watching the Pantheon rested on the Spanish Steps and absorbed the atmosphere of Rome. Tossed Lire into a fountain, which guaranteed our return. Walked past the Tomb of the Unknown Soldier and Medici Palace. Saw a Rubens Exhibit and Ancient Roman artefacts at a museum. Missed meeting Swedish Ambassador Ulquist he was away. Rome Termini after restocking our food "Ciao" to Sera and Claire. Met Tony Strano, who is fluent in Italian and was heading our way.

24 Brindisi (SE coast of Italy) (a.m. to p.m. Tues. Aug 14)

Night train through southern Italy via Napoli and Bari drank wine. Spent all day in Brindisi plastic-strewn beach on

Adriatic Sea. Dinner at Golden Egg restaurant with half Swede/Italian Franco saw Magnus again (met him on train to Hamburg) ashe left Greece. Expensive ferry ticket and port taxes for ship to Korfu, Greece. Ferry ride on the open deck c. 10 p.m. to 5 a.m.

XI Eiltniki Dimokratia (Greece)

25 Kerkura (Corfu) (passed Albania - troubled nation) (a.m. Weds. Aug. 15)

Ancient city on island site of first naval battle (565 B.C.)

26 Aegis Gorgios (Weds. Aug. 15 to Sat. Aug. 18)

Stayed at Pink Palace resort; met Betina from Porto Alegre, Brazil just missed Colin Born, a friend who worked there and had waited discotheque with two meals daily, cheap bar, plates broken over heads, open veranda on beach, hundreds of English-speaking backpackers, volleyball, swimming, hiking, touchstone for EuroRailers. 'George' proprietor expensive and time eating moped incident with Nine and Fiona (we got lost, ran out of gas, split up, slept on beach, straggled back late a.m.) reminded of Lawrence Durrell's book on Cyprus Bitter Lemons.

27 Patras (p.m. Sat. Aug. 18 to a.m. Sun. Aug. 19)

Arrived after daylong boiling ferry ride with Betina and friend called Aunt Westy in D.C., got supplies, souvlaki, slept in station.

28 Athens* (a.m. Sun. Aug. 19 to p.m. Weds Aug. 22)

Train along Peloponnesian coast, through Corinth, across deep canal for c.$5. At night we had space on the roof of the Lozanni Hostel. Began our wait for money to arrive Korfu had done in our budget. Though city was terribly polluted, cheap food and beer, hot sun formed a group with Californian designer John, Irish robbery victim. Jim, Brazilian traveller Zaca,

Napolitan Fernanfo, an loyal Tony purchased some ropes for knot practice and sandals in old market. Toured the city extensively on foot: Olympic Stadium (Athens longed to host the hundredth anniversary Olympic Games), Ancient Agora.

Acropolis The Parthenon (designed by Ictinus and Callicrates 448 B.C.), The Erchtheum, Propylee, Temple of Athena Mike, Areopagus (roots of freedom of speech where Paul the Apostle spoke we saw demonstration)

Weds. Aug. 22: After delays and expensive calls, our money arrived! On Amonia Square, we ran into Rachel Moore, Ian Dalcimer, and Tom Burr from Lyford Cay/Nassau; they'd been on the islands coincidence! Visited Turkish Embassy with Tony and Zeca to inquire about visas Having seen John end Fernando off to Florence, Jim off to London, and Zeca to Turkey, Tony, John, and I made a fundamental change in out plans.

No more ferries or overcrowded Islands. Rather, Eastern Europe. We boarded the 'midnight express' from Athens to Istanbul, Turkey.

p.m. Thurs. Aug 22: Bought food in border town of Alexandropolous.

XII Turkiue Cumburiveti (Republic of Turkey)

29 Istanbul (once Constantinople home to Byzantine, Roman, and Ottoman Empires; Ataturk new hero) (early a.m. to late p.m. Fri. Aug. 24)

EuroRail Passes invalid; we bribed conductor, evading him in Istanbul early morning began walking tour, visited Bazaar, where we bought beautiful fez caps, vests, necklaces, earrings inexpensively, lost photo book toured Mosque of Hagia Sofia (built by Anthemius of Trailes and Isidorus of Miletus, 532-37 A.D.), Blue Mosque, and Mosque of Ahmed. I witnessed and heard noon 'Salat' (Islamic prayers) at Blue Mosque visited the Archaeological Museum bust and sarcophagus of Alexander the Great, conqueror of Persia after 327 B C.; other artefacts.

Hosted for delicious apple tea and conversation by carpet merchant. Saw a young man hit by a car and whisked away quietly and quickly.

30 Haydarpasa (on Asian continent different time zone, p.m. Fri, Aug. 24)

Ventured by ferry across the Bosporus Straits to Haydarpasa, led by Turkish acquaintance Serkan of Kayseri toured a yacht club, saw Black Sea, Sea of Marmara, and Istanbul by night people friendly and warm missed last train West: John had deadline for college, so we followed the train in a cab, racing through police barricades and over hills we made it, rewarding Serkan with a bottle of Bahamian 'Kalik' beer!

Greece (once more, this time passing through on our way North)

31 Thessaloniki (in Macedonia important province) (Sat. Aug. 25)

Heavy rains delayed two clays' worth of trains from Athens; crowds

XIII Socialisticka Federatiyna Republika Jugoslavija (Yugoslavia)

32 Beograd (Belgrade)* (p.m. Sun. Aug 26)

Train ride from Thessaloniki to Belgrade spent on floor of train in aisle with Germans, Swiss, Austrians, and Gypsies we drank Greek Ouzo and listened to the Grateful Dead with Thilos and friends (avoided paying). North of Skopje a truck with two trailers careened off a highway and through some woods before grazing our train and halting us for hours. In Belgrade we rested, meeting young and old Americans Marshal Tito a public idol still, after resisting Soviets since 1948 civil conflict, meanwhile, was breaking out in Kosovo Province p.m.

Sun. Aug 26 we made our way through Zagreb for Venice, Italy

Italy (upon return, we headed towards John's new school in Switzerland)

33 Venezia (Venice) (Mon. Aug, 27)

Celebrated my 20th birthday with Pilsner Urquell on way to Venice bedecked in Turkish clothes, and unshaven after three or more days in trains, we were thoroughly searched by Italian border Inspectors.

Showered and dressed up, we toured Venice on foot, Tony interpreting. Ran into Dion, a South African whom we'd met in Barcelona's Hostel visited a Dali exhibit; John bought me a gift shirt with Dali painting relaxed at Piazza San Marco. Toured St. Mark's Basilica, begun 1063 separated by water taxis a mad rush for train to Milano watched the famous 'Orient Express', which Mom and Dad had taken.

34 Milano (Milan) (Mon. Aug. 27 to Tues. Aug. 28)

After train through Verona (setting for Shakespeare's *Romeo end Juliet*), we arrived in Milano Centrale too late for dinner with Franchesca Grassi and family, residents of Nassau and Milan slept in station.

Tuesday was treated to warm reception, delicious lunch, at Grassi's Milan Cathedral, begun 1386, and fantastic Mussolini-era station.

XIV Suizzera Schweiz (Switzerland)

35 Lugano (p.m. Tues. Aug. 28 to a.m. Weds. Aug. 29)

John settled in at Franklin College for year saw Dara Ceratelli there. Gorgeous classic-mountain setting with Lago d'Luganc below. After tour of town, Giovanni Grass) (Franchesca's cousin) met us.

36 Como, Italy (friend Giovanni's home-town) (p.m. Tues. Aug 28)

In his British Rover, Giovanni took us to dinner at a quiet restaurant after a splendid meal; we toured old Como, in which are preserved ancient Roman fortifications, historic churches, opera houses, and homes. We toured the famous resort Villa d'Este or. Lago d'Corno. Late Tuesday we returned to Lugano to say goodbye and part Giovanni returned to Como, John remained in Lugano and Tony and I waited for a 3 a.m. train North to Munich, heeded back to Stockholm.

33 Stuttgart (a.m. Weds Aug. 29)

We tried contacting Swedish, friend Erik Ringvist in Heidelberg no go an American transport plane bound for Iraq crashed nearby; 13 killed.

39 München (Munich) (p.m. Weds, Aug. 23)

Spoke with, but were unable to see. Uncle Stefan Wahlquist reluctantly we decided to head East to Prague after a short stay.

40 Nürmberg (p.m. Weds. Aug. 29)

Passed through site of Longfellow poems and post-WWII war trials.

XV Ceskoslovenska Socialisticka Repubika (Czechoslovakia)

41 Praha (Prague)* (p.m., Weds. Aug. 29 to p.m. Thurs. Aug. 30)

On train to Prague drank Bohemian beer (16 oz. $50!) arrived late met army recruits (en officer, a dog-trainer) from Bratislava who gave us bullets end army cigarettes in exchange for a EuroRail map.

Were offered rooms in houses for $3-5, stayed in college of Franklin Roosevelt in Holesvice, across the Vltava River, for c.$3 my first bedroom since Barcelona, more than two weeks earlier!

Thursday a.m. made walking tour of historic Prague many book stores Wenceslas Square, site of the Prague Spring uprisings in 1968; overturned Soviet tank and famous statue of Wenceslas, (1361-1419), king of Germany, the Holy Roman Empire, and (later) of Bohemia.

Solidarity posters flew everywhere in the home city of President Vaclav Havel, Alexander Dubcek, and author Milan Kundera a city alive enjoyed a four-course meal in one of Prague's finest hotels: c.$5 each! Found a stolen wallet and passport above a toilet turned them in bought posters of Vavtav Havel, trinkets, food, ticket to Berlin.

XVI Deutsche Demokratische Repubiik (DDR) (East Germany)

42 Dresden (p.m. Thurs. Aug. 30)

Passing through from Prague was firebombed by Allies in WWII. Refugee camp along the Elbe River on the Czech border, white tents.

43 East Berlin* (cities essentially together by then) (p.m. Thurs. Aug. 30)

Bus through East Berlin; many buildings large and clean, others not.

44 West Berlin (less grimy, more fashionable) (p.m. Aug 30 to p.m. Aug 31}

Took metro to Zoologischer Garten, walked to Kurfurstendamm. Ended up sleeping on the steps of a friend of Tony's on Shluter Strasse.

Wrote sign: "Wir nicht Strafbar" ("We are not criminals") for residents.

Early a.m. Fri: began the day at a cafe, made an extensive walking tour of the cities, past Braitscheid Church to the Victory Column on Bismark Strasse and down to the Brandenburg Gate and the infamous 'Meuer' (Wall).

Merchants sold inexpensive, surplus uniforms, badges and art books Remnants of Allied occupation and segregation of the city till 1990.

At the Brandenburg Gate some protestors fasted and others completed a Paris-to-Berlin bicycle ride for peace as we watched energetic aura!

Strolled around in East Berlin, witnessing a historic signing for the reunification Germany made by both leaders near Alexander Platz.

We followed the Wall to Potsdamer Platz and Checkpoint Charlie (past where Adolf Hitler died in his bunker); great void clearings near the Wall we chipped and hammered at the newly defunct Wall, taking pieces walked far to find *Godenkstatte Plotzensee*, where many German prisoners of conscience were brutally killed before and during WII. Returned to Western Center Kurfurstendamm to see bitter Pink Floyd music film *The Wall*, which was powerfully pertinent in setting of Berlin returned to the station late in the evening and decided, despite the histories' vibrancy of Berlin in 1950, that we should head to Stockholm bearded a train for Whittenberge, then Hamburg, but at the last minute I saw a 'Whittenberge' southwest of Berlin on a map; we panicked.

With our packs on, we jumped off the train as it was pulling away; kicked door shut (so train wouldn't stop), and conductors applauded us!

Waited five hours in dreary Litchenberg station, East Berlin, for train to Sweden; young skinheads with knives racially harassed some travellers.

45 Sassnitz (rest on costly train to Baltic via Stralsund) (a.m. Sat. Sept, 1)

Sweden (in many ways a relief to return)

46 Malmo (Farmer's home area; southern Swedish coast) (a.m. Sat. Sept. 1)

Switch from ferry to intercity train to Stockholm through Lund, where Dad attended University, on the last valid day of my EuroRail Pass.

Stockholm (stayed with Farmer) (p.m. Sat. Sept. 1 to a.m. Tues. Sept. 4)

Intercity train to Stockholm on last valid day of my EuroRail Pass. Tony and I developed films, ate well, and saw Stockholm before he stayed with World Cup Soccer friend Jakob on Mon. Sept. 3. He intends to travel back to Melbourne, Australia, via Bangkok, Thailand, 1990/1991.

I was able to see Hansi Dantruth and was treated to dinner by Andreas Ade (a friend who had coincidentally been on our flight from New York!).

I flew back to Boston College via New York on Tuesday, September fourth. Before boarding the plane, I was forced to give up the bullets which Czech soldiers had given me. After

Eric Wiberg

John and I had weathered and savoured such a wonderfully intense month of travel together, it was difficult to leave Europe, and as difficult to adequately thank those who helped us.

Sailboat *Chebec*'s Atlantic Crossing May 10 July 1, 1991

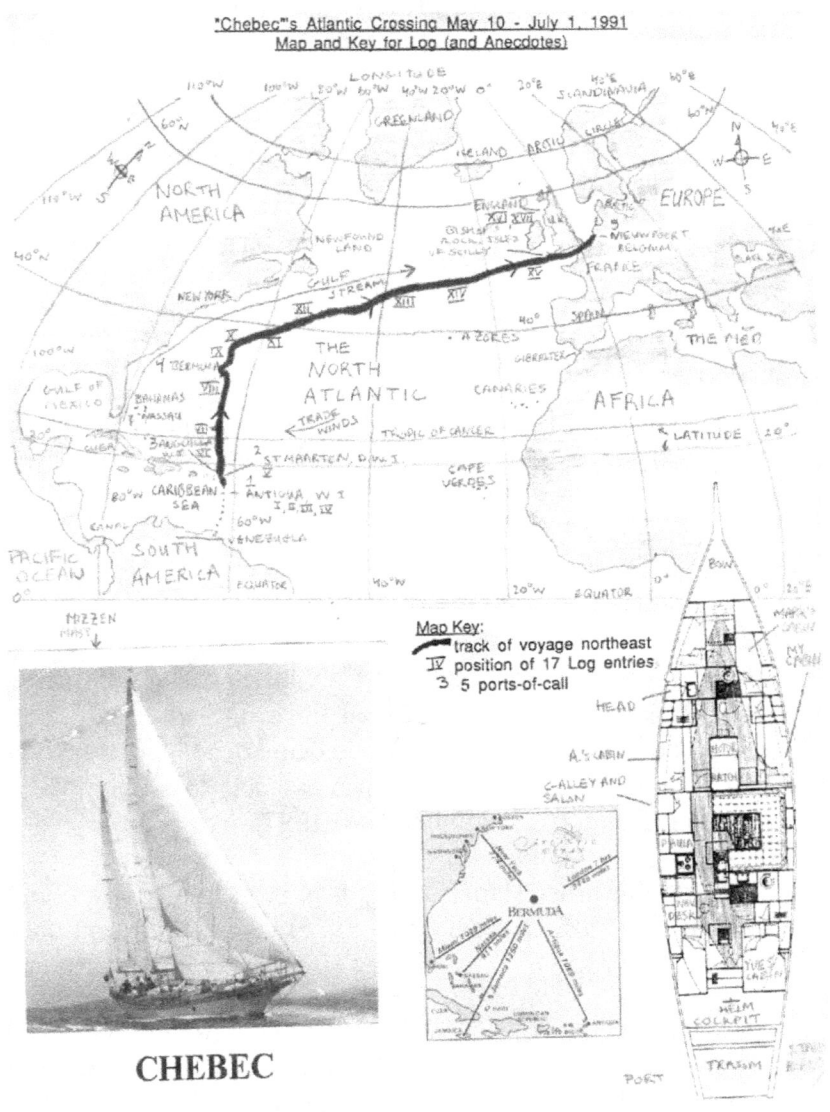

CHEBEC

Juvenilia
Map and Key for Log (and Anecdotes)

1) English Harbour, Antigua, West Indies: May10-16 (entries I-IV)
2) Philipsburg, St. Maarten, Dutch West Indies: May 16-19 (entry V)
3) Road Bay, Anguilla, West Indies: May 19-21 (entries VI-VII)
4) St. George's, Bermuda: May 27-June 6 (entries VII-X)
5) Nieuwpoort. Belgium: June 27-July 1 (entries XI-XVII, written in England)

The Statistics:

4.000+ nautical miles sailed. South to North 35 lines of Latitude: 2,000 nautical miles. West to East 30 lines of Longitude, 3,000 nautical miles and S time zones. 3 layovers, 5 ports, 7 weeks, 30+ days at sea, 100+ watches each (200+ hours at th9 helm: singing, fearing, smoking, working, reading...).

The Crew (in order of appearance):

Yves Henault, Nieuwpoort, Belgium Captain of *Chebec* Captain Splash (kitten), Antigua passenger, entire crossing Loco (Alexi), Cumanao, Venezuela crew/Mate, Antigua to St. Maarten Eric Wiberg, Nassau, Bahamas First Mate, entire crossing Patra, Amsterdam, Netherlands crew, Antigua to St. Maarten Grazie, Milano, Italy passenger, Antigua to St. Maarten Mark Aitken, Titirangi, New Zealand crew, entire crossing A., English Harbour, Antigua crew, entire crossing Paula, Antigua passenger, entire crossing.

Sailboats:

Ulysses, Colt International, and *Juana* Antigua.
Kermit and *Rock n' Roll II* Antigua and St. Maarten
Stormy Weather Antigua, Bermuda, (England later)
Loophole Antigua, St. Maarten, Anguilla, and Bermuda

The Crossing: We must sail and not drift nor lie at anchor. The Log (and Anecdotes):

ENTRY 1: DATE: Friday, 10 May, 1991, 19:32

POSITION: Airborne between Miami, Florida, and Antigua, West Indies (a free flight which I earned for giving up my seat on a flight months earlier)

WEATHER: sunset reddish and bright the first I've seen: In months!

ENTRY: Here ends a major phase. Here begins another. Vested with ambitious hope; riddled with answerless-ness. Bahamas below; just saw our home in Nassau pass under our starboard (right-side) wing. Flying to Antigua tonight. Alone. Nowhere definite to sleep. Finished my Oceanography final exam this morning in Boston. Sold some text books for cash. End of Sophomore Year.

Going solo. Looking to crew as far offshore as soon as possible. Looking to sail. Sail for the next four months.

ENTRY II: DATE: Saturday, 11 May dawn

POSITION: Aboard *Colt International*, moored in Falmouth Harbour, Antigua

WEATHER: Sunrise clear and warm. Getting hot.

ENTRY: Rose alone from the forward cabin, brewed up a coffee, and sit here on deck savouring coffee and a smoke. Day one. Gorgeous. Surrounded by hills. A harbour full of sailboats is becoming visible in the rising sun.

Discovered Bill Biewanga on the flight last night; he's done three Whitbread races around the world. We had drinks ashore I posted my resume (*Curriculum Vitae*). Bill will put me up until I find a boat sailing out. It's good to be back on board *Colt*. Good to be here. Boston behind me for over a year. Great relief. End stress. Start sun. Start sailing again. When Bill gets up I'll go ashore and "hit the docks" looking for a boat. Will there be any berths left?

ENTRY Ill: DATE: Sunday, 12 May 15:45

POSITION: Aboard *Chebec*, tied Nelson's Dockyard, English Harbour, Antigua

WEATHER: Winds 10-15 knots South/S.West

ENTRY: I spent most of yesterday, my first day, hitting the docks. I must have asked 50-70 boats for work, called some on the VHF radio, and left resumes everywhere. Found out who had left about everyone I knew. David, (who spent last season in the Bahamas), sailed for Falmouth, England before sunset. I fallowed them to the harbour entrance in the dinghy.

Another boat (which I swam out to) took on its last crew and weighed another anchor for Newport. They were offering $50 U.S. a day. This weekend nearly a hundred poets headed out stragglers of the Race Week fleet. Neal, Bear, and Mike…they've all left.

In the evening, I hit the Galley Bar, on Nelson's Dockyard (where admiral Nelson and fleet were based). A New Englander named Pete brought me a beer. Then Otto (Finnish skipper of *Rock n' Roll 2*) directed me to "Eve", a Belgian friend in his thirties, on one of the bigger boats, named *Chebec*. I asked for Yves and heard "come aboard!" Off with the shoes hat, and beer, and up the gangplank I went. His back was to me, his face in the shadows. A group of men were gathered round him He looked like Brando playing Kurtz in the film *Apocalypse Now*.

Yves: "Yes?" Me: *"Do you want help going across?"* Pause. "Yes. Welcome." Disbelief. Someone else: "Good boat good skipper. You're lucky." Pause. To Yves: *"I have five thousand miles experience."* "I've known fools with a hundred thousand miles. Welcome. Where is your beer? Have a Polar." I drank the cheap Venezuelan beer, dizzy with excitement *"Where to?"* "Belgium." *"How?"* "Direct." *"When?"* "Two days. When I get money." *"Who with?"* "Me, you, Loco, and Captain Splash." Fear. *"Aren't you the skipper?"* "This is *Kapitan Splatz*." My new skipper held up a kitten and smiled. "You're welcome. Move your gear aboard tomorrow." I did.

ENTRY IV: DATE: Tuesday, 14 May 08:00

POSITION: Aboard *Chebec*, English Harbour, Antigua

WEATHER: Calm, warm and humid, pace is slow and languid

ENTRY: Comfortably settled in on *Chebec*, though now it is only going to be Yves and I going across. I have had to weigh my options. While we were in a bar at Falmouth Harbour, 'Loco' (whose real name is Alexi), received an offer to be First Mate aboard *Pegasus* on a good monthly wage. He is a poor Venezuelan in his mid-twenties. He has worked hard on boats in the Caribbean for several years. The offer was too good for him to turn down.

We tracked down Yves in another bar, and they sat down over a drink and discussed his situation in Spanish, which vie all speak. Yves had in a way adopted Alexi, and was hoping to show him Europe. But he knows Venezuela, and how important a wage is to Alexi. Alexi will send his mother and family most of the money. Though sad, he let him go. Alexi will rendezvous with *Pegasus* in St. Maarten.

Sailing life is so tenuous. There are sailors here who have been living on the docks for months, and others who never stop and are paid highly. In a moment, plans change. Some pack it in and return to land. Fish out of water.

A young Englishman (who crewed aboard *Chebec* from Antigua to Venezuela and back Yves' only charter so far), scurries around the harbours on a tiny collapsible bicycle, which is splashed with paint. A local girl told me that he had arrived almost a year ago with a large sum of money. In that time, she told me, she had not known him to change his white T-shirt or wear shoes.

He spent so little, she told me, that the man who cleans up broken bottles for tips at the Galley Bar gave him money for food. He told me one afternoon that he had a seat on a British Airways flight back to London that night. I asked him what he would do, as many don't leave. His greatest concern was how to get the bicycle on the bus to St. John's and on the plane.

Most have sailing life seep into their bloodstream forever. These two harbours in Antigua are the Mecca of sailors from all over the world in the spring. The charter season ends, and the yachts congregate here to celebrate the end of the winter season with Antigua Race Week; many sailing races and even more drinking. Then they silently pack up their gear, gain and drop crew and hangers-on, hoist sail, and go off in every direction.

The American boats tend to head North to Newport and New England for a summer of chartering and cruising; many call in at Bermuda. The European beats (like *Chebec*) make for ports in Europe Gibraltar and the Mediterranean, Portugal, France, England, or the Baltic, calling in at Bermuda or the Azores on the way. Then, in November, (after the hurricane season), they sally forth again, heading back to the Caribbean. From Gibraltar many head back to Barbados and up through the Leeward Islands via the Canaries or Cape Verde Islands. A triangle sailing route has evolved: heading from one charter season to another. *Stormy Weather*, (a classic 1936 yawl which we crossed in league with), has averaged more than two crossings a year for more than a decade.

Drumbeat lost someone overboard East of Bermuda. Most of the casualties never make the press. They come with the territory, which is the boundless sea. I'm a rookie at this, and three people have been killed in passages of mine. The world often doesn't understand. Press coverage might bring regulatory attempts, imposed by people who don't know the sea from their elbow (like Congressman Silvio O. Conte, a Boston College graduate...).

One doesn't tell all in the sailing world at least not to those outside of it. I'm trying not to tell all; to 'spill the beans'. A. shall remain A., Yves Yves... There's only so much one can say when probing the sensitive nerve of sailing life. For many, it becomes religion. For many life. Some sailors still wear gold earrings, either for rounding the Capes (Horn, Good Hope), or to pay King Neptune at the gates of Atlantis. The more 'yachty' might wear red trousers for crossing 'the pond': the Atlantic. I don't own a pair.

One cannot know all in sailing, experience speaks for itself. I once heard a 'salty' skipper describe a sailor who claimed to know it all have all the answers. The skipper described him in a word: "scary". He didn't trust him as far as he could throw him (which I'm sure would be far!). The more one lives on the oceans, it seems, the greater one's respect for them. The greater the fear. The stronger the addiction. There is reason why many wives have tried to keep their husbands from the sea. (Nowadays there are husbands trying to keep their wives away! There are many distinguished women sailors, record holders and professionals: A. Davidson, C. Francis, N. Milnes-Walker, K. Cortee, F. Arthaud, N. James, T. Edwards, T. Aebi...)

Life around these boats becomes for the most part idyllic; free from pretensions, crammed with sunshine, sailing, and exotic stories. Communal bodies of people intermingle; bonded not my nationality, race, religion, or gender, but by a real sense of living. It is a community of the sea; one, which has whittled down lo these last few bastions; one, which nurtures itself; one whose members nurture each other. They revel to no end when the going is good (during peak season), and settle down in the off-season. In Antigua Summer is off-season. Those that remain are stragglers, dropouts, or just taking their time. We stick together; when one is low on money or cigarettes, the others share. They've 'been there', and know what it's like.

Juvenilia

People's fronts, which may work in New York or Paris, are seen through in minutes here. A smooth-talking drug dealer from New York, who carried a suitcase full of hard drugs, was found out within hours of arrival. The law is relatively low-key in the sailing community, but v/hen it strikes ii does so with a bite. One can bend some rules, but should adhere to the almost sacred, unwritten laws of the sailing world. Breaking laws like carrying illegal substances brings disgrace to, and anger from, sailors.

The police may make a round of the yachts looking for illegal foreign workers. A friend was captured with a dozen other non-Antiguan day-workers painting a boat. They spent the night in jail, but their captors, unsure what to do, let them free. Occasionally the police might follow a skipper's request to remove reluctant crew. Other offences are more serious. You don't want to have drugs on a boat, which are easily impounded; the skipper arrested. With picks and fire-axes police or Coast Guard will tear a boat to shreds looking for drugs, it's always best to keep boats 'clean'.

Most sailors live relatively simply, working and drinking in their own world. There are two general groups of sailors, cruisers and racers. The very good are both. That happens less; with new boat designs (tiny racers, heavy cruisers). There are the professionals who crew racing boats or skipper boats on deliveries. The larger, high-budget boats have professional crews. Some of them joke that there are two helms; one tor skipper, and one for the owner (which is disconnected, they joke). Many good owners are also apt sailors. Others that may not sail should be thanked for their patronage.

Others, like Yves, are willing to give the young and willing a chance with no real wage In my case, it's not that I don't work Loco and I have been, busting our backs making *Chebec* shipshape; clean and in working order it's that I am being paid nothing. But the adventure and the living expenses make it worth it when earning initial mileage. I need to get to Europe anyway; for school and to meet up with *War Baby* in July. In two months, I should save some $2,000 U.S.; for free travel, room and board. When Yves goes hungry, I go hungry. People are always there to pitch something in.

On Sunday evening, we hiked to the top of Shirley Heights, across the harbour, for a local tradition. Drinks from the morning onward, and at sunset one of the most beautiful views in the Caribbean. From Shirley Heights, you can see Guadeloupe and Montserrat, and, (facing inland), much of Antigua. An unforgettable evening, with live Calypso music wafting across the harbour.

Loco's departure was quite a blow to Yves, and will alter our plans. Yves and I will have to take to boat across ourselves. *Chebec* is a 19.5-meter (85-faot) ketch, sporting two masts, a full set of sails (English - Ratsey and Lapthorn), fibreglass hull, spacious 4-meter beam, and 2.4-meter craft. The first of a dozen French custom graph *Chebec* designs, her teak deck was Said in Taiwan, and her instruments (Brookes and Gatehouse) in England. *Chebec* weighs some 35 tons, is powered by a Gardner engine, and registered to St. John's, Antigua.

Yves and his boat are strong and seaworthy. They are a good pair. *Chebec* has survived some 16 Atlantic crossings, and Yves almost as many; as skipper or Mate. His previous crew said that he let them sail the boat, and I knew when not to. It is a very large, heavy boat with sails that have to be handled entirely by hand, hanking them on clip by clip. Unlike other, high-budget yachts, *Chebec* lacks roller-furling sails, an EPIRB (Emergency Position Indicating Radio Beacon), and her SatNav (Satellite Navigation System) fluctuates.

Her decks are full teak and strikingly beautiful when clean. Like her undersides, (which had accumulated inches of algae, weed, and creatures in the course of months a- berth), the deck was in a sad state when I boarded. My first images were of a large steel wrench, which had rusted its shadow onto the deck near the windlass at *Chebec*'s distinct bowsprit. It never rested there again. The hose, which pumps salt water from a fixture on deck, had lain in the sun for months, it seemed. Its plastic coating has melted neat concentric circles onto *Chebec*'s exquisite deck. The forward running lights were skeletons of rusted wire and nuts. On Yves' orders we drilled new ones on.

The inflatable dinghy was in a sad state; it dangled off the bow half submerged. I rowed it over to marina and scraped the muck off of its underside, bailed it out, and inflated it. The cockpit and its lockers were a study in contrasts: shoes which guests had left months before, cigarette ash and beer caps littering its sole (grating), children's toys intermingled with varnish, brushes, and halyards. An unused outboard engine, full scuba gear, (I tried this underwater, only to learn from a dive professional that it is dangerously outdated and I thought it was my lungs!) Propane tanks for the stove we have enough of, which was good. They should last almost all the way to Europe. As with pumping the bilge, changing the propane tanks is done manually in the often wet-cockpit two miserable chores.

Basically, *Chebec* is well fitted; it is just a question of sorting and finding its tools. The previous owner, who sold it last November, had obviously been a meticulous and precautious skipper. I enjoyed the challenge, which *Chebec* presented me. I enjoyed the leeway I was given, and, for a while, I enjoyed bringing the crew together to get her going. Normally you would need at least four crew to sail it effectively, (though sailors race boats its size single-handed around the world some nonstop!)

I think on this heavily it is a tremendous responsibility. I don't envision money coming of this, I do envision Yves and I entering a European port after more than a month at sea, direct. It is too much to resist. We wandered to the patio of a bar after Loco decided to leave and sat there long after closing. Yves is worried about the turn of events, I looked him squarely at said: *"I'm with you. I'm with you all the way."* I think he's hoping to pick up crew along the way I know that he wants a woman aboard. Yves' money came through from Europe yesterday Provisions in St. Maarten are cheap, and we may find more crew there.

On Mother's Day I called home and told my mother that I was going to cross the Atlantic virtually single-handed. The last time I tried that, i ended up on her doorstep three weeks later, in the middle of the night; bleeding and barefoot. We sail for St. Maarten tomorrow.

ENTRY V: DATE: Friday, 17 May 01:00

POSITION: *Chebec*, moored off Philipsburg, St. Maarten, Dutch West Indies

WEATHER: Gusty; winds at 20-30 South/S. East, 25 % chance of rain

ENTRY: What a voyage! 16 hours from English Harbour, Antigua to Philipsburg, St. Maarten: we set sail just after midnight on Thursday, arriving at 18:00 that evening. Passed E. of Nevis and St. Kitt's, W. of Barbuda and St. Bart's. A good voyage of about 100 nautical miles; brisk winds of 20-30 knots, gusting to 40. (One nautical mile is equal to about 1.2 statute, or land, miles. A knot is a nautical mile per hour.) Steady following seas; the boat held up beautifully.

I am now First Mate of *Chebec*; the second-in-command. The crew has shifted considerably since I signed on earlier this week. There were nine of us, including Splash the cat, during our first voyage. Loco has left. Mark, a New Zealander, in his early twenties, showed up on *Chebec* in Antigua looking for a berth back to London after backpacking in South America. He is fit and smart, and has sailed in the South Pacific. We welcomed him. The day he walked aboard I went with him to the shack he rented from a woman on Falmouth Harbour. He stuffed his goods into his backpack, we moved it aboard, and by afternoon we were working on the running lights. We gave two women lifts to St. Maarten; "Grazie", a photographer from Milano, and Patra, Yves' friend from Amsterdam.

Getting out of Antigua was rather more 'political' than I would have liked. We took on fuel, water, and provisions and

Juvenilia

anchored in English Harbour. In the afternoon Yves went ashore while a diver cleaned our underside. After sundown the wind picked up, and our anchor began to drag. On radio and in dinghy we tried to hail the skipper, to no avail. In danger of wrecking ashore, we lashed to a smaller catamaran. Close to midnight the catamaran's skipper threatened to cur us loose rather than wash ashore.

Desperate, though unsure enough of myself to start the engine (which Mark was stilt repairing), I went ashore to find Yves. His Mends, worried for us after hearing Loco calling on the radio (*Ulysses, Ulysses, Chebec*), pointed him cut. He was sitting along the harbour outside the bar, surrounded by talkative sailors and locals. A dramatic scene was unfolding. I nervously noticed that A. (the bottle-cleaning Antiguan) was prancing about holding my passport and all the ship's papers.

Yves was arguing with the bar manager about taking care of the girl, named Paula, who apparently was debating whether or not to come with us. She had few legal papers and little money. I told Yves our situation. He said not to worry; that the wind wasn't strong enough for *Chebec* to drag anchor, and that he would return shortly. Partly relieved and partly in despair, I returned, hoisted the dinghy on deck, and waited for our captain

With moments to spare, Yves returned to *Chebec* with an entourage of well wishers in dinghies. Songs were sung, farewells said, the anchor and sails hoisted, and off we set. Yves had convinced the two Antiguan employees of the Galley Bar; Paula and A., to join us on our voyage across the Atlantic. We all bid Antigua a poignant farewell under the midnight moon. Yves set a course due North West and receded below, not to be seen again until before we made St. Maarten I pulled night-watch with Loco while the others rested, then trimmed sail for a dawn squall. Patra and I plotted the course at the navigation station.

Yes, Yves lets you sail his boat.

ENTRY VI: DATE: Tuesday, 21, May 10:40

Eric Wiberg

POSITION: Road Bay, Anguilla, West Indies (Anguilla means 'serpent')

WEATHER: Winds 10-15 knots, gusts to 25, seas choppy outside bay, rain

ENTRY: Arrived 18:00 Sunday 19 May less than half an hour ahead of *Loophole*, which sailed with us from St. Maarten. Her crew, including Pete and padre, (a Santa-Klaus-bearded Englishman on his way around the world under sail are good company. Together we provisioned cur boats with water, filled our diving tanks with air, and cleared customs. *Loophole's* skipper is friends with Yves, and they have made a change or plans. Shall set off for Bermuda later today.

Road Bay is the place of locals, and sailors during their stay are locals in their own right. We dropped anchor in the glassy bay within an hour of sunset it was clearly visible in twenty feet of water. Mark and I swam ashore, evading the gaze of customs agents anchored farther out. The sun set in our faces as we basked in the sound of a local 'jump-up' reggae band.

A pack of Marlboro cigarettes go for $1 U.S. here. I made $4 by diving up and selling more than a hundred feet of anchor rods (chain) in St. Maarten. I sold it to a South African, who will try to survive hurricane season alone on his boat. He needs it more than I. I have few financial problems as I have hardly any money. Yves does not pay his crew; we all receive room and board and a free crossing *Loophole* caught two large tuna sailing here, and A. prepared one of them for us. Tasted great.

I have my own spacious cabin, forward of our comfortable salon, (where Paula sleeps), it is intended for charter guests, fitted with lockers, a bookshelf, two bunks, access to the head (or toilet), and a hatch leading to the foredeck. Mark is in the forepeak cabin, A. in the Port (left) side cabin, and Yves in the skipper's cabin at the stern of the boat, within access of the cockpit. We gain the deck (through the galley and salon), through

Juvenilia

the main companionway at midships. Sails are kept on deck before the mast, with the fenders. Most of the ropes and gear are stowed in lazarettos, (lockers), in the cockpit. The large transom at the stern end of *Chebec* holds our gangplank, the cat's litter-box, our fishing gear, and the inflatable dinghy. We fly the Antiguan ensign from a stay (wire supporting the Mizzen mast).

We four sailors hold six hours of watch alone per day. I relieve Mark at 06:00, give the helm to Yves at 08:00 (often later, as he navigates and calls on the radio), and then take it from 14:00 to 16:00, and after dinner from 22:00 to midnight (the 'graveyard watch'). We are forever on call, however, and often a day's work far exceeds six hours. Dishes are to be done, the boat cleaned, the sails set and altered... Even at anchor in this idyllic bay, we spent the windy night fending off an abandoned cargo ship alongside,

ENTRY VII: DATE: Friday, 24 May 09:35

POSITION: Longitude 62 degrees West, Latitude 23 depress North about halfway between Anguilla and Bermuda. A voyage of c. 1,000 miles.

WEATHER: Kicking up a good 20-25 knot winds S./S.W., following seas

ENTRY: On starboard tack, heading 15-20 N.N.E., Departed Sandy Island, Anguilla, for Bermuda 16:00 Tuesday, 21 May. The five of us (Yves, A., Mark, diving on the reef: "Sea you in, Bermuda!" Arranged hailing times on Single Side Band (SSB) radio. When possible, these radio calls became an formative end fun contact, sometimes as often as twice e day.

We 'bumped' lightly a few times before weaving outside the coral. Squall meanwhile brewing. We are averaging 150 nautical miles a day: have covered 500 of the 650 nautical miles on the Rhumb Line (an imaginary straight line connecting them), of which we are keeping 'above' (upwind).

Getting into the blustery Trade Winds from the East. Finally, out at sea again! Bluewater sailing! Offshore at last!

ENTRY VIII: DATE: Monday, 27 May 10:00

POSITION: Several miles due East of St. David's Light, Bermuda

WEATHER: Placid, windless, calm, humid

ENTRY: We missed Bermuda! We finally have St David's Light within sight. Spirits high after hitting a low this morning. We were due to have sighted land by dawn, after nearly a week at sea. SatNav is down; we are relying on ships for positions. Hailed *Baygone* bound for Puerto Rico at 03:00 Tues., *Vinashi* bound from New Zealand to Belgium (which made Yves and Mark happy) 15:00 Weds., British Warship bound for Virgin Islands 04:00 Thurs., and freighter *Saray* abound for Nassau (home!) at 12:00. We keep our eyes peeled closely for ships, and Yves rewards us with cigarettes for spotting one. Spend warm days on deck reading, listening to music...

Am tracking our progress on my chart. Crossed the path of last summer's failed crossing attempt twice. Bad omen. By dawn we figured we'd missed Bermuda altogether. *Loophole*'s crew by new hangover and asleep in St. George's Harbour. I stayed up all night; A. and Paula alert as their first real passage nears its end. Seas flat cairn. Under power. Failed to hail an aeroplane overhead I was on the bowsprit, and Yves on the radio. Bermuda Radio told us all to be sure to be at work on time.

At 08:00 Yves altered course to W.S.W. A wise decision. An eerie arc in our wake for only distant whales to observe. A was devastated when we told him we were missing Bermuda and heading straight for England. Bad joke. Food getting lower. Excitement on Mark and my watch when Tiger Shark hit against Port bow. I ran along railing towards bow while he grabbed for his camera. Lost hold momentarily when shark whacked against the Starboard quarter beneath my feet, it was a real fright, though

Mark almost took some great photos of me being eaten alive by a shark to send home!

Captain Splash adds wonderful merriment to our strangely comical screw-up. As Yves predicted, she smelled land long before we saw it. She went into a frenzy of excitement, circling the boat in seconds and chasing me around the deck, much to Mark's displeasure, who was asleep below us. Paula's shorts, which hang from a stanchion, serve as a lively plaything for Splash. Who could worry with her frisking about? Shortly after we altered our course, a white Bermuda Longtail Dove circled our mast and then led us directly to land past Kitchen Shoals and towards St. George's. Now I help Yves guide us ashore, having transited Bermuda six times under sail. We are nervously excited, and toothbrushes and combs surface after days of misuse.

ENTRY IX: DATE: Sunday, 9 June 23:00

POSITION: Lat. 37° N., Long. 62° W c.300 miles North of Bermuda

ENTRY: We only just narrowly avoided a collision with a Bulgarian merchant ship, which passed less than a mile from our Port side. In general, as with the crew of the Soviet ship *Ivan Kiriev* (who spoke with us at length), relations with merchant vessels remain congenial. Since our arrival in Bermuda on May 27, and in particular on the first segment of this leg of the voyage, morale has not been at its highest among *Chebec*'s crew.

We lingered at both moorings and docks in St. George's Bermuda for ten days, until our departure at 20:00 on Thursday 6 June. They say that ships and crews rot in port. Even in our arrival we were detained. The first thing we read in Customs was a sign reading: "Any information on , lost overboard from *Drumbeat* May, between Tortola and the Azores, please contact ". Encouraging, (it was not the first such notice I'd read, though normally they find the body.) Discrepancies involving Paula's passport (and Captain Splash' right to go ashore) left both confined to quarantine aboard.

Captain Splash earned her name once over when she slid out of her tether and splashed into the harbour. I was called through my hatch to save her. Later Mark and I had the honour of selecting for her the most ivory sand we could find in Horseshoe Bay. I felt warmly received on my return to Bermuda. Less than a year has passed since I sailed from St. George's. Little had changed. I was able to procure odd day-jobs in order to afford the basic amenities such as Bourbon Cream Biscuits.

I had the fortune to meet Stephanie, a scientist at the Bermuda biological Station. Within an hour of our arrival from Anguilla (where she has lived) I helped to rescue she and her moped from the harbour. While on the phone home, I watched her swerve to avoid a group of tourists and ride directly into the harbour! Fortunately, she was unhurt, so I finished my conversation, hung up, and walked over to see if I could help, ignoring the frantic tourists, we used *Chebec*'s gear to tie a rope around the moped and dive up her keys. Then Stephanie hosted those who helped in a harbour side pub. From then on. she treated *Chebec*'s crew with utmost kindness, lavishing upon us luxuries such as ice, biscuits, hot food, and good company. She also showed us showers and washing machines. A very special person.

Captain Dick Murphie was especially considerate; upon our departure. he gave me a package "not to be opened until the second watch after the $2,000^{th}$ mile from Bermuda". (I followed his instructions, and was heavily rewarded by my favourite Bourbon Creams. I could afford to indulge in one after each watch from then on. On really bad days I ate two and hot buttered rum!)

The days in Bermuda were strained by finance, deadlines, and chores, but lightened by Stephanie and our sailing brethren. Paul brought *Stormy Weather* alongside us, and would play the accordion at sunset. He picked up a talkative Californian as crew (who later tried to strangle Paul, and was 'put down' by the rest of the crew). The day *Stormy* sailed for France, Yves, Paul, and both crews had a final lunch together. Someone stole

Paul's last cigarette before he set off. Then they climbed aboard, motored up the harbour, pointed out of its mouth, and hoisted sail. An elegant sailboat, *Stormy Weather*. I don't think they used the engine again till France.

(We were supposed to catch up with Paul in Brittany France. On certain mornings during the crossing we would hear him translating French weather reports into English. Unbeknownst to us, Paul really did take *Stormy* from Bermuda up into the ice-packs of Newfoundland on his way to Francs. The purpose was none other than to chip ice from a berg for his Gin and Tonic. This he and his all bearded crew actually did! I saw him later on the Solent in England. From what I heard, he ended this year's Fastnet Race in recurring pain from an air crash injury (he earned R.A.F.'s highest honour). Along with Warren Brown, skipper of several *War Baby*s, Paul is one of the most experienced, renowned sailors in the North Atlantic, I wish him well.)

There was, of course, lots of socializing and new gossip in Bermuda. Too much. Tempers flared, backs were bitten... Bermuda Harbour Radio called for the First Mate of *Chebec*, which made me cringe. They drilled me on safety equipment, *Chebec*'s particulars, etc. Apparently, we had slipped through their bureaucratic net and they wanted 'the scoop.' I hardly gave it to them, though they were congenial enough. Someone asked me if *Chebec* was my 'yacht.' No, it's not mine, and no, it's not a 'yacht'. *Chebec* is a sailboat. I help to sail her.

Various people pushed their way aboard and dropped their life-stories on our laps, which at times was obtrusive of them. An Australian woman offered to film us into an advertisement for Bermuda for $500 U.S., which never came through. Though she wanted *Chebec* above all others. I'm not sure we were 'clean cut' enough. Over the phone I learned that Manchester College, Oxford, had accepted me to 'read' there, starting in October. Most people would not believe it when Yves told them; especially the British, who didn't seem to want to. Our ragged looks evoke both arrogance and envy.

The four days since our departure have been very trying. On a stormy evening we pushed off with *Loophole* from St. George's. *Loophole*'s first Mate caught his jacket on *Chebec* while pushing off from quarantine dock and was stuck with us. We gave him back, which is just as well he spent 14 weeks at Cambridge. To the entertainment of us all, Mark performed the Kiwi All Black rugby team's Maori war dance in full volume on the foredeck.

After a final beer together (a dozen or more of us, including the customs man!}, we blew our horns, saw Pete moon us, put on our running lights, and headed for the channel. At the entrance, the two skippers addressed each other like true gentlemen, as though entering a door. C., *Loophole*'s skipper bid Yves to take *Chebec* through first: "After you; beauty before age!". Yves responded with "No. I insist. Age before beauty!" *Loophole* went through first. They were our last words shared in person.

Few times in my life have I been so profoundly moved. Scared might be the word. I'd left that harbour for Portugal the previous summer and never made it. Sombrely, I tied up our ensign, dug up the harnesses, and tried to prepare for at least three weeks of very trying, very true, sailing. It has proved a gruelling voyage. Within hours we were separated by *Loophole* (we never saw her again). We pushed northwards, beating against heavy wind and seas, to catch the Gulf Stream.

ENTRY X: DATE: Monday, 10 June 21:06

POSITION: Latitude 38° N Longitude 61° W.

ENTRY: Today is the glorious celebration not only of Yves' 35th Birthday, but of *Loophole*'s skipper's, C. Rasmussen, begun exactly a decade earlier. I made the cockpit by my watch at 06:00 only to find that I was not needed. The autopilot had been activated, the engine purred, the sun shone, and sea spread before us as flat as the pancakes upon which we feasted tor breakfast. By that time, we had polished off at least one bottle of Gosling's

Black Seal rum, and were savouring Mark's infamous Gin and Tang's. We even had a few beers stashed in the cooler. It has surely been a sumptuous day.

We exchanged happy birthdays and verbal flirtations with the mixed crew of *Loophole* who ware by then well on their way to Horta in the Azores. (*Loophole* is a 48-foot Swan racing boat, *Chebec* a cruising boat. Based in the tax-free Channel Islands, *Loophole*'s tender is named *Deduction*, which should tell you something!) In the afternoon Mark and I hung a hammock from the forestay to the mast and served Yves drinks in it. He wore a massive sombrero and enjoyed seeing Mark and I wiping the varnish down with fresh water, which was therapeutic.

Towards sunset we gathered around Yves (we are all a decade or so his junior), while he sewed the damaged Spinnaker and staysail. We rummaged through Yves' books. I queried him for explanations of French *L'estrange Voyage de Donald Crowhurst,* while Mark, A., and Paula learnt and practiced Spanish from the books that Padre of *Loophole* had left aboard. For dinner, we supped on roast lamb with mint sauce, potatoes, and vegetables, finished with fresh fruit, and celebrated with a bottle of champagne. Though we had only a few Polar beers, we were true to our motto "Let's get Polarized!" (Yves' birthday proved to be the calm before the storm: never again did that crew have it so good.)

ENTRY X^I: DATE: Saturday, 15 June 05:00

POSITION: Lat. c.42° N., Long, c.46° W (lying on my bunk in my cabin)

WEATHER: Entry explains itself

ENTRY: 1,120 n. miles N./N.E of Bermuda, 1,900 miles from Bishop Rock. Scilly Islands. England our next point of land. We are presently running downwind aboard *Chebec* under bare poles, with only the Yankee and Mizzen sails up. We are making 8-12 knots; sometimes all 35 tons surf down the waves at 15-17 knots! The wind is blowing a steady 40 knots, with gusts as high as 60. The seas are blown in sheets of spray against us. On the illustrated guide to the 11 stages of the Beaufort Scale, we are experiencing the worst: Force 10-11. Yves reports that they were blowing to 67 and beyond earlier this morning. This is hurricane force wind.

We are making very good speed east on a course between 80 and 95 degrees, which is good. This storm has been building up for more than two days. We are now in the North Atlantic, crossing the Gulf Stream. The water is cold and grey. There are still 4 active crew Yves, A., Mark, and myself. Paula is understandably queasy, and Captain Splash doesn't know what to make of it. Her litter box has been washed overboard. Seas are 20-30 feet, curling over behind our transom. Awnings ripped. Genoa blown, as is the Spinnaker and stays'l.

The second time the crew holding the Genoa sail blew, the crack of noise followed by clapping sail was so violent that everyone was woken. (It first blew at 15;00, 24 May, and was 'repaired' in Bermuda at great expense.) The second time, I was on watch, at 07:00, 9 June. We were making good speed in a brisk wind of 30+ knots, which was too much for such a light sail. (I think it was a Number 1). Neither Yves nor I wanted to stop a good thing, however, and at the slightest alteration of angle to the wind (I was confessedly struggling to light a hand-rolled cigarette) it tore at the clew, where the sheets are attached. The sail shredded, and made a tremendous noise. The boat slackened speed noticeably.

I put us on auto helm and replaced it with the sturdy little Yankee sail, which is the only sail to survey the voyage undamaged. Our conspicuous may well starve. (A few years ago they found a starved man off the Azores who had spent one month alive, one dead drifting on his way from Bermuda to the Azores on a heavy, steel boat.) Meanwhile, all goes well. Eric.

ENTRY XII: DATE: Sunday, June 16   21:00 GMT (Greenwich Mean Time)

Juvenilia

POSITION: Lat. 44:15° N., Long. 39:50° W. on *Chebec* headed for Bishop's Rock

ENTRY: Today has to have been one of the shit days of the voyage. I'm afraid, after 1 1/2 months and 2,500 miles. During my shift from 6-8 a.m. Yves and I discovered that we had: blown the Main halyard; the sail was whipping on deck, not lashed blown (torn) the stays'l.

Torn the teeth out of the mizzen boom and a main preventer block and destroyed (flayed) the awnings and the covers for the varnished rails.

So far we have blown the Spinnaker twice, the genoa twice, torn the Mizzen sail at spreaders and head, and torn the hanks out of the stays'l.

One morning, after dawn, Yves and I lowered the remaining sail to do repairs, I at the helm, Yves on the foredeck. Kneeling on the deck at the bow of the boat, he asked me to bring her up to windward so that he could lower a sail. I brought *Chebec* directly into the wind and was absolutely shocked to discover how huge the seas actually were. Going downwind (as we had been), we almost seemed to drift. Facing the wind, our huge boat was left half out of the water for whole seconds before literally smacking down in the trough of a swell. It was like crossing a reef in surging breakers in a Boston Whaler (small motorboat).

The boat has been under a lot of strain, especially during the last few days, with a full gale blowing. Boat-speed during the gale ranged from 8 to 13 knots apparent (not considering the 2-3 knot Gulf Stream current). Waves are 25-35 feet in height huge coasters down which we surf. Rogue waves fill our cockpit, tear away our garbage, mangle our transom, and put us ankle and knee-deep in swirling cold North Atlantic seas.

Today I put in more than eight hours at the helm. I am constantly called on deck. I clamber desperately through the hatch above my bunk, from which I can see the sails. On a moment's notice I toss on my jacket and foul-weather oilskins, pop the hatch open, clamber over my books, seal it shut, and shimmy on my butt (like a crab) along the deck to the cockpit.

Worn safety harness once changing sails on the bowsprit in pitch dark and heavy seas, clinging half submerged to doused sails. (Took them 45 minutes to find Jim in the Bermuda Race. He was comatose. He lived. Lucky.) Otherwise it is too much bother. It oughtn't be, as we take the helm for two-hour spells entirely alone. Many a time do I rest with a knot in my stomach. Many a time must I lay down for ten minutes in full gear, thinking about the coming hours on watch.

In the storm we must put our full body weight on the helm, hoping that *Chebec* doesn't breach (turn towards the waves and roll ever often fatal). Shoulders ache. Hands swollen. We didn't expect the cold. A. wears paper bags on head, hands, and feet. Foul-weather gear hardly ever comes off, as it is so cold. Certainly my feet have remained clad consistently for more than a week.

I have an infection festering on my left foot from a scratch in Anguilla, but have not braved a look at it. Too c-c-c-cold to take off boots and socks. (C., of *Loophole*, had warned me of it in Bermuda. I should have listened. Finally, the night we arrived in Belgium, I attacked it with my Swiss-army knife and needle; a Zippo lighter and liquor for disinfectant, I won't tell you what I found, but it stopped festering, and only left a scar.)

Often it is a problem to reuse your replacement and control the boat at the same time. We must really rely on each other to remain fit and sane. A. carries a knife with him on watch. He says it is to cut away the lifeboat for himself if and when we roll over, pitch-pole (bow under), or suffer a knockdown a consoling thought. I severed our fishing line when the boat turned around up to windward and bade like a cat biting its tail. I had been talking with Yves in his cabin, steering with my foot. The truth is, if we go overboard, chances are that the boat will go over.

Juvenilia

ENTRY XIII: DATE: Sunday, 23 June 16:50 GMT

POSITION: Lat. c.48° N,, Long. c.12° W.

ENTRY: We are about 300 nautical miles S.W. of Bishop Rock, which is c.350 n. miles from cur final destination; Nieuwpoort, Belgium. ETA June 27. I am still very pleased to be at sea, to be sailing, and finally to be completing and Atlantic crossing. I am joyful with anxiety towards moving to Europe. Seeing my sister and Gustaf in London. My Farmor (father's mother) in Stockholm miss my parents and brothers.

Am reading Kundera, Marquez, Hesse, Tristan Jones, Conrad. We listen to tapes of the Bee Gees, the Gypsy Kings, Carlos Santana, Jaques Brel, Paul Anka, Mark's Peruvian Andes music. (The compact discs, of course, would never play in the rough seas, and even the stereo must be lashed down). Sometimes we try to use the autohelm (Cetrek: Danish built), though this exasperates me, as it is difficult or unmanageable in a heavy sea.

Life has become trying aboard, as I suspect it is apt to on any passage of 3 weeks or more, especially with a crew selected randomly, on the 'spur-of-the-moment'. Mark is a comrade who helps me remain sane simply through communication and understanding. We are like brothers. I am being paid absolutely nothing, which worries me.

An added stress has unfortunately come to me through A., a 28-year-old ex-smuggler and addict. Not only had he fought cheery old Loco in Antigua, but had roused legal and local trouble in Bermuda to the extent that his farewell from the Wharf Tavern in Bermuda was "good riddance the asshole is gone". Of course, A. being one of us, we stood behind him.

A good hunk of our limited budget went towards 'repairing' our SatNav in Hamilton, Bermuda. The SatNav failed from the first to give us a proper reading, and we again rely upon passing ships. Celestial navigation with a sextant is of little use,

177

owing to rough seas and more than two weeks of perpetual clouds and drizzle. To brighten our days porpoises dance in the wake of our cow. We whistle to them and gaze at their sleek, chocolate-brown forms.

Another relief comes from passing vessels, from which Yves is a master at extracting our position. He is fluent in French, Dutch, Spanish, Portuguese, English, and German, which make communication easier. One French Captain, astounded at seeing *Chebec* in the open ocean, premised Yves that he would return to rescue us if called. Conversations begin with "Merchant Vessel, Merchant Vessel, this is S/Y (sailing yacht) *Chebec,* or "Ship off to Port…can you see our lights?"

Yves takes pride in telling them that his crew is Kiwi (New Zealand), Bahamian, British (Paula). Antiguan, and Belgian, Paula, and A. have shared lives in Antigua, and understand each other well. Yves, who navigates, cooks dinner, and takes the helm, bears a real brunt of the work. I try to give him extra time to sleep, but in the cold even this is not easy. He has contacted family and friends in the SSB radio some as far away as Argentina.

The refrigeration ceased to function at the end of week one. Another casualty is the crew head. (Having lost nearly twenty pounds, I have absolutely no use for this item during the last two weeks of the voyage!) I have showered once since my arrival in Antigua more than a month ago. I haven't shaved, as Mark and I are having a friendly beard-growing competition. He is winning the sideburns, I the goatee. Except when Paula offers a little trim, our hair remains untouched. Whereas before we might venture a salt-water rinse on deck, we are now lucky to heat up fresh water below for a dry-bath. For the first month I didn't wear socks, belt, trousers, or a shirt collar. Quite a break from Boston! Now we dress for the cold.

An interesting distraction which helps some people (or perhaps I am the only one!) remain sane at sea, are mirrors. The mirrors aboard serve more for introspection than for vanity. They are a mark a standard by which we can judge ourselves. As before, I didn't know anyone I sail with. It is almost necessary not to share too much of yourself on a boat, as it often becomes more of a barrier than a bond. In these circumstances, the mirror becomes an important median for reflection.

You can just stand before it, 'dumb' without even focussing on your face or the foul-weather jacket (which glows around your neck like a halo in the dark), and lose yourself in thought, as if in silent communion with yourself. The mirror in the head is near one of our two portholes, which for much of the crossing is buried under water. Looking out of it, you can see the deep ocean beneath, as though in a submarine. It gives an eerie reflection when closed, and when open allows much water to gush in.

A source of some/much of the frustration among the crew in our crossing is definitely lack of food, or scarcity of such. In Bermuda we could not afford to 'top up' on either provisions or fuel before departing. By the close of the second week we are completely out of: eggs, milk, butter, sugar, coffee, vegetable oil, jam, honey, crackers, fresh meat, vegetables, and, of course, cigarettes and booze (the last of which were expended on Yves' birthday party).

Like some other sailors, we contemplate smoking tea leaves, but as we can only drink water or plain tea, and our rolling papers are wet, we haven't gone that far between dinner at c.21:00 and the following 21:00 we are rationed to 2 slices of Yves' home-made bread, sometimes with cheese, at others with a bit of soup. Dinner is normally pasta or rice.

Last week I accosted A. over his obvious theft of food. He was coming off morning watch and taking huge bites from our daily loaf of breed. I called him a thief. I shouldn't have. Suddenly he drew a long kitchen knife from the rack and jabbed it at me threateningly. He held it to my throat, saying that he was going to cut me, kill me, poison me, and cut my eyes out. I looked up from my book, which had become a blur, and told him to put the knife down.

I began to 'read' again. Highly agitated, he pressed the knife harder to my throat. I looked up at him and told him with surprising honesty: "If you drew my blood, I'll kill you. On the spot. With my own two hands."

At this point Paula, shrieking intervened. She pulled A.'s arm down, and with it the knife, yelling at him furiously. A. went into his cabin. Paula told Yves, who decided that the threat could not have been serious. Paula, my age, lives aboard according to her own routine, separate from ours as sailors. She bends a much-needed ear to our problems and provides a relieving break from the stress of operating *Chebec* safely through those conditions. I am indebted to her strength of will and tenacity. More than once has she set matters straight for me, as I wouldn't have been able to do.

I remember with remorse Stephanie's parting reminder in Bermuda; that every so often vessels alter course for Bermuda to drop off the bodies of crew murdered at sea, and imprison the murderer. Never have my hands shaken so much at the helm of a boat as when, moments after A.'s attack, I climbed up the companionway and relieved Mark for two hours.

ENTRY XIV: DATE: Monday, June 24 12:36 GMT

POSITION: Day 18: 150 nautical miles to Bishop's

BBC radio has been telling us where to shop, what music to listen to, and that we must be on our way to work or to party. We have also been told that another Gandhi has been shot to death in India.

ENTRY XV: DATE: Tuesday, 25 June 20:00

POSITION: Day 19; Longitude 7^0 West, Latitude $50°$ North

WEATHER: Grey, breezy, fog, and drizzle

Juvenilia

ENTRY: LAND HO! Just after my 14:00 to 16:00 watch began, I deciphered through the fog and drizzle the faint trace of an outline of land, and a flash which I was hoping would be the by now infamous Bishop Rock, island of Sicily, England. Strained as they ware, my eyes did not deceive me.

For a few moments, I laughed gently to myself indeed almost silently. I smiled a smile that would have made a Cheshire cat envious. Smug was I. I savoured that moment to myself for a little while before sliding the hatch to Yves' cabin open and probing: *"Yves?"* "Yes?" He was sleeping. *"I think I've sighted land."* Pause. "What makes you think so?" Pause. I think to myself. I couldn't resist: *"Because I am looking at it, Yves."* He came to see for himself. (Before, when we sighted a ship, Yves would hand someone the helm and say; "I must confirm my position." Once I replied, *"You, Yves, are Captain of Chebec, cook, and navigator. There. I have confirmed your position. Now take the helm back".* He laughed.)

The others heard Yves and I talking. There was a murmur in the main salon.

I whispered my secret to A., who was the first to pop his head up. In the wave of a vision all our tensions were dispelled. We danced. We laughed. We dreamed aloud. Once, in the thick of a storm (when the halyard snapped and the Mainsail fell), Yves had bellowed; "My boat is being sailed by three five-year olds!" Well, upon the sight of land, this was truly so. We were giddy with excitement. Within an hour A. was serving us all hot rice and vegetables. We wrapped ourselves in motley garb and watched the dark coast, lit up occasionally by a white triangular sail.

Though it would still be an arduous three-day sail up the heavily trafficked English Channel, we could afford to be people again. And oh what a relief it was! Today has truly been one of the happiest days of my life when we unfurled our mouldy Antiguan flag. Its golden sun seemed to bring cut the real sun from behind the clouds. After two weeks of grey, we welcomed the warm sunshine as a long-lost friend.

We bore down upon a tiny Belgian sailboat and hailed it. The fist people we'd seen in almost a month a man and his wife popped up. A.'s first question was whether they had any cigarettes. They didn't know what to make of us. When Yves asked them in Dutch, they responded quickly, swinging round to pass us a packet of Belgian Belga cigarettes; no fewer than 25 to a packet!

I clambered half-dressed out of my hatch; saw them give A. the cigarettes, and hailed them back. In a dash, I fished out of my cupboard the last remnants of a bottle of Gosling's Black Seal rum, which Stephanie had brought me in Bermuda. When they came under our extending transom again,

I handed the woman the bottle, which she clutched happily. She scampered below with it; he set a course for the Scilly Isles, behind us. They were living and sailing aboard a tiny wooden boat, on the bow of which they had hand-painted a name like *Orion*. I wished them luck.

We spent the day welcoming glorious sunshine, warming ourselves, and drying garments. Against the charming haze of land we made out the outline of an impressive hermaphrodite brig *Tail Ship* on its way to Wales for toe regatta. Tonight, we whisk past the dark silhouettes of merchant ships, peacefully eliding along the Cornish coast, savouring the womb-like presence of land around us.

ENTRY XVI DATE: Wednesday, 3 July 12:00 GMT

POSITION: In transit via train between London and Oxford, England

ENTRY: We arrived aboard *Chebec* in Nieuwpoort, Belgium, at c.18:00 GMT+2 on Thursday, 27, after almost

Juvenilia

exactly 3 weeks at sea (21 days virtually to the hour). Captain Splash having had a run-about on terra firms, we made our way to warmth, Duivel beer, and Belga cigarettes in the KNYC; the Royal Yacht Club at Nieuwpoort. Though I can't honestly say that in my state its 'Royalty' didn't mean a damned thing to me, we were treated hospitably, and Yves fed us well.

We were just in time for Yves' One Ton Cup World Championship charter at $1,000 *per diem*. I arrived in Belgium after nearly seven weeks of gruelling and fulfilling adventure absolutely penniless. In the three or so days that I remained there, preparing *Chebec* for its charter, I hadn't the money to make a phone call to nearby Brussels or the Netherlands. In the course of the voyage Yves had given me $7 ($3 in St. Maarten and $4 in Bermuda) I wasn't about to ask for more.

We spent one afternoon hosting a retired commodore on *Chebec*, though I didn't lift a finger. And we didn't lift a sail. Everyone got a try at the wheel, and we only hit two boats while docking. It was quaint. Someone asked me how we managed in the "terribly rough" weather of the preceding days. I was reminded of the tanker captain whose first question upon sighting us in the midst of a gale 2,000 miles from anywhere asked us: "What are you doing here?" I felt like telling him: *"Doing here? Doing where? We've just become lost during a sea-sail!"*

On Sunday, 29 June I staggered aboard the 2 a.m. ferry from Oostende to Dover, having hitchhiked from Nieuwpoort. Yves footed the bill. My odyssey aboard *Chebec* for the meanwhile was over. We had been at sea more than thirty full days; I had donned my gear a hundred or so times From South to North we had sailed across roughly 35 lines of Latitude, totalling more than 2,000 nautical miles. From West to East we crossed thirty lines of longitude; some 3,000 miles, and six time zones. The sum total of our actual mileage from English Harbour, Antigua, to Nieuwpoort, Belgium exceeded 4,000 nautical miles.

In the harbour at Oostende I noticed a grand square-rigger berthed down the quay. After two months of immersion in sailing, 1 couldn't help but ignore it. But a sailor doesn't escape sailing so easily. She was the *Pogoria*, out of Gdansk, Poland, bringing wealthy Canadian students to Cape Town, South Africa. In September, after two more months at sea aboard *War Baby*, we tied alongside her in St. Malo, France, and got to know most of her crew.

Because when we headed East of Bermuda, our course effectively went off my chart, and I created an ad hoc one on the reverse side of the original. As we neared our final destination the dots connecting our course became closer and closer. It crossed the Greenwich Mean Time date line near Hastings and Dungeness on the morning of our 21st day. (It was my coldest and most miserable watch of the voyage. Currents virtually stopped us.)

Finally, at 23:59 of Wednesday 26 June, my line, which had followed more than 4,000 miles across from the Atlantic, ended off of the French coast. Thor Heyerdahl ended his account of the RA Expeditions by saying that if he had done nothing else, he and the crew had made a line across the Atlantic on a map into a real voyage on RA, his papyrus raft. I finished the voyage without a line to support it.

ENTRY XVII: DATE: Saturday, 16 November 1991 18:33

POSITION: Crouched in front of the computer, Manchester College

WEATHER: Exceedingly grey and foggy dangerous weather to bicycle in

EVENTS: Epilogue: Bermuda? I would say things are bad there, but Somers and the crew of *Sea Venture* settled the island in 1609 only because they wrecked ashore. (They liked it so much that they built a boat out of the wreck to keep going West the America!) Well, times are bad. Hurricane Grace ravaged Bermuda earlier this month. According to Bermuda Harbour Radio (yes, the same!), several boats were dis-masted or sunk during the hurricane: *Rascal V* and *Orca* dis-masted. *Cygnus* and *Anna Christina* (95 feet) lost. Probably more. Merchant and cruise ships deterred. Air-service halted.

This is not new to Bermuda, or many other islands (been to Tristan da Cunha lately?) I worry for Dick Murphie, who has spent years repairing his sailboat *Maja* after she was wrecked by a hurricane. He planned to re-launch her this autumn. I hope that he (and she) have weathered this hurricane. Though registered there, *War Baby* is fortunately not in Bermuda. She is on her way to New Zealand and the Antarctic.

As far as I know, Yves and his crew (which may or may no! include Paula and A.) are on their way back West across the Atlantic to Antigua. Mark returned to Auckland in June. (After several years of travel and an Atlantic crossing, his mother insisted he return.) Captain Splash is, I'm sure, sorely missed by his follow-felines in Antigua. Either that, or they will bite the fur of her tail off once more, and force her into English Harbour with a 'Splash'. Good thing Yves was listening, he's picked up most of his crow in the same style, and 1 am grateful for it. If Yves gives me the chance to sail aboard *Chebec* again, I couldn't say no.

I've neither spoken to, nor heard from, any of the crew of *Chebec* or *Loophole* since our crossing. They now live in a sphere distinct from my own. It is a sphere into which anyone is welcome, but which one only attains by being there. By living in it.

Dream dreams, then write them. Aye, but live them first!

Samuel Eliot Morison, *Sailor-Historian,* 1887-1970

From a statue on Commonwealth Ave., Boston

Eric Wiberg

Travels in The British Isles, France, Belgium, and the Netherlands, 1984-1991

Juvenilia

Travels in The British Isles, France, Belgium, and the Netherlands, 1984-1991

1.   Ireland: June August 1984 (age 13). Flew Nassau/London/Cork, drove to Parknasilla, Sneem, on the Kenmare River, County Kerry. Lived in cottagewith Frank, Mrs. and Dr. Baensch for six weeks. Fished and boated extensively on Kenmore River with Jim the hermit. Caught Connor, Pollock, and Salmon. Hiked in hills, Killarney Lakes, around Spraigue fort, to Tralee

2.   England: March 1988. Choir Tour as Organist Assistant, Saint George's School, Newport, Rhode Island. Route: Flew Boston/London, drove/sang in Cambridge, Peterborough, Bury St Edmund's, Stanford. Birmingham, Wolverhampton, Coventry, Oxford, Southwark, Greenwich, London. After tour stayed with sister Ann in London for a week. Flew home to Nassau, Bahamas.

3.   England: Summer, 1985. Flew Stockholm, Sweden/London, to stay with Allegra Fitzgibbons and family for several days. Drove to Buckingham shire for the annual jaguar clay pigeon shoot. Stayed in their villa, at Pusey Manor, Pusey. (July '91: Allegra, friends, and I drove to Henley for rowing regatta).

4.   The Netherlands: Summer, 1990. Train from Stockholm to Groningen with brother John. Stayed with Han Kolff on Niewstadt for several nights. Drove to their shimmer home of Oldengaerde, then for sailing rally in Sneek. On to Amsterdam a few days later, spent 3 days in The Hague, then Kolff home in Rotterdam. Early August went on to Paris and South via Bruxelles.

5.   Coastal England and Belgium: Summer, 1991.Aboard S/Y *Chebec,* a 65-foot ketch registered to St. John's, Antigua, Captain Yves Renault of Belgium hailed Bishop's Rock, Isles of

Sally on Tuesday, 25 June 1991. After three weeks at sea sailing from Bermuda. Spent three days negotiating the English Channel via Start Point, the Needles (Isle of Wight), Hastings, Dungeness, Dover, and Dunkerque. Arrived in Nieuwpoort, Belgium on Thursday, 27 June. Hitchhiked to Oostende on 1 July, took ferry to Dover.

6.   England. Ireland, and France: 2.000+ miles aboard *War Baby*, S&S 62-foot sloop, Captain Warren Brown of Bermuda, July to September, 1991: train Dover/London1 July, stayed with Ann and Gustaf. Visit to Oxford, and then train to Lymington on 7 July. Met up with *War Baby*, and 10 July voyaged to Weymouth, Plymouth, and Dartmouth via Salcombe. Ran afoul of a trawler off Dartmouth, returned to Lymington for repairs Scotland voyage called off.

Second voyage to Dublin. Ireland, via Weymouth. Plymouth, and Falmouth, England. Arrived Howth, off Dublin, in early August. Sailed Howth to Crosshaven, off Cork. Rendezvous with Story family. Sailed to Glandore, visited Don Street and family. Then to Kinsale, Baltimore, and Fastnet Rock. Returned to Lymington England mid-August via St. Mary's, Isles of Scilly, and Plymouth. Flew to Stolkholm in interval between crews. Returned to *War Baby* late August, new crew. Sailed for Channel Islands via Cowes, Isle of Wight. Made Alderney, the Guernsey and St. Hillier, Jersey. Celebrated double Birthdays (Warren and I May 21st!) in St Peter Port. Guernsey with *Witch of Albion, Daisy Bates*, and *Panic Major*. Stocked up, sailed for St. Malo, Bretagne, France. Several days there with *Pogoria*, then Brest, France. Voyage ended. Rented a car for driving tour of Douarnenez, Quimper, and Concarneau. Flew from Brest to Paris for several days, then home to Bahamas Paris/Miami/Nassau mid-September.

7.   England: Moved to Manchester College, University of Oxford, for full academic year 1991-92 (my first Winter in Europe!). Live in Warrington Hall, on the corner of Holywell Street and Mansfield Road, across from New College and in the

heart of Medieval Oxford October 1991-June 1992. My parents, sister Ann, and Gustaf visited in mid-October. We drove North to Blenheim Palace for the day, then Stratford-Upon-Avon for Shakespeare's birthplace and home, Royal Theatre. Tour of country in car.

During time in Oxford numerous trips to London via train. A note-worthy round trip on Guy Fawkes' Day, October 1991. Rented a car with Manchester College students Charles (from Lewes), Patrick, and Kent host Charles driving. Drove South-East to Lewes, in Sussex (via Brighton), for the annual Pope-effigy burning ritual (till past midnight) for which they are infamous. Met an American friend of brother John's while there.

8. Scotland: December 1991: Bought one week ScotRail RoverPass for £29 with Mark Robertson, Australian student at Merton College, Oxford. Made Glasgow via London and Carlisle. Train North to Crianlarich, where we disembarked to hike with three burly Scotsmen. Hiked to Bridge of Orchy (drinking from a bottle of Scotch) to find pub closed. Hiked over hill and dale to Loch Lyon via Fleming estate, opened the pub. Ate and drank for hours. Train to Fort William from Bridge of Orchy. Next day bus to Kyle of Lochaish, then Uig, Northern end of Isle of Skye. Train to Inverness for night. Tram to Aberdeen, then Dundee and St. Andrew's via Leuchers. Stayed in St. Andrew's with student friends for three days. Train to Carlisle via Edinburgh and then London. Mark returned to Oxford. I stayed with sister Ann in London, then flew

London/Miami/Nassau on Dec 15 Returned Oxford in January 1992.

Eric Wiberg
A Brief Wander Through East Africa, March April 1992

A Brief Wander through East Africa
March-April 1992

Outline of Route: Mombasa, Kenya to Zanzibar, Dar es Salaam, and Mbeya, Tanzania. Then Karonga and Chitipa, Malawi to Nakonde, Zambia. To Dodoma, Tanzania, via Iringa and Mbeya. To Arusha via 'Dar' and Moshi. To Nairobi, Kenya, via Namanga. To Kilifi, on Kenyan Coast, ending in Mombasa.
Expenditure: Return airfare £320 British. c.$600 for over 3 weeks: average daily budget of $15-20 (or less) feasible. Many, many thanks to my parents!
Modes of Travel: Bus, 'Matatu' (public bus - cheap and crowded), Dhow, (sailboat), train, Taxi/impromptu charter, hitchhiking, bicycle, foot, canoe...

Juvenilia

A Brief Wander Through East Africa, March April 1992

Outline of route: Mombasa, Kenya to Zanzibar, Dar es Salaam, and Mbeya, Tanzania. Then Karonga and Chitipa, Malawi to Nakonde, Zambia. To Dodoma, Tanzania, via Tringa and Mbeya. To Arusha via 'Dar' and Moshi. To Nairobi, Kenya, via Namanga. To Kilifi, on Kenyan Coast, ending in Mombasa.

Expenditure: Return airfare £320 British. c. $600 for over three weeks: average daily budget of 415-20 (or less) feasible. Any, many thanks to my parents!

Modes of Travel: Bus, 'Matatu' (public bus cheap and crowded), Dhow (sailboat), train, Taxi/impromptu charter, hitchhiking, bicycle, foot, canoe.

Sunday, 29 March 1992: Stockholm, Sweden, to Athens, Greece, via London

Dawn in Stockholm. Grateful to Farmor (my grandmother) for hosting me (and to have been reminded to 'lose' as hour!), I set off. Fly Stockholm's Arlanda to London's Gatwick Airport. Lunch with sister Ann and friends in Chelsea Gardens. Return to Gatwick by 16:00. British Caledonian (a British Airways subsidiary) Flight KB242 departs 16:43, arrives in Athens c. 22:00.

Departs Athens at c. midnight. Local for Mombasa, Kenya. Thanks to a friend's introduction, I am invited to join Captain Tim Parrot and Nigel Reid in the cockpit of Caledonian's *B757*. Fully laden with fuel (as it is less expensive than in Kenya), We barrel down the runway, over Piraeus Harbour, and across the Mediterranean Sea towards Egypt.

Monday, 30 March: Athens to Mombasa, Kenya

Dawn breaks over Africa, illuminating Mount Kilimanjaro off to stir board, it becomes visible, in its snow-capped brilliance, to us in the cockpit. Sparsely scattered clusters at thatched huts spot the plain below, sending trails of grey smoke drifting upwards. Ahead a seemingly endless stretch of gentle coast stretches in either direction, giving way to the Indian Ocean. Beyond the horizon lies India and Australia, which seem far away from East Africa.

The nine-hour flight from Athens, Greece, has taken us over Cairo. Egypt, Khartoum, Sudan, and Nairobi, Kenya, to Mombasa. The air traffic controller welcomes us and guides us in with a heavy German accent, reminding me that within the century Mombasa had bordered German East Africa, which is now Tanzania. He guides Nigel, who is at the throttle, and Captain Tim to the landing strip of Moi International Airport, Mombasa.

British Caledonian nudges into its slot and halts between German, Swiss, and French charter-flights (which I am told have only recently beer, allowed access to Mombasa). Nigel and Tim, calm and confident, remove their headphones. I have had the fortune of sharing both take-off and landing with them. For such an exhilarating introduction to Africa, I am grateful.

Disembarking (typically last) I wade through the crowds of holiday makers, clear immigration. I by-pass baggage collection and stroll into the thick humidity. Lonely Planet's 'travel survival kit' to East Africa and my 'OstAfrica' map are already ruffled in my hand. On my back is a tiny daypack, formerly appendage to a Dutch Army pack, purchased in Oxford for £5. At about three cubic feet, it holds all that I bring medical/toiletries kit, diary/log, small camera, 1 pair of trousers. 2 of shorts, 1 shirt, 5 T-shirts, pillowcase, 3 paperbacks, undergarments... (My shoes, the heaviest. items, I will no longer even use).

Changing U.S. Dollars into Keynian Shillings, I venture my first Swahili greetings: '*Jambo*' for 'hello' and '*Asanta sana*' for 'thank you'. I hail a taxi into Mombasa and secure a single room at the New Britania Hotel (off Digo Road and across from the Post Office), for about $6.

After a dazed wander around town, I buy water and rest till the afternoon. Then *"Tusker"* beer at lively hotel fear, where I meet Samuel M. Towards evening we clamber aboard *"Matatu"* (public bus) to his residence just Worth of Mombasa. There I meet Patrick Kiania a musician, and his housemates, students, and relatives, including Francis and Judy later, Samuel guides me back to the hotel, where 3 sleep soundly.

Tuesday, 31 March, Mombasa, Kenya

Spend day wandering streets of Mombasa, including Fort Jesus and Dhow port in old town, where I search for a Dhow to exotic Zanzibar, off the Tanzanian coast. Reserve place on deck, clear through with immigration and District officers, customs, etc. Wooden-building, colonial bureaucracy. Hot. I pay off my guide. Visit Swedish Consul, Mr Heilman, who is friendly and helpful. Browse in market and buy bracelets. In the evening spoil myself with European cuisine at the Oceanic Hotel on the shore.

On the terrace I meet two young women, who propose that I take thorn on a tour of the nightclubs along the coast. After dinner, I return to my hotel for money, only to miss our rendezvous in the Flamingo Club. In retrospect, this is just as well, as they were almost certainly prostitutes. According to the Taxi driver (who drove me there and waited), I would most, likely have spent way beyond my daily maximum of $30-40 taking them all over the coast, and would have been lucky to afford a taxi ride back to Mombasa. Return to hotel. Sleep. Write depressing poems by candlelight.

Wednesday, 1 April, Mombasa and aboard the Dhow

In the morning, I walk down to the Dhow docks in the Arabic old port. Check in with immigration officer; no need to return till late afternoon. Wander around in Islamic Old Town. At a food stall I meet an injured young boy who guides me through the city. Buy sandals for each of us (Mine are a Maasai tribe design, made from strips of rubber from a truck's tires. They are called *Nginyira aka* in Kikuyu meaning sandals in which men tiptoe after women, Kangangi, a Kenyan friend at Oxford, later tells me. I wear these sandals from then on.)

I buy the boy a belt for myself; a *'rasta'* cap and coconuts (which the man cuts and ties on a string for me). Farewell to my young companion. I buy water and bread in a store, and retain to hotel. Give one coconut to an Italian back packer apparently stricken by Malaria (as is another guest). I check out, and am giver, a warm farewell by bidding adieu to the Kikuyu women who run the hotel, two Americans, and Ziggy; a Dhow captain from Lamu. On the way to the Dhow I check in at the Swedish Consulate, where they are having difficulty sending a FAX to my parents in Nassau.

I am ready for my travels to begin in earnest. In sandals and T-shirt I hopefully look, less 'green'. Pause for a swim on coast, where haircuts and smokes are being tad in the afternoon sun. Having left it on the shore, my coconut is diligently returned by several boys. Along the shore I pass the Mombasa Club, where a cluster of *'Wazungu'* (whites) bask beside & pool.

At the Dhow port I meet Olivia and Kate, English girts who were teaching on a remote island on Lake Victoria in Uganda. Boarding our Dhow in the evening, we forge places for ourselves to sleep on the dock. That night police prevent the Dhow from leaving, as it is dangerously over-laden with people. The end of the 40-day Muslim Ramadan fast is impending and many Mombasan Muslims are sailing to Zanzibar to celebrate Idi-al-Fitr, or Idi Day, with characteristic feasts and festivities.

Thursday, 2 April: Dhow from Mombasa, Kenya to Zanzibar, Tanzania

Delayed again in morning when they clear us off of our Dhow in order to re-stow our things and filter paid passengers. Meet Nigel (English) and Graeme (New Zealander), each a very experienced traveller, on the deck of a nearby Somali Dhow while we wait for ours to ready itself. Not far away on the crowded deck of a Somali Dhow, a woman gives birth, is taken ashore.

We are startled to see the Dhow push off with our things, only to realize that they are performing 'sea trials' in the harbour for the police. Finally push off in the evening beautiful sunset. The night is spent restlessly cramped on deck, in light rain and jolting swells.

Friday, 3 April: Dhow to Zanzibar, Tanzania

Pass Pemba Island to Port, with Tanga, Kenya, and Sagamoyo, Tanzania to Starboard. We have Zanzibar in sight by late morning, by which time I am dehydrated and sun-burnt to a crisp. Feel nauseous and weak. Still green. My companions; veteran travellers of East Africa, seem to be fine.

In Zanzibar we grapple for our gear, including Graeme's bicycle. We clear Customs and Immigration, and I stagger to a Taxi, which takes me to the Africa House Hotel. Ridiculous £20 for one night, in single, without running water. Nigel, Olivia, and Kate come by for lunch. In the evening, I go by their hotel, the Warere Guest House, and we stroll through Zanzibar town, buying dinner as we go.

We meet our Spice Tour guide 'Mitu' outside Sinbad's Restaurant, and plan a tour the following day unless the moon is sighted over Mecca. Wander around the Floating Restaurant and Old Town at night. I stagger back to the Africa House bar, on a veranda overlooking the coast, where I meet two Dutch geographers from Madagascar. Sleep.

Saturday, 4 April, Zanzibar Town, Zanzibar, Tanzania

Check out Africa House, move into Malindi Guest House, near the harbour. Love it; clean and well-kept Muslim place. Luxurious single, though costs $15. Plans to go to Spice Tour called off. Calamari lunch in the Fisherman restaurant with Olivia. In the afternoon Graeme finds a BBC transmission of the

Boat Race, in which oxford beats Cambridge. From the Warare Guest House, Zanzibar, we hear the sounds of London.

The sighting of the moon over the Mecca means the festivities begin in earnest. At night, the celebrations begin. We wander along the many food and entertainment stalls contentedly. Roadside meals are '*Chipati*' (thin, fried dough), small bread loaves, meat kebabs, or octopus washed down with sweet spice teas or strong coffee. Good and very cheap.

Sunday, 5 April: Zanzibar Town, Zanzibar

Enjoy day long Spice Your, explore flora and fauna of the island with Mitu as guide, including the market, cathedral, slave dungeon, Sultan's Palace, and Fiji beach. A Frenchman moves out of Nigel and Graeme's room in the Warere, and I move in. Triple room, single bed, $5. Dinner with Nigel and Olivia at Sea view Indian Restaurant.

Wander through part during Idi festival. Despite light rains the well-dressed townspeople and visitors intermingle happily, many of the girls have painted feet. I end up talking with young children and a serious-student along the wall Omar leads the conversation, mostly about school. They study several subjects and languages at ones in Primary School. Walk home across town alone, pleased, though with upset stomach.

Monday, 6 April: Zanzibar Town and Jambiani Beach, East Zanzibar Island

Early morning Graeme sets out on bicycle across island to East Coast. Nigel sets off via ferry to Dar es Salaam and the train. West, I meet with chartered Land Rover, which carries a British couple, a German group, and French girl, and I to the East Coast, across the island. After a bumpy ride we make it to the coast, calling in at Paje and Bwejuu settlements before jumping off at the Shehe bungalows on idyllic, palm-lined Jambiani Beach.

Very relaxing day on the coast, with a walk a mile out on the sand banks at low tide, followed by two hot meals. After dinner and reading, late night talks with British travellers, American students, and German punks.

After midnight, Mr. Shehe himself escorts me to the communal Matatu into Zanzibar Town, departing at 2 a.m. He introduces roe to his mother and family, and relates the values of his clean little community. Asked about the scarcity of dogs, he explains that as a result of a recent government anti-rabies campaign, most domestic animals had to be shot.

Tuesday, 7April: Jambiani to Zanzibar Town to Dar es Salaam, Tanzania

Arrive on the bus from Jambiani beach in Zanzibar Town c. 5 a.m. Walk to Africa House, then Warere to say goodbye to Kate and Olivia, Scramble to make ferry. I can't find my entry form, and almost miss the ferry. At the last-minute an understanding immigration officer lets me through. New ferry skippered by Australians. Tired, but eager for mainland.

Arrive in Dar es Salaam late morning. Disembark alone, in heavy rain. Stagger around town with my gear, sweating. Try to locate a black-market intact, but make the costly mistake of taking an easier offer from a smooth-talking confidence man. Am robbed of $50 U.S. by two of them in a back alley while others look on knowingly. Long story in itself, but the dismal afternoon continues. Lonely, vulnerable, sad.

Costly taxi leaves me at the TAZARA (Tanzanian - Zambian Hallway) stations, where I discover that I've been robbed of almost all my Tanzanian money. Noble Omari N. steps in and helps me through the afternoon. A walk to a bank; closed. A ride into town; no refund forms for stolen traveller's cheques. The Kilimanjaro Hotel teller claims they haven't money to refund stolen cheques (said as she changes $100 bills into Tanzanian!)

Finally make it back to the station less than an hour before train departs.

Omari and friend Dashin secure me a bunk in a First-Class cabin. Omari is greeted with respect by all. A real saviour. Then, as if the day hasn't been enough, I spend the night tending off the unwelcome advances of a gay Ugandan student. When woken by his hands on my back. I decide to disembark in the next station. Except for securing ticket on TAZARA train to Zambia, it has been a miserable day. I determine to arm myself.

Wednesday, 6 April: Dar es Salaam, Tanzania, to Karonga, Malawi via Mbeya

Thinking I have time to kill (wrong!) I disembark train to Mbeya with a large group of back-packers (mistake), disregarding my ticket for Nakonde, Zambia. Make it to border, where I am selected (from a group of some 30 back-packers who charted a bus there) and detained. Forced to bribe my way through and have health certificates falsified rather than hitchhike back to Mbeya via Tukuyu, where Nigel is visiting his birthplace.

Crossing frontier into Malawi, I rent a cycle and catch up to two fellow-Swedes (I travel on my Swedish passport); Tobias and Mattias. We hitchhike c. 15 kilometres to the Malawi checkpoint, where men with long hair have it cut off by border guards with knives (or whatever is bandy). Women's birth-control pills and certain guide books also banned. Spend night in Karonga, on the northwest tip of Lake Malawi, with Swedes and Canadian gin in the Kenkenuou Guest House for about 6 Kwacha a single.

Thursday 9 April: Karonga to Chitipa, Malawi

After banking and a walk to lake Malawi with Tobias and Mattias, I spend the day trying to hitchhike west to Chitipa. Alone. Little luck. Must make Mpulungu, Zambia, on Lake Tanganyika, by Friday evening or Saturday morning to make the

Lake Tanganyika steamer (vintage 1914) M/V *Liemba* up to Karonga, Tanzania Not. On roadside meet Samba and Agness, Malawian students. Observe chain gang. Hear gravel plant dismiss its labourers by 'gonging' a truck wheel hung from a tree.

Meet an 'African Doctor' also in transit to Chitipa, from where a truck deposits a filthy young back-packer on the roadside opposite. He is an Aussie, and his story deserves heed. He has spent a week trekking from across Zambia, through Chitipa on the Malawi frontier, to Karonga. Arrive Chitipa late with African Doctor. Help him with his many things (portable office), and am welcomed to share his mud hut. Sleep, absolutely exhausted.

Friday, 10 April: Chitipa, Malawi to Zambia, return to Chitipa

Frustrating but enlightening day spent, trying to get out of Malawi. Greet the rising sun with a tin hill of intoxicating 'Malawi beer' (maize and millet fermented in rainwater), with African Doctor Sanfolo Ngambi and Mr. Benson Nyondo. Later we drink Malawi Whiskey, purer and more potent. The drought has badly damaged the maize crop, and they cannot offer food.

Mr Nyondo (Benson, though he is, at age 62 a revered village eider on the Zambian side) offers and proves to be an indispensable and loyal guide Mr. Nyondo helps me across the border into Zambia by mid-morning. No vehicles going into Nakonde, on border with Tanzania. Most of day spent trekking to and from iambic in the unforgiving sun, drinking choleric water or Malawi Whiskey. Am introduced to many village or hamlet elders, and fed '*sumi*' (maize hash) by Mr. Nyondo's daughter, and meet her children; Ndlodire, Jeremia, Love, Lutamio, and Tensono among them.

Fruitless search in evening for vehicles heading into Zambia. A spanking new pick-up truck pulls up, and two White South Africans give me a pack of invaluable Camel cigarettes. I didn't climb in. They headed North at full speed and music blaring. Met an aspiring writer serving as a border guard outside of the almost military base of a Malawi youth organization.

At night, I finally relax a bit from my ill-fitting high-strung exasperation by sharing several drinks and meeting volunteer workers. Chitipa boasts no fewer than 16 dialects among some 1,000 (?) residents; a motorcycle, and maybe 2-3 cars (most vehicles are government-owned). Spend night in Council Houses, Chitipa after exhausting day.

Saturday, 11 April: Chitipa, Malawi to Tunduma and Mbeya, Tanzania

First thing I try to do the next morning is 'get the hell out of Dodge' guided by the border poet and cleared the previous day by the immigration official, who was most helpful. Jump on first vehicle heading North, which is a commercial *Matatu*. Standing clinging on its frame roof, we skit across the plains in view of gorgeous spacious mountain ranges and valleys to the Tanzanian frontier.

Guided on foot across the Titi and Sangwe Rivers into Tanzania. Road again. *Matatu* to highway leading to Tunduma. Arrive in Tunduma late afternoon via *Matatu* (which breaks down on a hill, forcing us to walk). Clear immigration and customs in Nakinda, Zambia, and Tunduma, Tanzania. (To do so I walk into Zambia from Tanzania with a Malawi exit stamp from Chitipa to get a Zambian entry stamp from Chitipa and exit stamp from Nakonde. Then back to Tunduma, Tanzania in order to get an entry stamp, though I never officially left!)

The officials are tired but helpful; it is through them that I learn the impossibility of achieving my goal of making Lake Tanganyika with my remaining time and money. Here ends my plan to continue in a deck-wise circle from Ckitipa to Mpuluagu, Zambia, up Lake Tanganyika, through Kigoma, Tanzania to Uganda (via either Burundi and/or Rwanda or across Lake Victoria via Tabora, Mwanza, and Bukobe Tanzania), ending a sweep of some half-dozen nations from Kampala, Uganda, to

Mombasa via Nairobi. Another time, Travellers have told of often planning, but never making, the Lake Tanganyika ferry.

Meanwhile, Nakonde and Tunduma are outposts swarmed by 'truckies' in transit, border guards, prostitutes, and black-marketeers. Crest-fallen, I clamber into another *Matatu* to Mbeya, Tanzania, my grandiose plans having completely fallen through. Cry silently in *Matatu* and am consoled toy maternal women who offer peanuts. I arrive in Mbeya Sato, and scrape up funds for a ridiculously expensive ($10) single suite.

Meet a young Spanish woman, Miriam, she is on her way to Malawi from Lamu. Her company over food and drink is much appreciated. Court her to no avail. Ironically, I miss the simplicity and hospitality of Chitipa, from which I fled so urgently. Write letters (never sent); sleep for a few hours.

Sunday, 12 April; Mbeya to Iringa, Tanzania

Board bus at 5 a.m. from Mbeya to Iringa to the North. Breakdowns and terrible heat feeling good, but fatigue eroding me. Afternoon in plaza of Iringa seem the only '*Wazungu*,' and it dawns on me that I may have more hard currency in my pouch than many of the villagers earn in a year. Meet. Richard K. in the Medina Restaurant. He informs me that the definitive soccer football match between the Shaba Sports Club and tie African Youth Club happens today in Dar es Salaam: respective red/white and yellow/green banners abound. Fluttering from vehicles. (The African Youth Club wins).

Richard is escorting a new acquaintance from his father's funeral with typical hospitality. An English Fisheries agent and African colleague board my overnight bus from Iringa to Dodoma. On bus begin to tool ill exhausted, cramped, dehydrated, and sick to stomach.

Monday, 13 April: Dodoma, Tanzania

Arrive in Dodoma before dawn. Exhausted and feeling very ill. Rent room at Ujiji Guest House. Buy knife in a long-sheath and local handicraft such as wooden whistles. In a Tanzanian bank I meet Chris Gilbert, a Canadian also in his early 20's; at some 6 1/2 feet a student and Toronto barman. Chris has legged X-thousand miles in more than 7 months and 2 trips through southern Africa, mostly hitchhiking. Survivor of the Namib and Kalahari deserts end a frequenter of Victoria Falls, he is also a veteran of African hospitals, (...the beginning of lasting companionship).

From the bank, we wander around to pick up rare Dodoma wine, cassettes of Swahili music, and water. Chris had found the bus from Dodoma to Arusha unsafe and unsound (and had ejected himself accordingly). We agree to go in together on the bus to Dar es Salaam, then a train to Arusha.

Feeling ill, I return to ray single room to rest. There, my own growing discomfort and nausea is compounded by the heart-wrenching groans of a seriously debilitated child who has been left to claw his way around the courtyard outside ray window under the merciless sun.

For hours his screams and grunts, haunt me, following me when I shift into the latrine. He crawls around and defecates outside my window. The lodge-keeper is unmoved. Out of this comes my most bitter and despairing writing, poetry, and drawings logged on the trip.

Towards dusk Chris and I rendezvous for the bus to Dar, which turns out to be pretty hellish for both of us. I try vainly to eat before we set off. Our legs are quite long, and like any bag larger than my own, fit nowhere comfortably. Again, there is a child sicker than I; rigid on his father's lap in the seat in front of mine. His face is sallow, eyes sunken and bloodshot, nose running.

Tuesday, 14 April: Dodoma, to Dar es Salaam, Tanzania

The trying overnight bus ride is redeemed by my managing to rescue the sick little child. At a typical wayside stop, serving various burnt items for travellers to devour, the child wanders away from his father, bus, and all.

The driver a master of his own realm is set to poll away. As the fatter frantically rummages through the market, I find the child standing dazed on the fringe of the bush. Desperate, I hoist him on my shoulder, put him on the 'revving' bus, and run to alert the father. This done, to inquisitive shouts of passengers, we set off.

Chris and I arrive in Dar. We split up to take care of business; banking etc. Receive and send Fax'es from Swedish Embassy Consulate, then on the street, I make my new club *cum* knife known, and continue on my chores unmolested.

In the Salamander Cafe (aptly named, as *'Salame'* is a peaceful greeting in Swahili!). I meet Hans-Erik. He has had immeasurable experience in the game reserves such as the remote Selous Game Reserve and the Ngorongoro Crater, where he worked with wild game let various films in the 1950's and since. Based in Arusha, he is European-African, fluent in the languages and dialects of the region a real sun-weathered, self-professed holder-on.

On way to the Dar train station, Chris and I take diversion to view the sprawling tropical city from the roof of a government building. We observe an impressive Presidential cavalcade of beige Mercedes. (Chris has this ritual before). Very fortunate to be given tickets for 3 Second Class cabin on the train to Moshi by a German traveller. Spend luxurious night between Dar and Mosh, passing Bagamoyo. We make our way northwest towards Arusha and ultimately Nairobi, Kenya.

Wednesday, 15 April: Moshi and Arusha Tanzania to Nairobi, Konya

Chris and I wake to coffee and breakfast-in-bunk with Mount Kilimanjaro looming snow-capped over us. Good time.

Arrive in Moshi before noon. Followed off train by very 'green' Danish student/tourist. Board *Matatu* for Arusha. I feel constrained in the company of the naive Dane, as we attract the greedy attention, which I haven't experienced since Dar. Stalling to avoid him upon arrival in Arusha, I am the last passenger to try to disembark into the crowded town plaza.

The bus-boys target me; one cross-checks me with his upper body as I try to seep down. Meanwhile, a second pushes himself over behind me while he and a third rifle through my pockets and grope at my upper body. By this time instinct kicks in the fear hits shortly afterwards Grabbing my vulnerable pocket and stomach firmly, I thrust forward with one knee, unbalancing the thief at my waist. When he is upright. I check him against the bus, as he had done to me, and step off.

A few strides away I regroup, am again heckled, and stride away quickly. Finding Chris, I tell the Dane to piss off. The 'elders' who observed the robbery attempt leave us undisturbed, and I am convinced that had they have taken action; it would have been against the thieves. (Such is a silent morality, which we would see articulated later in 'mob justice' in Nairobi).

Chris and I enjoy a meal of my favourite *'wali ng'ombe'* (rice and beef), and I wrap my pouch around my body and crotch with three strings. Safe. We wander around Arusha, disappointed as it is mid-day of low season and a few characteristic *'safaris'* (which simply means 'journey' in Swahili) are under way. We are, despite general lack of people and good shopping, able to buy good postcards, *'Kanga'* wraps (popular and much-used by the women), and cheap Tanzanian cigarettes and coffee.

We return to *Matatu* station by 6.40 p.m. and board the first *Matatu* which, within ten minutes of departure, swerves, without brakes, across the read and crashes through a well and into a ditch. A woman beside us is injured, and some passengers bleed from fortunately shallow cuts. We were buffeted by the bags and passengers. Disarray.

With surprising calm and resignation, Chris and I pry ourselves and our gear free of the wreck, bend to a knee among the throng of onlookers, take photos, and return to station. As we walk away the police are pulling up. Grateful to be free of the wreck, and that injuries were limited, we return to the *Matatu* station.

There we board a second *Matatu,* which takes us through spectacular scenery and wildlife like the Serengeti plains just North of us. I jokingly call this the Matatu Safari'! (Unlike very dear charter '*safaris*', we observe ostrich, zebra, gazelle, giraffe, impala... for a pittance!). Arrive on Kenyan border. In Namanga, at dusk. Ease through customs and immigration. Formalities are handled by the flame of my lighter, as electricity is out.

In no-man's-land between check-points we change money (the black-market is increasingly being rendered defunct by the easing of exchange controls). We charter a cheap taxi into Nairobi with a Maasai tribes woman, passing more wildlife as we go. Chris secures us a place at the Iqbal Hotel, Latema Road, and Tom Mboya Avenue the strip of ill-repute. Modern Green 24-Hour Bar, on Laterna Read, has been open all day, every day since 1963. We chat with young Kenyan women and fascinating Somali students who are deaf. To communicate, we use sign language, drawing and writing. Only just resist the allure of Virginia, who (I am later told) is a 14-year old prostitute.

Thursday, 16 April: Nairobi, Kenya

Very fortunate to catch stores and banks open before Good Friday. Chris and I do our banking shopping and chores etc. (Ali at the Iqbal Hotel (named after his cat) does our laundry!). We call in at the Thorn Tree Cafe, Stanley Hotel, to leave notes to travelling companions (Nigel later found mine there). Good lunch at the Malindi Dishes restaurant, Gaborone Road. Reasonably quiet night, good dinner at the Trattoria Restaurant.

Still resist Virginia, as has been my practice throughout. We are told by a pharmacist who studies the health of prostitutes moving between Bukobe, Tanzania, and Nairobi, that between 70-80% of prostitutes in Nairobi carry the HIV virus, which can lead to AIDS.

The tragic crash of a Kenyan Air Force jet into a residential area, killing some 50 people, jolts the city. At night, in a spate, isolated incident, mob violence erupts across road from Chris and my hotel room. A group of some three thieves attack and stab a taxi driver for his earnings.

One of the thieves is immediately trucked down by a vigilante mob. In the uproar we see him run towards and crutches a road sign in front of a dimly lit alley. The sign sways and jerks. He is being beaten senseless and stabbed by the mob, who try to set him afire. Prevented from doing so by moisture, they drag him down the muddy alley by his ankles, kicking his head as they go. Venturing down the alley, Chris and I learn from witnesses and Taxi-drivers that the mob was trying to lynch hire when the police took him away. Quietly, we fade out.

Friday, 17 April: Nairobi to Mombasa, Kenya

In the morning Chris and I foresee our paths diverging. He wants to hit the coast and sun for his remaining few days. I have social contacts and chores to follow up on while in Nairobi. Chris must try for his Aeroflot flight to London on Thursday, I for my Caledonian departing on Monday. We agree that he will set off by train tor Mombasa that evening; with or without me. I hitchhike west into the comfortable suburb of Ngong by myself. Busy day trying first to track down fellow boston College students studying in Ngoog: make contact, no more.

Visit the Karen Blixen Museum; the Yarm in Africa, at the foot of the Ngong Hills, which opens her (AKA Isak Dinesen's) 1937 novel *Out of Africa*. There seems discomfiture among fellow-passengers that I should take the *Matatu* (and not a Taxi, which other 'tourists' take) from Ngong back into Nairobi. Pass the City Morgue, where crowds await news of the airplane crash victims. The papers claim that in the city morgue several thousand bodies remain in state, some unclaimed for up to four years.

Try calling home, it nearing Easter and Mother's Day. Leave a note for an eminent hotelier in Nairobi. Beginning to mesh my life in Oxford and 'society' with that of traveller, and to become uncomfortable doing so. These feelings are compounded in the modern setting of Nairobi. Final decision to either stay and make something of college students and contacts there or, again, 'get the hell out of Dodge' and hopefully rendezvous with Chris for a jaunt to the coast.

In a mad rush to the station and a push to get tickets (in which 'fresh' tourists vying for First Class and paying by Eurocheque, complain that I am too close to them!) I make the last train to Mombasa. I have the good fortune not only to find and rendezvous with Chris, but to share a wood-panelled, colonial style Second Class Cabin. Good ride, in company of Mark, a friendly New Zealander living and working in Kenya. Wildlife outside windows and Tusker Deer inside. Good meats served aboard.

Saturday, 18 April: Mombasa to Kilifi, Kenya

Arrive at dawn to Mombasa. Chris and I do banking and shop for T-shirts. At mid-morning, we take Matatu to Kilifi on North Coast. In Kilifi Village share a room in Tushaurine Lodge. Have a good swim along coast of deep harbour, which is spanned by a modern Japanese bridge. 'Charter' a dugout canoe which Salim, a local fisherman, rows across strong currents.

In the harbour lies anchored a British luxury yacht, which I'd seen twice in Dar es Salaam. Inside the sheltered harbour lies one of the largest bivouacs of sailboats on Africa's East Coast. This renowned feature of Kilifi Harbour has admittedly been a craw. The sailor in me leads us through swamp and mire to the local boatyard cum yacht club; the Swynford Boatyard, headed by the amiable and known Philip Mason, who welcomes us.

Though uncomfortable at first (indeed overwhelmed by New England and British accents and swathe of European faces), I am introduced to and ease into conversation with a friendly writer, Ian Hughes. Chris fades out, leaving me with many drink tickets. It being Easter Weekend, there is a festive piss-up, for which I forsake food, and end up the worse for it. Meet interesting sailors, intelligentsia, residents, expatriates, Mertonians (a college in Oxford) deep-sea fishermen, and contemporaries. They drink as any Bahamian might I feel quite at home, though the setting contrasts sharply with those of my travels.

Am kindly dropped off in the village by residents my age, among them Peter. By nightfall, however, I am feeling completely drunk, and collapse in my bunk, regretfully missing a planned rendezvous with Peter and friends and the evening's festivities. Chris explores the local nightlife with Simon, a friendly competitive dancer working with our lodge.

Sunday, 19 April: Kilifi to Mombasa, Kenya.

Am woken by the melodious chorus of Easter hymns wafting from churches in the village, interspersed with Muslim chants being broadcast from the Mosque. Spend good morning writing c.100 pages in my trusty diary (a gift from Amanda). Token self-portrait photo, and reflection on trip. Very hung over. Chris returns late in toe morning, accompanied by a local girl, who is apparently accomplished at Karate. We learn from Simon that her fiancé willed himself to death on the prophecy of a local 'witch doctor'.

We finally head on foot for the beach, with Sato (the previous day's canoeist), as our friendly guide. Tense at first after a difficult walk around private properties; we relax on shore near the Seahorse Hotel. The auspicious wealth of expatriate homes and heavily guarded pleasure boats (lived upon at anchor), draws uncomfortably parallels with Nassau and the world awaiting upon imminent return. The jet-skiers and pleasure-boaters (and in an eerie sense), we seem strangely incongruous. We return to the village before dusk.

Though it has provided a relaxed interlude, I am happy to finally head out of Kilifi, which I do with a tongue-tying farewell from Chris and Salim. Board the *Matatu* back to Mombasa, alone. In the evening, I check into New Palm Tree Hotel, Nkrumah Road, Mombasa. A few beers downstairs and with smokes in all room. I offer a farewell address on my veranda to two English girls, who really don't seem to be listening.

Upon return to my single room, I assess the whole trip; ups, downs, and all, and surmise that it's been damned good, and well worth it. General sense of accomplishment. Sleep.

Monday, 20 April, 1992: Mombasa, Kenya to London, via Athens.

Very early rising. Taxi to Moi international Airport, where massive lines and long wait with complaining '*Wazungu*'s welcomes me back to the European world. Board British Caledonian c.10 a.m. (not 71). Good flight to Athens, complete with music. Spectacular views of endless desert, lake Turkana, White and Blue Nile Rivers, Eastern Samara Desert, and both the Red and Med. Seas. Sad to be leaving, though. Rueful return to Athens. Refuel and we're off. Flight over snow-capped Alps. Meet Joanna, who was on my flight down, and spent most of her three weeks in idyllic Lamu, on the North Coast.

In London share a cab back to Ann and Beth's flat. Happy reunion with Ann and 'news', including barbecue. During my stay in London check in at the Institute for Tropical Disease at St Pancras Hospital still must take anti-malarial tablets. Eventually must return to Oxford, unshaven, sandalled the works!...Back to reality (?)! Africa!

You Can't Get to Mpulungu from Here

The rainy season is descending upon central Africa as I wade into the soothingly cool waters of lake Malawi. Two fishermen, standing chest deep and throwing their nets, eye me curiously; a filthy young European getting wet. We smile at one another warmly, exchanging casual greetings in Swahili. Though it is a dialect from the faraway coast, and not of this vast interior, I am still fresh from among the Swahili; the coast-dwellers. Facing the expanse of lake, I overhear clearly "*Wa-zungu*" a universal word for Europeans for non-Africans.

I am relieved, I won't let the lingering fear of malaria or bilharzia keep me from this cleansing in the frothy surf; this long-sought baptism. Bilharzia. The insidious bloodworm abounds in another, un-swimmable lake which beckons to me to the West. It is Lake Tanganyika, stretching along most of the frontier of Tanzania, formerly German East Africa, some 300 miles (and three frontiers) distant.

Making it to Lake Malawi from the East African coast has been an accidental triumph of my trek into the interior. It has only slaked, and not quenched abucolic travel-thirst which whets and tingles the back of my throat. I am giddy with the taste of this, the first of three major lakes in the region. As though eyeing a row of exotic decanters from counter height, I crave these bodies of water.

Though I've made good time to the first lake, I'm still trying to force Lake Tanganyika into my vision of the precious days left no me here. With less than a fortnight remaining of my solo jaunt, this exercise increasingly resembles fitting the wrong pieces into a puzzle, which I have mapped across my mind. A sailor accustomed to making islands across water. I find myself seeking lakes across land. My first objective obtained, I stand chest-deep in it, gazing across Lake Malawi, unravelling and revising these imaginary charts. Here, in central Africa, of all places. I find myself obsessed, of all things, with boarding a boat.

The next lake promises reprieve; upon it I will find a vessel. More than a vessel, the Lake Tanganyika ferry is an enigma; its own ghost resurrected, it is evidence of its own history. The Germans had transported it piecemeal from its

Juvenilia

factories to the shores of Lake Tanganyika in 1914, constructed it there, and launched it as the proud steamer the *Graf von Goetzn*. Then came the war. The Germans showed their determination that if they couldn't retain, then the British wouldn't gain this; their African anomaly. Rather than surrender the lone flagship of their landlocked fleet, they methodically greased and scuttled the steamer in the depths of Lake Tanganyika.

Clearly anxious for the prize, the British bought salvage rights to the steamer from the Germans in 1922, raising and restoring it during the ensuing years. By 1925 the steamer, re-christened the *Liemba*, resumed her service of Lake Tanganyika. Since then it has been skirting along the coasts of Zambia, Zaire, Tanzania, and Burundi; delivering mails, goods, peoples, assorted cargo.

Travellers and their purses are offered sundowners on the first-class rail, or sunburns on the third-class deck. Now, every twoweeks the *Liemba* disembarks and takes on passengers in a port named Mpulungu: Mpulungu Zambia. It is the port of call nearest to Lake Malawi, and it is Mpulungu, and not Karonga. Malawiu, where I am, that holds my attention.

Mpulungu: The name alone presages a blossom of fresh images, which tickle the very fibre of my imagination. Each mention of the place precipitates an intangible spall bursting ever me; so many gossamers of mystique floating downwards; daffodils, parachutes; netting. Increasingly, Mpulungu ensnares me. It escapes feature on all but the most detailed of maps; it emerges among private company and in travel lone as though from a chrysalis, hovering above (or within) the conversants, flitting its delicate phantasmagoric wings across our eyes.

Mpulungu: There, a cluster of the hardiest adventurers and travellers congregate, responding as though to a silent siren; drawn there as though by scent. The curls of grey smoke (effusions from the steamer's reverberating funnels) leave a vaporous trail across the water such as jets leave across the skies. This call, unsounded but not unheeded, seems to promise a rendezvous; with experience. It allures these wanderers from afar. Then it holds them there within its spell, waiting on anxious haunches. Release is weather permitting at best.

In Mpulungu, a fortnightly exchange of dreamers. I am prepared to make it there. I want to exchange this terra firma, for the gentle sway, the vertebraeic shudder, and the misty smoke of a steam ship under way. The next ferry is due to push off from there within a week, and I'll be damned, as I surrender my ankles to an unknown feast of amoebae, if I'm not going to make it to Mpulungu by then. I figure I know how to get there, only the lines on the map sort of thin and trail off in its direction...

My German map of the region (called simply *Ost Africa*) indicates that the roads between here and the Zambian frontier, and, from there to Lake Tanganyika are only "slightly inferior" during the rainy season. In some regions, it takes winter and snow to deter travel, in others oppressive heat, in central Africa it is the rainy season, and it is beginning to seem that in it renders not only roads, but one's estimation of travel "inferior".

Problem is, time's getting short. Problem is, I've already been diverted. I hadn't planned to make it to Lake Malawi. The train I had been on from the coast was scheduled (and I was ticketed) to brush near enough to Mpulungu to backtrack there within a day. During my first night, though, I was woken by the slither of fingers down my back towards my rump. I jolted awake, throwing off my cabin-mate, a student at Makerere University in Uganda, whose affection I did not share. I decided to disembark at the nearest station Mbeya, Tanzania, on the frontiers of both Zambia and Malawi. My cabin-mate was downcast, I insisted, the train pulling away from my little pack and I into the mist of sunrise.

It took me a day of hitchhiking, chartering an old cycle, and hiking with other travellers to make it to the shores of Lake Malawi to find that I was dissatisfied. To find that I would rather be in Mpulungu. This morning the pelting morning sun illuminated farewells as a cluster of travellers pushed off for southern Malawi, I for Zambia. One lake the more, I figured; one country the more. Besides, I have trouble backtracking from a toilet, let alone an arid Zambian plateau. What 1 needed was a body of water. Lots of it. To remind me where I am. And here I am.

My trek to Mpulungu begins in earnest outside the gate of a cement compound on the road from Karonga to Zambia. The wait at roadside is characteristically monotonous. I'm hitchhiking, and hitchhiking is a bore when there are fewer than three vehicles in a morning. I squat roadside with baby-toting children, jovial elders, and silent labourers. The heat hums. Young women in colourful wraps and children mutter "*Wazungu*" in passing and giggle shyly. A chain gang trudges by, kicking dust. The prison guard, a Mr. Henderson, welcomes me to Malawi. He seems bemused that I should be here, waiting among Africans for transportation which few of them have faith will materialize.

The afternoon drones on. Shortly after the gonging of a wheel suspended from a tree declares lunch hour in the compound, the distant buzz of a vehicle shakes me alert. I stride into the road; it is a car belonging to the Ministry of Education, servicing the remote village of Chitipa, on the Zambian frontier, with teachers. I figure I'll be chosen for a ride. I'm wrong; it speeds by, curling dust around us as it passes. All that I can see of it recedes down the track is the outline of chairs strapped to its roof. Disheartened, I return to the shade of a tree, surveying those that wait with me. I feel that by expecting the only ride of the day, I have in some way betrayed them.

Among the sparse group arrives a fascinating entourage. Two porters march down the wide road led by an elderly African man dressed like a commanding officer. The porters deposit his cases, sacks, a collapsible table, and a chair under our tree. Then they saunter away together. Their leader is dressed in the type of clothes you might imagine Field Marshall Montgomery wearing while off duty. An army-green sweater covering a collared shirt complements his dark brown trousers and scuffed leather shoes. He wears a smart military-style peaked hat, and a thin rectangular name-badge is pinned to the chest of his sweater. I nudge towards him. It reads simply AFRICAN DOCTOR. African doctor. No more. Though familiar and at ease, he stands slightly back from the company, as I do, and is treated with an old mixture of respect and disdain by those waiting for us. Though intrigued, I settle down to wait.

Towards mid-afternoon, the first vehicle of the day pulls in from Chitipa. It is a massive truck, boasting at least eight wheels. Dozens of people are packed standing or crouched asleep atop the loads in its truck bed. Most of the passengers clamber down. The driver calls out that he will return at dusk and pulls away. I am resettling into my torpor when I notice something odd across the road, where the truck had been. It is a small military backpack not unlike my own. It is unattended. Fearing more closely into the bush beyond, I espy the back of a slender young man. He is filthy; covered in dust and a dark brown, but his hair brownish-blonde shag gives him away: *Wazungu*. I have to catch myself from calling out. He is peeing.

An African nearby nudges me towards him. I hold back, reluctant to disclose my surprise. I am at a loss. Beside me a vendor sells refreshments from a worn cooler. I've been drinking costly sodas through the afternoon. The other traveler strides across the street and buys three little plastic bubbles (like the baggies they sell goldfish in) filled with a local concoction. They are a fraction the cost of a soda. He shows no sign of wanting to talk. I break the stillness with English:

"How long did it take you to get from Chitipa?"

"Two days." Two days? But my map says that it's just up the road! Then, the inevitable:

"Where were you before Chitipa where did you start?"

"Mpulungu." Mpulungu. Damn. He's already been.

I feel irritated, react nonchalantly, and shift my queries to where he's from: Australia. How long has he been travelling this way? a couple months. Where is he headed? Lake Malawi. Then, Mpulungu again. How did he get there? The old ferry; the *Liemba* all the way down the length of Lake Tanganyika. How long ago? He'd gotten off the ferry when it had polled into Mpulungu almost two weeks before. But where has he been in the meanwhile? Traveling. But where? To here. He has spent the past twelve days traversing what I plan to cross in less than a week, and he looked the worse for it; gaunt, dehydrated, exhausted, the works.

Of course, I don't want to believe him. It can't be true. The Australian is impatient to get away from me. I can hardly forgive his lack of interest. He asks me nothing. He is looking for some other passengers who were taking a different route to Lake Malawi on the condition that the last one there buys the beer. It has taken him twelve days. I'll never know who arrived first. Shouldering his pack, he trots away. My eyes burn through his back, bitter with his forthrightness; his rude denuding of my ambitions. He has stripped my travel plans; my itinerary as it were, of its veneer of efficiency, and drawn them into his own mythic, timeless realm. I return to my wait, stewing.

On the precipice of dusk, I am shuddered awake by the squeal of eight tires. The truck comes to a halt within inches of my feet, which are sprawled into the road. The roadside beneath the tree springs alive. I know the rules. Every man, woman, and child for themselves. I have no problem with that, snap awake, spring blithely aboard and crouch into the truck bed, tucking my pack between my knees.

While people are still shuffling around getting settled, the driver begins revving the engine in preparation to leave. Then I hear the old man in the dignified army-green outfit calling irritably. I look over the side of the truck. His porters have abandoned him, and he stands there frail, with his pile of goods. Almost reluctantly, a youth on the ground helps him pass it up to me. As the treks of the truck wheels begin to roll forward, the

African Doctor pulls himself up and perches against his belongings gratefully.

The truck pulls away into the dusk and begins weaving along hairpin twisting unpaved trails, over rudimentary log bridges, and across the hills towards Chitipa. In a light rain, the moon rises and hold still and motionless against the sky. We are jostled around in the truck bed, occasionally stopping along the forested track to deposit passengers and their gear. I rest. Heavy rains wake me as we near Chitipa towards midnight.

The truck halts, and the same rules apply. I look to the African Doctor. He is an old man, and frail, and in Chitipa after midnight, in heavy rains, he is without porters. I help him offload his goods, shuttling them onto the nearest verandah. In at a kitchen at the village center he treats me to a hash of maize, which we eat with our hands. For the African Doctor, Chitipa is home until duty calls him on another medicinal tour. He welcomes me to share his mud huts, which are thatched in local maize-stalks and padded in caked mud. I accept. I put my back, to work, carrying the better part of his traveling office upon my shoulders through winding trails only wide enough for one pair of feet.

The moon shines, and by watching his back scurrying into the darkness, I am able to keep up with him until we arrived at his abode. I laugh to myself, struggling across a scraggy plain, carrying a stranger's belongings to a stranger's home in the dead of night. Here, my bearings begin to slip. I virtually savor my resignation; nowhere could seem farther from here than Mpulungu right now. Finally, I am able to lie down and rest, on a cattle skin stretched across a wooden frame, inches off the floor. I sleep soundly, giving myself over to a host for the first time during my jaunt.

Roosters awake me to a sun fully risen. I stumble outside the empty hut into a drizzling rain. The Doctor is explaining his saga to a family in a nearby hut, and I quietly follow a trail to the communal outhouse; a thin circular hut surrounding a hole. The African Doctor returns, and the introductions begin. Waiting to

Juvenilia

meet me is a man chosen by the African Doctor guide me towards Zambia. His name is Mr. Benson Nyondo, at age 62 already a great grandfather, a friendly, loyal man.

Before seven in the morn I've been introduced to the local brewers; women dispensing paint jugs full of Malawi beer: a potent brew of maize and millet grain fermented in rainwater. By noon the three of us are quite drunk. At around mid-morning Mr. Nyondo and I begin my quest for Mpulungu, which is seemingly more and more distant by the hour. Finishing a second jar of Malawi beer, we buy a small bottle of distilled Malawi whiskey, and walk to the village centre of Chitipa.

Chitipa is a true frontier settlement; very much home to its residents, very much a no-man's-land to travellers. It is a dead end of sorts, but very much alive, with some nineteen dialects spoken in and around the village. At all hours, people trek in from adjacent Zambia and Tanzania for their potent maize beer. Vehicles do not carry passengers like myself across the frontiers. It seems that a three-day layover along its dirt roads is a comparatively brief stay. About the only way out of Chitipa is net atop an axle, but rather atop your own two hips; on foot.

Resigned to this, Mr. Nyondo and I spend most of the day trekking into his native Zambia, meeting members of his extended family along the way. We eat and drink well, despite the crusty aridity of an evident drought. After a hike of several miles across flat but bristly territory we cross a dried-up riverbed to the Zambian checkpoint on the border. Here I plan my escape to Mpulungu, but no one is there. I read and sign the register, noting that in the past month the only travelers to have cleared were two Dutch and one German cyclist. Determined, I cross into Zambia. The border is little more than a rickety gate on the winding road to nowhere in particular. There are no more vehicles on one side than the other, meaning there are none on either side. Mr. Nyondo eyes me laughingly from the other side of the gate, I feel betrayed, bitter, disoriented. I feel tricked. I can't hike to Mpulungu alone in this heat. And yet there is no other way. I begin to feel profoundly lost.

Mr. Nyondo guides me back towards Chitipa. Backtracking. I all but give up. The hours, the days, the ventures, become a blur. Even my words become slurred, since no one understands English beyond one syllable. I communicate with no more than the inflection of a hum or intelligible murmurs, which indicated approval, disdain, thanks, and disbelief. Each day, indeed, each hour, makes me more anxious to leave Chitipa for Mpulungu. And with each hour (realize that it is never going to happen. You see, Mpulungu is elusive.

My experience is proving more African than I might have expected. Slowly I slip into surreal delusions of matterless-ness; a sense of having no location, a sense of almost not existing. Without bearings to prevent them, these delusions draw my attention and imagination away until I can conceive of myself as little more than one dirty little dot on the face of the planet, as obtrusive as a sundial, but less useful, standing out against time and history. I don't belong, but I can't imagine myself anywhere else.

Sure, I make it out of Chitipa. After so many days that they seem like weeks, I literally cling to a vehicle clearing through the Malawi frontier, the driver all the while yelling at me, me hanging onto the frame of his truck bed with the other Africans. They keep trying to dump me along the way, in the valleys and villages of no-man's land telling me I can't get out; I can't cross the borders. The driver finally stops and pushes his young nephew towards me to be my guide, and together we traverse both the Titi and Sangwe Rivers back into Tanzania.

I find a road again, and try to make it back to Zambia to Mpulungu, but an understanding, elderly border guard tells me that it is futile, and pushes me back .I climb into a truck going back East, and cry and cry and cry, because I'll never make it to Mpulungu, and two women, one beside me and one across from me, offer me peanuts to cheer me up. I climb out of the truck back in Mbeya, Tanzania. In a hostel near the bus depot there is the first *Wazungu* I've seen in weeks, it seems, but I can't speak to her, only murmur and inflect. I retreat to my room, where, lying in an

Juvenilia

empty bathtub with a cigarette hanging from my lips, I carve into the chalky wall a map of Africa with an "X" over Mpulungu, Zambia, and the inscription "You can't get to Mpulungu from here."

Yacht *Stornoway*'s Trans-Pacific Voyage 1993-94

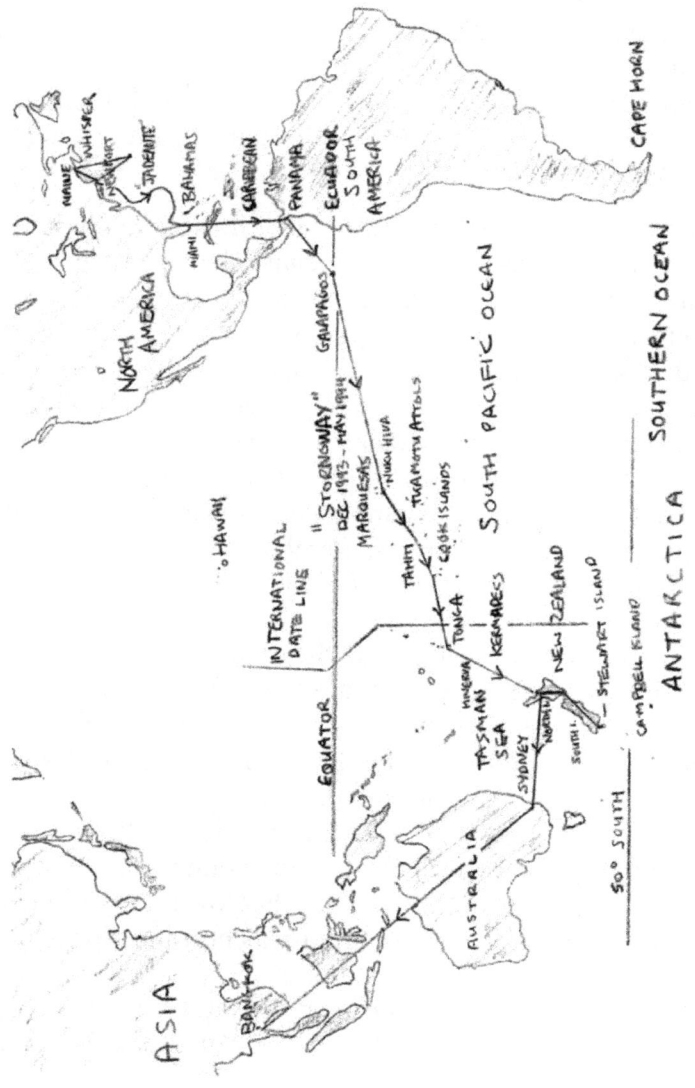

Eric Wiberg

Yacht *Stornoway*'s Trans-Pacific Voyage 1993-94

S/Y *Stornoway*, Greenock, Scotland, 68' 1962 Camper & Nicholson Burma-Tank 12-Meter Ketch Trans-Pacific Panama-Galapagos-Tahiti-Cooke-Tonga-NZ 1993-1994.

There are many ways to tell this tale. The best, I've found, is to let it tell itself. For our voyages together aboard the 70-foot Vintage sailing ketch *Stornoway* took on a life of their own. And they infused the lives of the dozen or so sailors, landlubbers, students, cooks, and friends who took part with recollections both bitter and sweet, for that was the nature and the scale of the undertaking.

While flying home from school in New England family in Nassau, Bahamas, I espied an elegant yacht from my airplane portal. I had a life-ring 'round my feet' 'cause I'd just helped deliver e 52-foot sloop frost my selling bass of Newport, Rhode Island, USA, to Florida, via the Bahamas. It was the autumn of my 23rd year, and I'd just finished a decade of schooling, which had taken me from the Bahamas through New England to England. Frustrated at not having pulled a. career or foreseeable future out of my formal education, I'd begun to see myself as a bit of a 'peacock', in all it's useless flamboyance and plumage. And again I sought the consolation of ay escapes to sea.

Mistaking the 'elegant yacht' to be my boarding school's research ketch, the St. George's School R/V (research vessel) *Geronimo*, run by my friends and sometimes employers, the Comnetts, I went down to the docks to say hullo. Alas, in her berth lay nestled an entirely different vessel with entirely different prerogatives. It was the classic Scottish 12-meter design sailing yacht (S/Y) *Stornoway*, bound not to tag turtles and sharks in the southern Bahamas, but towards New Zealand, to effect repairs to her ageing Burma-teak hull and topsides.

Stornoway had set off from Fort Lauderdale, Florida, that October, with a crew selected at the last minute, after years of preparation end half a dozen or so drop-outs from their original captains and crew. Returning to the docks with ray older brother John. I was able to briefly meet her owner, Chris, and to give him my sailing file, which catalogued several thousand miles of mostly amateur, but lately professlonal, sailing voyages between the New England, the Caribbean, and Europe. The only woman of the five aboard at the time, a spritely wee lass with long dark hair named Tina, read my resume and promised to contact me from Panama in the near future.

At the time, *Stornoway* was in shambles, with a random crew running here, there, and everywhere, trying to top up on diesel fuel (what true 'sailing' ship, needs diesel? we rationalized), in an effort to get under way. John and I turned our backs on her and went home. She pushed off for Panama, calling in at Port Antonio, Jamaica, along the way. Discussing the possibility of sailing aboard her with ray parents, brother John, and our house guests from New Zealand (friends of John's (and mine) from Nantucket), we agreed that it sounded a bit uncertain, even dubious, and left it at that. 1 went on to secure work, through my sailing agents, aboard power yachts In Palm Beach, Florida, that November.

It came in the form of a facsimile message (Fax) sent from Panama and forwarded by my father in Nassau. I was just completing my apprenticeship as a toilet cleaning: crew of big 'snazzy' power yachts, on which I had never worked before. I was unhappy; I'll transcribe the offer as verbatim as I can manage:

Letterhead: Yacht *Stornoway*

Port of Registry: Greenock, Scotland

Dear Eric,

We have studied your resume and are interested in employing you as First Mate aboard *Stornoway* on the coming voyage.

The original Mate will be removed. The craw has gotten rotten, without leadership or authority, and we expect you to whip him into shape a bit.

You will have your own cabin and private head (bathroom).

All we can offer as a wage is $100 U.S. per week.

We have been stuck in Panama awaiting batteries and repairs after a recent lightning strike, but would like to push off soon - hopefully before December.

We need to know if you can join us ASAP. We will cover your flight to Panama. Also return airfare from New Zealand.

As soon as you arrive we plan to set off westwards. From Panama to the Galapagos, the Marquesas Islands, Bora Bora, and Tahiti, French Polynesia, then the Cook Islands, the Kingdom of Tonga, Fiji, and New Zealand's Bay of Islands.

Expect to arrive In Auckland, 'City of Soils' by mid-February, 1994. Before the cyclone season.

If you are interested in this 'voyage of a lifetime', please let us know.

Yours. Chris and Tina, *Stornoway*, Colon, Panama

...Galapagos, Marquesas, Bora Bora, Tahiti! ...I was sold! Mate? Whip the crew into shape? Fine! I'd been Mate trans-Atlantic before, on a 65-footer, and had survived that one yay! Where do 1 sign up? When's the next flight to Panama?

Needless to say, I accepted.

I had a lot to leave behind. Settling up with (and closing) bank accounts in Palm Beach, Boston, and Nassau was the easy part. Quitting the job I'd committed to was not so easy, but possible. That was done by Thanksgiving. I explained to my employer that it had been a lifelong dream to sail around the world (even alone, if I had/got to!) The morning after I received the offer.

It was the saying goodbye bit that proved the hard part. But I dutifully packed my bags, wrapped the Christmas gifts for family and friends, and headed home. Then a jaunt back to my half-home of New England. Flew to New York and spent half a week saying goodbye to my closest friends in Connecticut. Follow student and longtime ally. Rich would do fine without me for a year at home and law school. I was packing my school possessions from my uncle's basement and saying goodbye to my girlfriend Maureen in Greenwich, which proved heart wrenching. But we were stoic even cheery about it, and both parted to don our respective pairs of 'travelling shoes' I for the South Pacific, she to Thailand to teach.

The hardest, of course, was leaving home and hearth for so long having to say goodbye to a loving family, when we all knew there would be at the very least challenges and dangers ahead. But I'd spent about half a life leaving home, and we all figured I'd be back before long...

I left Nassau on December First.

Funny question to be asked I thought, as I boarded American Airlines' last flight of the day from Miami to Panama City. "Am I in the service?" whose service? The Armed Services, you idiot! Ahh...Of course. I'm going to Panama. I've never been. Didn't we invade there some time back? Indeed. I was in for a bit of a surprise, because the airplane was chock-full of fierce, GI-Joe doll looking guys, and tweed-coated, suave, spectacled, CIA-operative-looking types. The soldiers themselves locked like a sampling from Hitler Youth or Black Panther 'catalogue' and there seemed to be hardly a Panamanian in sight!

What disturbed me most was net being among soldiers and snoops they were just doing their job (holding a much smaller nation with a mighty important canal through it under their thumb), and I was going to do mine. What disturbed me was that I was considered one of them the soldiers with the square jaws, steely blue eyes, and six-foot frames. Though on appearances alone 1 seemed to fit in fairly inconspicuously, they shouldn't really be judgin' the old book by its cover, I figured. But then, what else would a 'gringo' be going to Panama for; there certainly seemed to be few tourists aboard!

Comforted by my anonymity, I settled myself into the smoking section, and enjoyed scribbling a spurt of Narcissism into my Journal. Fed by Gladys Knight and the Pips screaming into my ear about a "midnight train to Georgia", and offered numerous rum and cokes (*Cuba Libres*!) by the flight attendants (who probably thought I was about to face a dangerous, secretive mission and perhaps I was?), I was pretty smug on my flight down to Panama.

I'd settled all my belongings from school to my room at home. I'd painstakingly said goodbye to those closest to me, I'd managed to get Xmas gifts for everyone, and even done some shopping, on Chris' request, for *Stornoway* during ay brief layover In Miami. And I was going to join a massive yacht on another voyage! Yes, 1 was pretty smug.

My new employers made brisk personnel changes on my arrival in Panama! I met Chris and Tina at the Balboa Yacht Club that evening after an eye-opening cab-ride through some pretty third-world scenes (reminiscent of East Africa) in humid back-alley Panama. I'd managed to negotiate my weekly wages up to S125 a week with Chris, and he and I settled into an easy camaraderie, lapsing into lengthy conversations about some of ay loves and his hates: hoarding school: and the British Empire. Aside from that, though, the carpet was swept from under me.

For one thing, *Stornoway* was not the rust-bucket 'tub' she had appeared to be in Nassau. Though her wooden sides are worn and splintered, down below and on deck she is a first-rate, top-of-the-line luxury yacht, and I figured would have to be tended accordingly. Not so, though. The captain. Skip, disdained of my working aboard in port, saying 'save it for the voyage'. But the voyage seemed to be slow in the coming. And I was soon to witness a coup d'etat of sorts, to boot!

As agreed, the original mate, a young American named Tony who became chronically sea sick (an affliction to which I have yet to succumb) and constantly ran his mouth and rabble-roused ashore, was sacked the day I arrived. His neatly packed duffel bags wore tucked in *Stornoway's* spacious cockpit when I stepped aboard for the first time. Tony had been given his flight back to Florida at the same time he'd been given 'the boot'. What we aboard didn't realize, was that he was drinking away that return airfare in the adjacent Balboa Yacht Club, on the Pacific Ocean side of the Panama Canal, as I settled into my new cabin! And what a cabin it was, replete with a semicircular lounge area in the forward-most niche of the yacht, with telephone, intercom, speakers, and my own *ensuite*stereo-cassette-recorder! That was just the beginning   add three hatches, all opening onto *Stornoway's*spacious foredeck, and a cozy 'head' with private shower nozzle, hot and cold water, and my own mirror, and I was set!

All did not bode well in the rest of the yacht, however. Unbeknownst to me. Tony was not the last to go. Matthew, the young Australian crew (who had no sailing experience at all, but accepted the offer Tina had made him at a skydiving camp in Florida that fall) had become a problem. Having gone several months un-administered he become daunted and frustrated at the systematic, even perfectionist demands of yacht upkeep, in which he had no instruction. And they had spent most of their days 'rotting' in port, with tempers flaring, and arguments between Chris and Tina understandably not uncommon. For they had landed a hapless crew. Soon Matthew's dismay and decay became dis-temperate, though, and Tina discovered thinly veiled written threats against her, penned by his hand. He had to be gotten rid of   and was. He was flown back to Florida, thus eliminating the role of 'underling' in the onboard hierarchy, which had given Tina and I a shared 'inferior'. Suddenly I became the youngest, with no one under my command, except, possibly, her cat Davie!

Last of the original crew to go was no less than the captain himself. Disillusioned by their meagre progress, but bound by his word to continue, despite having lost the crew he'd helped to select, the American captain Skip understood from Chris that he was free to leave. He saw little prospect of the swift 'delivery' voyage, which he anticipated (planning to basically power across the Pacific, relying on *Stornoway's* Mercedes Diesel engine more than the sails). Skip opted to return to the States in time for Christmas. By 7th December, he and Matthew were on their way back to Florida; leaving Chris. Tina, and myself aboard. From five to three persons during my first week! The power structure was being shaken from the top, and I was left anxious about where I fell into it all. Relief was soon to come, though, in the form of an experienced sea captain and an old friend of Tina's an Englishman in his early fifties named McKay.

Captain Keith McKay signed aboard *Stornoway* on 7th December. He is a man of action confident and decisive. On 11th December, we set out on an overnight 'shakedown' (crew and yacht adjustment) voyage to the Taboga Cays. And on the night of Saturday, 18th December, we left behind a collage of 'yachtie' and 'Zonie' (canal zone) friends and pushed of westwards for the Galapagos Islands under cover of darkness, with mooring fees only partially paid, and our visa permits over-extended after two months in Panama.

Under way at last! Offshore!

Now we're talking about the actual voyage to much more my turf, and a damn sight easier to narrate than the interpersonal conflicts, which arose persistently aboard. In describing the upcoming voyage, I'll skip ahead a bit for the sake of brevity and say that the actual 'sailing' bit became the most enjoyable, if not the easiest, aspect of the months ahead. After all, once you have weighed anchor you're all set: you know who the crew are going to be, you know where you're going, and it's a question of pointing the yacht's nose in that direction. At least that's what I would tell newly recruited crew along the way. We all wish it were that simple, and perhaps it is. The major glitches of the journey were also the most intriguing, if not exasperating. They occurred not only in Panama, which had been pretty clear-cut, but in the Galapagos, in Tahiti, and in Tonga, as well. But all that's jumping ahead. In the meanwhile we've just left Panama, bound on 'Leg 1' of *Stornoway*'s proposed trans-Pacific crossing.

Our first major passage together proved several things: that *Stornoway* is indeed a mighty powerful, wonderfully rigged and balanced, classic, heavy-bur then, fully keeled sailing yacht, sluicing through the water rather than skimming on the surface of the sea. She veritably surges! Mighty powerful, with all manner of sail combinations to set. No engine needed, thank you!

Secondly, McKay is a real sailing master; a gutsy sailor of the old school, a man of charm and panache, self-confidence and good looks, and an impressive knowledge of yachts, their upkeep and propulsion, and their engines. His familiarity with owners, however, especially those that insist on remaining aboard while ostensibly giving someone else command (a questionable practice, at root, eh?), proved limited dangerously limited for upon the rock of Chris' expectations, McKay was in danger of running aground. He began right off by courting young Tina, thus negating Chris, to Chris' marked chagrin at least marked to me, who had to constantly try to alleviate tension and distract the distraught with weak, self-effacing humor. I was becoming the court jester aboard, and already it was draining me.

Thirdly and fourthly in the revelations of the voyage came our realization that yes, the roughly 800-mile route of Panama-Galapagos is a mighty unpleasant, wet and choppy slog, taking a week or so, and, gratefully, we were reminded that on a sailing boat, even the most disparate of characters can become jolly close companions, working and playing together to the merriment and satisfaction of all. In making this final point, I lay the bait. McKay led the way, and everyone became a player: we celebrated a crossing of the Equator on Christmas Eve while making our final approach to the Galapagos. And what a merry day it was. The sun shone through as we passed dangers astern and threw our inhibitions to the wind to become temporary thespians! Having played up being an 'Equatorial Virgin' to McKay (though in truth I wasn't all of us had crossed the Equator), I was woken from my slumber by Chris, dressed as 'the Jailer' of Equatorial ceremony lore, in black stockings, stuffed, no shirt, and a pair of handcuffs. I was cuffed and led astern to the transom, where McKay, in an ingenious guise as 'King Neptune' awaited the chance to punish his only crew, I was shoved to the deck and forced, after hearing a decree condemning me to virginity, to kiss the feet of a topless 'Queen Nefertiti'Tina, perched on her throne of a stool! They all took turns dousing me in rotten porridge and slapping me with freshcaught fish, all great fun, and we sailed into Academy Bay!

If our Equator-crossing antics were the highlight of out voyage, then our week together in Academy Bay, on the Island of Santa Cruz, was the most pleasant layover that the crow enjoyed together. Sailing majestically past passenger-laden cruise ships to drop two 'hooks' (anchors) in centre stage of Academy Bay was just the kicking off of an enjoyable week of Yuletide festivities. McKay invited me to join him clearing the exhausted crew in with the local port captain a corrupt tyrant of a man sitting in a part of soccer shorts in the Ecuadorian Navy base. McKay offered a Christmas bottle of rum ($5 in Panama), and I interpreted with my Spanish. Once released with a ten-day transit visa (a week more than officially allowed in the eco-sensitive islands) we headed off to the local bar and disco called the '*Cinco Dedos*', or five fingers, to put five fingers around a few cold local brews! During our first beer together McKay made a point of denouncing Chris m a 'doomsday blasphemer' who was holding Tina down, and he called *Stornoway* a Swan-Nautor (the Mercedes of yachts) 'wannabe'. Now McKay was entitled to his opinions of the owners, especially after a gruelling passage, but Icertainly didn't like him knocking the yacht, our home, and I could tell the seeds of trouble were ripe to sprout.

McKay's gripes didn't keep us from enjoying ourselves in Santa Cruz on the contrary, he's a lively, positive man overall, and led me on a number of exciting tours and ventures. Within the first night he had gained the company of an Ecuadorian woman who spent winters on the island, and starting the next day we all enjoyed a continuous stream of outings on a chartered motor launch. These included swims with the playful sea-lion pups, a romp with sharks, dives from cliffs into ravines, and long luxuriant walks and swims on Tortuga Beach. The nights were kept lively for me by encounters with Israeli, American, and Ecuadorian (part-German, as many Galapagans are), ladies: all fairly innocent fun.

I woke in the hovel of an overseas scientist to face the dawn of ray my first Christmas away from home over a 'Mexican breakfast' of black coffee and a cigarette in a cafe in the village. Quaint. Aboard we celebrated Christmas, New Year's, and Tina's Birthday in true style, with X'mas lights, champagne, wine, music, and gifts. On New Year's night I ventured to the annual open house held in the British Consulate's residence, where I was welcomed as an envoy of the most striking (and British) yacht there. The following morning, still reeling from heavy boozing and sleepless nights, we hoisted anchor and set sail for the Marquesas Islands.

It was the first day of the New Year: 1st January, 1994.

The rest of the story is bitter in the telling, so I'll be brief. What started with a minor altercation that ended in a major one. On Chris' insistence, McKay pulled *Stornoway* into what he thought was Post Office Bay, on the island of Santa Maria, for a night of 'rest'. He also was ordered by Chris to curtail his admittedly rigorous 14-hour-a-day watch system to provide more sleeping hours. McKay was livid. Next day he realized he'd actually anchored us off the port captain's office in Black Beach Bay, and he brooded in the Navigating Station all morning. At noon, he read us all a list of grievances from his signed entry in the logbook. He didn't like yacht and crew, and in as many words, wanted off ASAP. I wanted to go on deck and cut the bloody anchor chain. But, instead we all turned back for the capital on San Cristobal in Wreck Bay. The voyage would be halted.

Keith McKay quit and on Tina, Chris', and my insistence, he disembarked around the 7th of January, a month after signing aboard, and flew back to the States without a penny of his wages. Disconcerting to me, the whole experience shook all of us enraged Chris, tore Tina apart, and shook and tattled me. So, when some snivelling asshole of an Ecuadorian Navy mechanic took $50 from us for a part, ran with the money, and returned later to try to smooch Tina, I threw him and his mates into our dinghy, yelled at them in Spanish, English, and bloody Swahili, for all I remember, and took great pleasure in picking him up physically and tossing him into the surf alongside the Navy Jetty

Though we understood from an American couple who had moored their yacht there for eight months (to teach the locals English), that the Navy boys might have been itching to impound *Stornoway*, confiscate it ('gratuitous', or 'wanton' seizure, I think it's called) and turn it into a 'floating brothel' for officers, the port captain empathized with us. Enjoyed speaking Spanish with me, and saw me as the next-in-command, which, as mate, I suppose I was!

Chris and Tina were getting desperate, meanwhile, and well they should have the threat of being towed to tire Ecuadorian mainland following an injunction by either McKay or the Navy still hung over our heads. They had to find a new captain 'pronto', and on the cheap, clear him (or her) with their insurers, and get back underway.

They didn't have to look far. I offered my services as captain, having anticipated that thrilling moment of my 'first command' since before I'd even joined. And I made it damn clear that, if I weren't an experienced sailor or mechanic, at least I could navigate (point the bow in the general direction).

Chris at first laughed. But, really, the joke was on him. He was in a real jam, faced with losing at least the insurance, possibly his dream yacht. And if he weren't willing to take command of his own goddamn boat (his dream, HIS life), then he'd better be prepared to hand it over to the next bidder in this case a 21-year-old wise-ass with little grease beneath his fingertips, and still a bit wet behind the ears.

Chris submitted my offer, and my (fairly impressive) sailing file to his insurers via fax. They accepted. And within a week of McKay's unfortunate departure, so did he.

I found myself captain of *Stornoway*, the largest yacht I've ever sailed on; much less skippered! Chris might call the shots and use his veto power, but now my ass was on the line as well.

And I'd be paid not a penny more.

It was the first week of January. Things moved pretty quickly once I'd been given control, but still not as quickly as I would have liked. I'm an offshore sailor, not good for much else aboard, and I wanted to sail. My idea was to yank the hook just the three of us. And set sail. Not so easy. We had crew to recruit, roaches to fumigate, and navigation to brush up on, not to mention nursing Chris and Tina's wounded morale and containing my reckless anxiety to push off. So, we waited, we tinkered; we dallied, as was Chris' way. But we had little choice ultimately, an open ocean faced us. Nowhere to go but west.

I found Trevor in my favourite cafe in the town of Basquiero Moreno, San Cristobal, within a week of assuming command. I exercised (if not exceeded) my full authority to recruit him aboard as the needed fourth crewman to man the wheel and satisfy the insurers. Our only criteria were for a person who could speak English and stand behind a wheel for six to eight hours a day. Trevor way surpassed all expectations. He came aboard with me and found Tina topless on deck. He met and liked Chris. And he loved the cabin I'd relinquished to take over McKay's former cabin markedly more Spartan. But near the Nav. Station. Though he was meant to fly back to his backpacking in Ecuador, and later to his family in Vancouver, Canada, that very day, Trevor joined us. On the spot. A brave man. But then he didn't know any better. He'd never sailed anything bigger than a Hobie-cat. That was just fine, though we'd all had it with the 'professionals' and their ephemeral loyalties. We had to get on with it.

On the morning of 23rd January, we lit roach bombs through the length of *Stornoway* 's bilges and went ashore to await the results (what really happened was the emergency vents were activated, blowing the smoke overboard and draining the batteries). We returned and 'made ship' in preparation to voyage. That afternoon we hoisted anchor and ploughed out of the reef-strewn harbour to wishful farewells from 'Karl Marx' and Delfin: three French friends named Carl, Marco, and Delfin; the two brothers slated to sail to Tahiti, the girl Delfin to fly, having turned down our offer for her to join us.

Right off the bat, Chris and I had problems to knead out. *Stornoway* began leaking in the seams as we headed between the Galapagos Islands and out to sea on a 3,000 mile passage across open ocean to the Marquesas, slated to take three weeks to months. Chris said 'Nay' (stop it now, pull in to P.O. Bay. and repair), I said 'Yay'(we ain't stoppin, goddammit, we're finally gonna sail, and if I have to swim over to is pair leakage, I will!). Chris won. I nudged her into a darkened, rock-strewn anchorage of the real Post Office Bay and we hunkered down to do repairs. I swam along her hull and found no leakage, but noticing that we had actually 'bumped' some coral I quietly had us move her to a deeper anchorage. Chris and Trev, meanwhile, lightened the keelson bolts holding keel to hull, and Tina baked.

I set about learning more about celestial navigation(with a sextant)by talking to a Chilean 'yachtie' friend on the VHF radio, and running through a few actual star sights on deck with him.

Satisfied that *Stornoway* would leak no more (leak less, we all acknowledged), and concerned about whittling provisions, the four of us (and cat) set sail from the Galapagos at noon of the 25th of January. A month after our arrival we pointed our bow towards the Marquesas Islands, which are little more than pin pricks on the table-cloth of the world, the charts illustrated. For me, as navigator, the voyage would be truly a 'trial by fire'. For all of us, it would be a test of endurance, patience, faith, and tenacity.

My biggest problem with Chris wasn't 'what' he did so much as 'how' he did them delegating Tina to do the dirty work, and not piping up until the last moment. My biggest problem with myself was my head: it was big enough that for a while I really believed that as captain, I could tell the owners what to do underway!

At noon of the 2nd February, after crossing our fourth time zone since Panama, I hoved *Stornoway*, bringing her to an eerie halt. We were in the middle of 'frigging' nowhere, 1,500 miles into our passage and; at more than 2,000 miles from South America, as far from land as you can get on this planet, of ours. The tension had gotten pretty thick between Chris and I, with two consecutive evenings of 'Happy Hour' spoiled by he and I arguing in front of the other two over my navigation tactics. I simply took our route across the clock-wise rotating Atlantic aboard S/V *Chebec* three summers before, and flipped the whole equation onto the South Pacific, with its counter-clockwise rotating Humboldt and Peruvian Current, (not to mention the Equatorial Current and a favourable Tracks Wind boosting us along at astounding speeds of over 200 miles a day). I took us south through shitty conditions at the outset to burst us into favourable southerly conditions further down the line. Chris wanted smooth sailing the whole way. I couldn't appease him. We were both right. Only he knew his yacht, and her limitations, better then I.

So, on that surprising Wednesday afternoon we drifted a while, made peace, played peaceful music, transferred fuel into our starving tanks (from massive drums of diesel which Skip had secured aboard for Just that passage), and all but Chris jumped in for a swim. An age-old tradition, and a great morale-booster for the crew, with all flags a-flutter. Out a dangerous one. Too. We were to learn.

I plotted our progress meticulously on an Omega International Chart (the type I'd marked their Atlantic series off with 15.000 miles worth of my previous voyages) of the Eastern Pacific Ocean. Each noon fix (thankfully procured by satellite, using our trusty Global Positioning Satellite (GPS) system, and not the old sextant), with a little circle. After 17 of these daily circles, we neared the Marquesas Islands, still unsure of whether to hail Hiva Oa or the capital, on Nuku Hiva Island. I grew increasingly confident of our approach. Chris grew increasingly anxious. And he was right. On Tina's insistence, I was heading for Hiva Oa, burial site of painter Paul Gauguin. It would be a night approach on a perilous 'lee shore'. Chris finally drew the line, lost his temper, demanded a course alteration to Nuku Hiva, the administrative centre, and stormed into the cockpit, leaving Tina and I staring blank in the Nav. Station.

Finally, Chris had made a clear stand given me his first 'order'. I lucidly understood that Tina, having never seen the sea until boarding *Stornoway*, held no nautical authority whatsoever, and that my own authority was limited to the desires of Chris. I was merely a glamorized crew who busted his ass navigating. Though embittering (and the cause of hours brooding alone in my cabin, even of my determination to 'jump ship' like so many before me, in the Marquesas) I was also relieved that Chris snatched the mantle of authority buck; it was frankly getting too much for me. And my unpopularity with the crew was really getting me down. But at least I could still navigate well. And navigate 1 did, guiding us between Ua Po and Ua Huka Islands at night, without Chris's crutch of a radar to confirm them. We made a splendid dawn approach, bursting through the channel at sunrise, edging between Nuku Hiva's *Sintenelle d'Ouest* and *Sintenelle d'Est* islands to drop anchor in after a near-record passage of only 17 days, on Friday, 11thFebruary.

Juvenilia

I had the honour and pleasure of clearing yacht and crew in with the French Gendarmerie on Nuku Hiva that afternoon. We had to juggle near a dozen nationalities between us (USA, UK., NZ, Australia, Italy, Sweden, Canada, France, and loyalties to Bahamas and a few others) before settling on each of our 'European' backgrounds. We hoisted the appropriate courtesy and nationality ensigns, doused our yellow quarantine flag, and were formally welcomed into French Polynesia after having tiptoed to their back door by the only means imaginable: by sailing there!

We lingered only a week in the fabled Marquesas: the 'land of men' which Europeans soldiers had decimated and to which European and American artists and writers have fled: Gauguin, chanson singer Jaques Brel, author Herman Melville, sailor-writer and actor Sterling Hayden; even Jack London and Robert Louis Stevenson, not to mention Rupert Brooke and William Somerset Maugham have trundled through France's Polynesian Isles.

Trevor and I teamed up and went ashore. On our first evening though, we had a minor anxiety attack over his future, and the length of the voyage, and 1 got so caught up in the excitement of paranoid fears and recriminations about Chris (much as McKay had dene) that I fully blacked out at a cafe ashore. Having hardly slept a wink, and rarely ever for more than two hours, in two weeks, I passed cut the following morning as well, and had to lock myself in my cabin for two days to recover. I had taken my navigating too seriously, but it had paid off. We were safe. I sent a tonne of a fax off to family and friends, and conspired to abandon the ship to stay in idyllic Nuku Hiva.

It turned out that each of us had doubts and consternations. But the fears subsided to a manageable plane soon enough. Chris hosted us ail for dinner ashore meat at last! And Tina enjoyed her wine once again. Indeed, the couple enjoyed a fine French Valentino's dinner together ashore while Trevor and I monitored *Stornoway* in perpetual swells and the occasional squalls, which rocked our anchorage. Trevor and I escaped on several jaunts and hikes ashore, notably to the 'valley of the Taipevai', land of cannibals chronicled in Melville's travel adventure entitled TVPEE. No such luck for us asa Catholic church and groves of palms greeted us there. We all would rendezvous at American expat, and retired yachtie Rose Courser's bar and villas on the hill for 'happy hours'. And the hours become happier, as for the first time I had myself referred to, with Trevor, as 'the boys'. For I am a boy at heart, and I was glad to think Chris would become the adult that I felt he should've been all along. (Perhaps he had been, and I hadn't acknowledged?). Anyway, happily hiked and rested, we set off from Nuku Hiva for Tahiti on Saturday, the 19^{th}February, (as to leave on a Friday is '*Tabu*,' and unthinkably bad luck).

A short passage to Tahiti became an eerily arduous one after we'd used up all our fuel to power through the Tuamotu or 'Dangerous' Atolls, on which Scandinavian adventurer Thor Heyerdahl's *Kon Tiki* raft had wrecked in 1948. We skimmed past the low-lying lagoons and off-lying reefs into a glassy-calm and windless sea. Drifting for more than two days, we began to crack at the seams, and were even tempted to swim in the azure, radiant fathomless blue ocean enveloping us.

The swim ended in a shark attack and the madness was ceased by a swooping plane; so we plodded onwards.

Hallucinogenic nights spent sprawled across the decks in the oppressive humidity and stillness led to fits of near-hysteria under the moonlit sky. Trevor and I lapsed into fantasies about 'melting parsons' and 'strafing pigs' on some imaginary Romanian frontier, before being brought to our senses (?) by sunlight. Trev couldn't resist a swim, and I soon joined. Only when I was alone, though 30 feet under, mimickingTina and Trevor's facial expressions through the translucent water, did the shark trailing us decide in for his attack from the depths beneath me. One look at the triangle of teeth approaching me from below, and I was on the deck. Moments later he swiped to *Stornoway'* side, taking the lower portion of our ladder with it. (They say sharks close their eyes on attack).

Next, we were shaken alert by a French government jet buzzing us at low altitude. (having swooped from behind the sun) and demanding to know our registry, and if we were anti-nuclear activists. They came around again (for a better look at Tina perhaps?) before flying off for Tahiti. We remained drifting.

"...It's a long, long way to go!" Trevor and I were chanting our customized rendition of *It's a Long Way to Tipperary*, as sung by the captain and crew in the Gorman film *Das Baal*. Fortunately, Papeete is pronounced "Pap-Ay-Eh-Tay." So we rhymed as we thread a narrow, reef-strewn passage between Tahitian surfers and ferries (filled with ogling passengers) into Papeete Harbour, on the island of Tahiti, on Friday, the 28thFebruary, one month and some 4.000 miles since leaving the Galapagos.

To get to Tahiti, we were shaken out of our drifting torpor by lashing gale-force squalls, beating our way through the length of the channel between Moorea and Tahiti, past Point Venus. The only humour in our tempestuous 'rude awakening' came when each of us on the helm habitually brought the bow too close into the wind in an effort to stretch closer to the haven of our only city in months. The result was that we completed almost a dozen pirouettes, full 360-degree circles in mid-ocean, only miles from our goal. And the only justifiable lapses in seamanship were to retrieve Chris' straw hat, blown overboard and lost!

We spent four Fridays in Tahiti, and there is no end to what one could write about those rich, lore-laden days. Suffice to say that this sailor had never heard better tales, nor sunk to the depths of quiet desperation that each of us aboard did. Chris even took me aside and offered to pull the plug on the whole endeavour, flying each of us home, if I felt like giving up. For within a week of arrival, every one of us had made a solo expedition to the offices of Air New Zealand, asking the (prohibitive) sect of the airfare to Auckland!

But none of us gave up. We all received or sent mail, and those of us that needed it sought repose in heavy doses; smoking away mornings on abandoned yachts with abandoned sailors, dancing away sultry nights in seedy clubs riddled with transvestites, hiking the hills not only of Tahiti, but of *Presque'Isle* the 'Almost Isle', Moorea and Marlon Brando's private atoll: Tetiaroa, which Panama friend Patrick sailed us to. There was no end to characters and their yachts, either, but we had to push off before long, setting sail finally on 21stMarch.

The passage from Tahiti, out of French Polynesia to Rarotonga, in the Southern Cook Islands, was not only the shortest leg of our voyage, but also the calmest so tranquil and reassuring that Jimmy Cornell, author of World Cruising Routes and others have ventured to call it the 'milk-run' in the vastest of oceans. And rightly so. Though the wind never piped up beyond ten or fifteen knots, we made a steady five to six knots (nautical miles per hour: about 1.2 statute, or land miles) under various sets of light-windsails. We had lost our only spinnaker sail, a red antique appropriately nicknamed the Jalapeno, (blown out during a dawn squall on the Marquesas leg) so we'd expected of the whole pacific nudged us from our left, where only open ocean and Antarctica lay, and ahead of us English-speaking Rarotonga lay waiting.

On 26thMarch, a mere five days after pushing off from crowded Tahiti, we nipped into tiny Avatiu Harbour on the island of Rarotonga, and dropped anchor as one of only two yachts in the basin the other was coming from New Zealand, and bound to the Bahamas. The only other vessels were charter fishing powerboats and large merchant ships that ply the far-flung Cooks. Most memorable among them was *Avatapu*, Captain Nancy Griffiths.

An American 'yachtie' turned to lugging freight in the schooner. She and her husband ran *Nancy* weathered about every blow, personal and other, between losing husband and son in the Marquesas and beyond, nearly losing their yacht off Antarctica, and finally losing the schooner awash with a cargo of concrete in the Cooks. Now she and *Avatapu* had to keep at it.

Juvenilia

Our layover on Rarotonga was short and sweet. We weren't cleared in by customs and immo. (Immigration), as all the laid-back, Kiwi/Nov Zealand authorities were enjoying local sports events. So our layover was like a social call popping in, with no demanding repairs, to sample the island culture for a few days! Trevor and I sampled the local bars together, and everyone did as they pleased; dining ashore. Full-course or burgers, sending Fax's and phone calls all over, any time, developing film, and comfortably back among moderately priced, English-speaking venues. Tina even took Trevor skydiving!

In the absence of stamps in our greedy passports, Trevor and I purchased local driver's licenses, which listed our address as 'yacht *Stornoway*, Avatiu Harbour, Rarotonga', and wound up our errands ashore. Then a last beer with Nancy at Tori's bar, which is made from the wreckage of Sterling Hayden's former command (at the age of 23: Gloucester, Mass, to Tahiti), the schooner *Yankee*.

On 1st April (yes, April Fool's Day), we waited till all authorities had packed it in. hustled aboard after 1 p.m. and just as the local barflies were lining the waterfront at trader Jack's saloon, motored out of the basin to the barrier reef. Those in the bar could see us glide to a standstill, maybe even hear our main engine cut out, but they couldn't see the smoke emanating from our starter motor down below. The ignition switch, salt-corroded, had jammed, burning out our starter motor. As subtly as I could, I began unfurling our sails. I determined, and we all agreed, that there'd be no turning back. If sail we must then sail we would to New Zealand if we had to! 'Damn the torpedoes, full speed ahead!'

By pushing off for the Kingdom of Tonga. 1,000 miles due West, without an engine, and, more than a month later, pushing off from Tonga with the engine repaired and an extra crew, we really 'max'd' out on our already taxed potential as a 'shoestring' crew. The resolution to continue from Rarotonga, and set off from Tonga, with so many odds against us, in my mind won the day for each of us, and especially for all of us, in terms of what we could face together.

If our arrival in Tonga after a week's worth of a slalom-course slog around reefs, breakers, and seamounts proved a climax of Chris, Tina, Trevor, and my voyages together, then setting off from Tonga with swarthy Stefan in our midst, shooting narrow, wrack-strewn passes in the teeth of successive gallon, the threat of Pacific Cyclones and New Zealand winter as great as ever proved no less climactic.

And in light of all that, our solemn entry 'round North Head and into Auckland Harbour that May, in all the danger of a midnight storm lashing us, was little less than an anti-climax, because by then each and every one of us, even Stefan, who had sailed from Panama in *Sea Snake,* a much smaller sailboat, was if not rattled and shaken, bone weary, knackered, and right out frayed.

There was a month's worth of dallying and puttering in Tonga, yes, but by then we'd become accustomed to that. There were the nights fending *Stornoway* off the rocks of Tonga's windswept basin in Nuku A'Lofa, holding her off with brawn and mere strings ropes in the absence of the engine. And there were the carousel ashore, the lurid tales, the dark and secretive company, come there to escape something or another; whether on yacht or a plane, they all started to seem the same. For we were at our tether's end, each of us, by then, and so broke, to boot, that I was selling off sandals and lighters to buy cigarettes, and we all accepted gifts of food after watching the Ministry of Agriculture and Fisheries take our beans and rice.

So it probably came as little surprise to Chris, after readying everything to push off in the midst of a seething gale, that I returned from an all-night binge among Peace Corps volunteers, drunken in the arms of a Tonga woman, and declared that on a gut feeling I wouldn't be sailing with him under those conditions. I had long demanded, and expected, a more experienced, 'heavy-weather' sailor even captain, to join us for the notoriously dangerous final leg to New Zealand. But he tried to push the four of us out into it, and I refused to go. That evening, though, Panama friend Stefan, of Stockholm, volunteered to join us, and with him signed aboard and ticketed back by Chris, we pushed off, through a reef-strewn pass, to a warm farewell by more than a dozen well-wishers on 4thMay.

Stornoway and her crew berthed at Auckland's Queen's Wharf on 11thMayand after hours of interrogation by Kiwi customs and immo., we were left alone to toast one another, and *Stornoway* quietly. We rested in a back-packers lodge together for a few days, swapping photos and addresses. Then Stefan returned to *Sea Snake* in Fiji, Trevor to family In Canada (via Stewart Island and Hong Kong), Tina to family in Australia, and Chris to more work aboard *Stornoway* somewhere in New Zealand. They had made it. I'll make my way back to Nassau the long way, I guess, but I'll carry with me a burden of poignant memories and heart-warming worries, somehow filling the void where my boyhood once was.

Report on the Water Barge M/T *Titas* Round-Trip Nassau-Andros, Bahamas, April 2, 1995

At about 21:00 on 31stMarch, I met with Captain Alan of M/T *Titas* at the Arawak Cay water-storage facility, Nassau. I introduced myself and offered a letter of introduction from Mr. Lund, dated 21stMarch '95 passed on to me by my father, A. Wiberg. Capt. Alan was receptive to the idea of my joining *Titas* for a round-trip to Andros as an observer.

The captain photocopied Mr. Lund's letter, showed me to a cabin, the Purser's bunk, on the Starboard Quarter and graciously gave my brother, John, and I a tour of *Titas*: engine and control rooms, deck, office's mess, cabin, and bridge, including an overview of nav. systems. The ship is in fine and immaculate condition. I found the computer software, customized to *Titas'*needs and voyages, to be especially impressive. We agreed that I could return that midnight to push off for Morgan's Bluff, Andros.

I returned to the *Titas* at midnight with my bicycle and a daypack. The Captain introduced me to officer's and crew, including the Chief Officer, Chief Engineer, and Third Officer, all of whom made a fine impression and seem entirely professional seamen. The captain pointed out that the crew of 15 hail primarily from Croatia, the Far East, and Central America. There was no crew from the Bahamas. Morale aboard is very positive.

At exactly 01:00, *Titas* pushed off from Arawak Cay for Andros Third Officer's watch. The captain helmed her out using 3 primary engines: 2 astern, 1 bow-thruster. The weather was settled and the roughly 6-hour passage to Morgan's Bluff calm and uneventful.

By sunrise at 06:00, North Andros was visible ahead of us to the West. By 07:00 *Titas* began her approach into the range from the 'drop-off' to Morgan's Bluff. The range is marked by 4 sets of markers. The channel is only about 200-feet wide and the captain pointed out that with 100 feet of beam and the prevailing following sea, entry for the *Titas* can be difficult. It requires stopping on entering the range and a sharp turn to the port once inside. Shallows mar the channel on all sides. We berthed ahead of the Nassau barge to take on water and immediately 'hooked up' at 07:30.

Though the Nassau Barge, assisted by two tugs, pushed off shortly after *Titas*' arrival, a waiting self-propelled tanker, the M/T *Mini Lily* stood off the channel and lay at anchor until *Titas* filled up and pushed off some five hours later, at 13:00. This must have cost the waiting vessel 5-6 hours in lost lime and substantial operating expense.

Captain Alan pointed out that such losses were not uncommon, and suggested that the receiving station at Morgan's Bluff be improved by enforcing 1) faster turnover of vessels 2) improved maintenance of the facility 3) greater attention to repairs. He pointed out to me 1) damaged fenders, laying on the wharf 2) poor safety standards on the diesel station hoses left to soak diesel into the soil, no shelter for the pumps, 3) poor maintenance of the channel markers, at least one of which the *Titas'* crew had set.

My mission, as I understood it, was to investigate ways to improve and expedite water flow from the Bahamas Water and Sewage facility on Northern Andros onto water transport barges like *Titas*. One way to do this was to look for deficiencies in water flow while ashore at Morgan's Bluff during the hours between 08:00 and 12:30.

The captain recommended that I investigate the air-release valves and flow- regulating tanks, which area meant to allow air and other obstructions to clear the pump flow system from the W&S Corp.'s pump station on North Andros to the pier at Morgan Bluff, and, ultimately to shipboard. He felt that the destruction or neglectof these facilitates was slowing down the loading process, and that by repairing and improving them, the time needed to load *Titas'* capacity of roughly 3 million gallons could be cut by as much as an hour or more each trip.

I disembarked in Morgan's Bluff with my bicycle, and right away went to talk with the Water and Sewage Supervisor in the wharf-side facility there. Mr. Russell, speaking for Mr. Gibson, the Superintendent (not present on Saturday), gave a positive account of water flow from the pump station located roughly 2 miles down the road, in the Loew's Sound area. Giving a rough idea of water supply in North Andros, he summarized that the well fields themselves operate from trench and tank water-collection systems, which drain fresh water from four trenches, dug in the earth into several holding tanks, or 'sumps'. Theses drain on the principle of gravity (see illustration). Only then are pumps needed, he said.

Then the W&S Corp. operates pumps from the well fields, some distance away, to get the water to two massive holding reserves at Loew's Sound. Of 16 pumps at the wellfield, 12 were operational at my visit. This seemed adequate to maintain a level of 6 million gallons held in two large collection basins at the pump station facility, which I visited.

I then rode my bicycle to the pump station in Loew's Sound and spoke with the manager there. 1 gathered that a Mr. W. Pratt is in charge there, and the facility seemed well run. I was told that the pump station uses 3 Diesel and 2 electric pumps to transport water through 24-inch bore pipes, which run along the road, roughly 2 miles to the ship wharf. These Caterpillar engines maintain a flow rate of 50 to 60 pounds pressure, enabling the water to flow steadily to the wharf and the ships.

Mr. Russell cited a rate of 1 hour and 40 minutes to fill the *Mini Lily*, capacity 727,100 gallons. That volume, in 100 minutes, indicates a rate of 7,271 gallons per minute, or 436,260 gallons an hour. At that rate, of just under half-million gallons and hour, it follows that *Titas* would take 5-6 hours to fill 3 million gallons.

The rate was being maintained; I was told, at about 50 pounds, while *Titas* was being filled. I understood that a second barge could be filled simultaneously without reducing the rate of flow, but this effort was not being made to fill *Mini Lily* at the same time as *Titas*, though dockage was available to do so.

It seemed to me that two things which could reduce the time of layover and increase the volume of water being pumped aboard at Morgan's Bluff were not being cone though they could be. The sight of the *Mini Lily* standing off the channel, useless, for 5-6 hours seemed to be an obvious waste of manpower, time, and money, especially given that she could have entered the channel, berthed, and take on water during that time, without disrupting either *Titas* or the water flow either at the facility or water level at the ump station's holding tanks. In this case *Mini Lily* lost time; next it could be *Titas*.

Indeed, surveying the maximum capacity of the wharfage facility at Morgan's Bluff, it seems that two vessels of

Titas' size could feasibly fill with water at the same time, as the holding tanks ashore offer 6 million gallons and claim to be able to disgorge to the wharf at a steady rate without lowering their water levels, which are replenished by the W&S' Corp.'s pumps at the well field.

Secondly, I investigated the air-release valves along the route from the Morgan's Bluff wharf facility to the pump house, on the captain's suggestion. I found that despite claims at the pump station that the air-release valve system was operational, the release-valves I saw were inoperable. One, near the wharf itself, had apparently been smashed by a car, and has not been repaired. A second, along the road, was in such a state of disrepair, with rust and general corrosion, that it seemed to have blocked up. It was a 2-foot high mound of rust, which it appeared, could be easily repaired or replaced.

The captain told me that he had filed a report to IPS along with photos pointing out this deficiency, and pointed out that by repairing these valves, flew could be increased and time reduced, thus saving substantial time and money for the water transport company the effect of $30,000 a month even, he said, by knocking of an hour or more of operational costs per trip.

In this vein, the captain also claimed that a 'regulating tank' at the pump station, designed to release air and obstructions along (the pipe-line from station to wharf, and thus reduce the risk of rupturing the pipe itself, was also inoperable, and had become filled with water, where it should be a regulating tank with pressurized air, I was told. However, since 1 was unable to inspect this tank 1 cannot confirm its state, though I assume that the captain has a valid point.

The interest of the captain and his officers seemed firmly with improving operability of the vessel and water flow in favour of the company (IPS). The captain, 1 understand, has been on this run tor some 5 years, has developed a good standing and cost-cutting trust with the Pilots of Nassau (allowing him to pilot the vessel in), and with the maritime community on the whole.

The first officer, I understand, has been with the vessel since Cadiz, Spain, some years ago, and also seemed an efficient, professional, and dedicated officer.

Having toured the area on bicycle between 08:00 and 12:00, met with as many relevant persons as possible, and visited the facilities dock-side, the pipeline along the road, and the pump station at Loew's Sound (but not the well-field, some miles in the interior of Andros) I returned to the *Titas*. At roughly 13:00 the tanks were filled with the required 3 million gallons, the pump station alerted to turn off pressure, the pipes from shore to vessel disconnected, and *Titas* cast off for Nassau in the shortest time possible.

On pushing eastward out of the range, it was noteworthy that the *Mini Lily*, which had been delayed 5-6 hours awaiting a chance to get into Morgan's Bluff to take on her cargo (possibly an unnecessary delay), seemed most eager to get into the wharf, and by passed the outermost marker, in ballast and with low draft, before *Titas* herself had even cleared the range. This indicated to me that the Panama-flagged vessel's captain was impatient with the time and money consisting delay, which may have been avoided. *Titas* proceeded westward from about 01:30 to 19:30, entered Nassau Harbour without event, and berthed again at Arawak Cay to disgorge her cargo and resume her cycle again.

The Bahamian-operated barge and tug, a less efficient operation more susceptible to weather and delays (and, as a tug-barge combo., more dangerous), seemed to have laid up at Arawak Cay and ceased operations for the night. This uncompetitive delay may have been due to it being 'Saturday night,' the Captain suggested it represents a second approach taken by one of *Titas'* competitors, the first being the pushy *Mini Lily*.

From my brief, roughly 24-hour stint aboard *Titas* for her standard water run Nassau-Andros, I can summarize that the following seemed to be operating in an efficient and professional manner: 1) M/T *Titas*, her captain and crew. 2) The line-handlers and port facility a: Arawak Cay disgorging *Titas* cargo. This includes the Nassau Harbor Control and Pilot's Association. 3) The Bahamas Water and Sewerage's 6-million-gallon water stowage facility and, presumably the well fields, which supply them.

From my brief visit, I would summarize that the following facilities and management could be improved: the ship's range lights, diesel pump station, fenders, and berth age coordination at the Morgan's Bluff facility (the option that the facility be managed by a separate entity/company would still require liaison with W&S Corp. and may be cost-prohibitive).The pipe running between the W&S pump station and the wharf namely that the air-release valves and 'regulatory' tank at the station and along the lint might be improved to expedite flow of water to shipboard.

Otherwise the operation seemed to flow smoothly, and for the time being the ability of the Andros station to provide and almost limitless supply of fresh water to vessels waiting to transport them to Nassau has not come into question. The system could continue as it does without great loss using the *Titas*, a superior vessel with largest capacity.

It is noteworthy that Andros has been described, by locals and guidebooks, as "an island of water" and the largest Bahamian island at that. Apparently, the well fields can yield a steady flow of water not just 12 inches from off the top. But apparently provide drinkable water as deep as 80-90 feet. If water quality remains good and can be 'harvested' consistently to a depth of even 20 feet, the volume of water available to be collected and shipped from Andros to other islands seems steady and consistent.

The issue is not the source so much as how to improve the efficiency of piping the water from the shore-side facility to the shipboard tanks in the shortest time and at the least expense, which would improve the service offered by the transports, and thus revenue earned. There seems room for improvement in this area.

Eric Wiberg

Summary of Round the World Trip, February - March, 2001

Here is a brief summary of that trip my fourth round-world, which took me to 10 countries: South Korea, New Zealand, Fiji, Singapore, Malaysia, Thailand, Sweden, Norway, France, and back to the USA, between 29th January and 14th March. (the first was 1993-94; a half year voyage across the Pacific, NZ 5 months, then SE Asia, the second trip was annual leave from Singapore 1997 eastbound and the third annual leave westbound).

The 2001 trip (a free ticket utilizing 140,000 Delta Miles, most of the, kindly shared with me by Dad)between 29th 30th January: Drove my old VW from Newport Rhode Island to Kingston, missed my Amtrak train, chased the train to Old Saybrook, Connecticut, parked and boarded. Stopped in New Haven CT to interview at Yale law, retrained for NY. Stayed 1 night in NYC, at Veronique's, and shared a limo the next morning she for La Guardia and Nassau, me for JFK and Seoul.

Two days fling to get to New Zealand. Met an interesting travelling companion Rob Panek, who grew up in Eastern Bloc (Poland), immigrated to the States, and was determined to do an around-the-world trip. He mixed a business trip for his NY state engineering firm with a trip from Korea to Oz., Singapore, the mid-East and Europe and has since made it back safely to his family in NY.

Seoul was freezing and lots of snow. We lay over at Kimpo, which will be replaced this month by a new airport at Inchon. Within a week of my arrival, workers from the Daewoo plant in the south instigated serious riots. Fiji another mere layover at Nandi *enroute* to the wedding in New Zealand. Stayed long enough to learn to say 'thank you' in Fijian: "*Vinaka Vaka Levu.*"

New Zealand: Arrived 4p.m. Long time getting the immigration. Had a Hertz rent-a-car waiting for me, but friend Littleton Glover skipped our rendezvous in order to fly. I drove 5 hours non-stop, using right-hand stick shift and driving on the left, through 50 km of winding mountainous roads and running over one opossum to reach Gisborne, on the NE coast of the North Island, by 10p.m.

The owner of the motel took me to a great pub in Gizzie (Gisborne), which is owned by the bride's (Peppy Streeter), relatives. 1 was the first one there and had a great time. By 11p.m. or so the rest of the wedding party gathered, and I saw the groom, good friend Chris Jones, and old friends from Singapore days, plus a few new faces from Connecticut (where Chris hails from) and NZ.

Three days of excellent partying and festivities with the wedding gang. Lots of good soul-searching conversations with my 3 roommates and others in the wedding group Deep sea fishing one day, picnics another, and every evening 3-star dinners with lots of speeches.

Saturday, 3rd February was the actual wedding downtown, followed by a superb dinner and dance at the Streeter's farm outside Gisborne, overlooking miles of gorgeous farm valleys during what was for them a long, clear warm summer evening. Partied it up till about 3 a.m. Music provided by a Brazilian who owns a house in Gisborne (about US $20,000 to buy, he told me) and commutes to NZ during out winter.

The day after the wedding most of us including Morten (Danish. also in shinning in Singapore) headed off to explore, and Littleton Glover, from Singapore and London days, and I drove rent-a-car to Auckland, where we checked into an excellent service apartment overlooking me harbour. Littleton, who works for Goldman in London, fitted most of the till!

Littleton flew to London the next day and I moved to my old haunts at Quean Street Backpackers (dorm room, US$10 a night) to see the city again and pack for 2 days. Caught up with fellow sailors, did a look around for *Stornoway*, (my first command, which I skippered to NZ from Galapagos in '94), and went shopping in my $35/day car for used books for the rest of the trip. Itransferred unneeded clothing, books tree to my duffel, shipped it home to Newport for about US$70, and prepared to go back to backpacking.

p.m., 6thFebruary, after a good piss-up with live music at the Downtown Backpackers I boarded a flight to Fiji, not arriving Nandi till 11p.m. At no point during the trip did I buy or read a guidebook, and so it was a relief to find another traveller, a German backpacker ('Gen')'winging it' on his own. Instead of drive 4 hours and US$100 to Suva (I wanted to see the Yacht Club, but Suva, the capital, is sail in political turmoil), Gert and 1 shared a cab to a good local hostel, where dorm rooms were a VERY cheap US$2-3/night.

Had a few beers and slept very humid but not many mosquitoes. Next day gorgeous and clear, caught up on reading, and in the afternoon went with Gert via bus to see a rugby game advertised as the 'International Series between Fiji and South Africa'. Even though it turned out to be a friendly match between Nandi's 'Holiday Inn Harriers' or something, and the Durban wildcats (?), it was a good game and a strong showing of Fijians and police. The fresh-squeezed bottles of juices were among the best (and cheapest) I've ever had.

At our hostel, I met an older American sailor who I had met and talked with in Newport RI two years before. He bad owned Irving Johnson's famous ketch *Yankee*, that he used to discover the wreck of the Bounty, and to teach sailors like Sterling Hayden the ropes. Small world.

Next day look part in a day-trip on Captain Cook Cruises to an island an hour off of Vanu Levu, near where *Castaway*' was recently filmed. I spoke with the fleet manager at HQ and also the captain on the bridge of their motor ship, however, we was net too chatty turns out, the week before they had moored his ship improperly, and it grounded and sank...oops! The island was beautiful snorkelled with giant clams, gorged on food and beer, and enjoyed the company of Anna, a Gentian gal who works, ironically, with ANA (All-Nippon Airways). The other passengers included an Australian Vietnam Vet and his wife, half a dozen elderly blind people on holiday, a gay couple in the hotel industry, and honeymooners who complained about their room.

Returned to our hostel, rested, played cards, ate, and watched TV with Gert and Anna, and boarded a midnight flight back to Seoul and then on to Singapore. Seoul was uneventful the rioting did not hit the capital for another week.

Singapore, 9thFebruary: Ahh Singapore. After 3 years of living there and 2 1/2 years away (in the [cold] States). I was there about 5 days. Most of the nights spent partying, most of the days spent catching up with old friends and work mates from my happy years there (September 1995- August 1998), spent working in tanker fleet operations with a US-Norwegian ship-owning outfit.

Greg Blakney of Canada and his fiancée Mimi hosted me at their lovely pad on One Tree Hill Road (where I first stayed in Singapore). A lot of good old friends and work mates made the effort to rendezvous and do what we always did go out drinking with me. Among these were Peder and Joanica (Denmark and Spain), Marius Hagen and Nina, Situ Kittelsen (roommates for a year), Morten Gronberg (NZ wedding roommate), and many other familiar faces.

Quite by chance ran into Nina Kurth of Finland and Screne Chee, from way back. And at Sentosa saw Rob and other cronies from beach-volleyball (and drinking) days. A few had defected from Singapore, but many seemed to have returned. I only missed the "brat pack" Esben, Mark Sherwill, Tom and Co., who are tied up in bachelorhood in Bugis, I understand. Everyone says that so much has changed, and while I saw a lot of new buildings and a few new clubs, the core and essence of the

Singapore I knew seems to have altered little in the 3 years since I left. That was reassuring.

I paid my respects at my old workplace, where Trond, KH, Capt. Khawar and Harald gave me an excellent reception and a nice long lunch, and also visited a Maritime Law conference under way there, and, my head throbbing and pockets much lighter than when I arrived, I boarded a train for Thailand. Morten hosted me for the last night. I took KMT (Malaysia's National rail service) to Kuala Lumpur on the 14thFebruary (Valentine's), and lay over at the beautiful station there to await a late-night departure I stayed at an Indian gentleman's back-packer's at the main station, and caught up on email, etc.

I didn't want to spend much ante in either Indonesia or Malaysia, because I disagree with Matahir's management of the country he's run for 20-odd years (he jailed his right-hand man 2 years at-n accused him of sodomy, and had the Police Chief beat him up personally). This was justified some weeks later when local Muslim "toughs" rampaged through a poor section of KL, killing about 5 ethnic Indians. Only the *Herald Tribune* reported those killings.

Indonesia was simply too volatile an impression borne out by Gert, who had a travelling companion's throat cut by a mob run amok in Ambon 2 years ago. (Gert managed to escape to an army camp).

I boarded the 1st-class sleeper of KMT's overnight train to Hat Yai Thailand late that night and was happy to share the cabin with an Englishman who had fought the communist insurgents during the so-called 'Troubles' in Malaya in the early 1950's (I went to college at Oxford with Jonathan Gurney, whose grandfather was the last British Governor of Malaya, shot to death in a road block at about that time).

At dawn, we cleared out of Malaysia and into Thailand, which was no problem. On the train was a Japanese girl who spoke fluent English and was very chatty, and a Thai fellow (track worker, I think) who insisted on wearing a Swastika on his cap (?) it wasn't even the Falun Gong symbol, but the real thing.

En route to Hat Yai (where I had been, in southern Thailand), I befriended a Thai rail worker based there and some young backpackers who were also going to Krabi. The Thai fellow showed us to a travel agent, and we all booked a mini-van for the 3-hour trip to Krabi, stopping along the way for some good noodles. After hitting the ATM in Krabi, a young Kiwi girl, two English girlfriends, and I chartered a long boat to take us to my favourite spot in Asia Rai Lay Bay.

We arrived late 8p.m. but were able to secure expensive bungalows (aircon, Thai Baht 1,050, or US$25), After a characteristically good dinner at Rai Lay Beach Bungalows (my favourite after numerous visits from Singapore) and a fire show followed by acrobatics from the girls, I enjoyed a fine sleep in my own bungalow. At that point I was waiting for Veronique and Ed to arrive from the states.

I'm breaking my promise to keep this short. Between 15th February and 3rd March, I stayed in Thailand, either at Rai Lay Beach (2 weeks) or Ko Phi Phi. Most of those 18 or so days were spent 'chilling'; sleeping late, reading, swimming, taking about 5 showers a day, and doing nominal physical activity. Exceptions were a short walk to Na Phrang beach, south of Rai Lay cut on the same peninsula, a hike to the bottom of a lagoon, an attempt at rock climbing with Californians Blaine and Jennifer coaching Steve of Canada and I, kayaking in the area, and finally snorkelling off Ko Phi Phi.

The main activities, for me at least, were reading, eating, drinking and sleeping. The average day began with a late brunch, around 11 a.m. over the "Bangkok Post" (2 days old typically), continued with a swim, more reading on the beach, maybe a catch-up on emails, a first beer around 6p.m. to sunset, a cold shower in my Bht750 (US$18) single-bed, fart, no-hot-water bungalow, another relaxed read by candle light on my balcony fronting the main path dissecting the island, and then dinner around 9 with companions or alone.

The best part of the weeks in Thailand, for me, was without doubt the excellent company that I found there. The first five days I kept a twice-daily vigil for my friend Ed, from Block Island, to disembark from the Phuket ferry (we had a rendezvous at Rai Lay of the I4th). Then I learned he wouldn't be coming at all. From the 14th to the 21st I bought tickets and lined up to meet Veronique at Bangkok, but on the 19th I learned that she wasn't coming either. Other friends from Singapore couldn't make it, but they told me ahead of time. So, I naturally turned to look around me for company, and was not disappointed in the least.

Rai Lay has changed in only one significant way since when I last visited: in a nutshell, it is more 'bourgeoisie'. Bungalows in the high season are now booked via internet or phone months in advance, for up to months at a time. The average age has shot up to mid-thirties. There are lots of families. There are even business outings (tour groups). There are far fewer dread locks, though. Rai Lay thankfully still boasts of a core of seasoned rock climbers, who give the place some sense of validity from bases at Diamond Caves and Thong Sai Beach.

I won't embarrass them by going into too much detail, but I was very fortunate to have met a few good people in particular, Steve G. from Canada, self-employed and on a two-week holiday, my age and educated as a lawyer, was the best buddy I could have hoped for one morning he even saved to "Bangkok Post" for me. Together we did several hikes and attempted the climb. One hike, around the steep coast, ended with both of us and all of our gear up to our necks in water.

Another great success on the companionship front were Blaine and Jennifer, who hail from Marin County, California. Great conversationalists, sweet and understanding. We all hung out and did a lot together, particularly during the day, both in Rai

Lay and Phi Phi. It was they who dared to teach Steve and I bow to climb!

Probably the happiest few days were when South African Gary and his friend Collin (both veterans of various wars in Southern Africa) and Steve and I teamed up with gregarious lawyers Kristin and Sidcel (pronounced Cecil, hers is a Norwegian name) from Oslo and Tromso respectively. Together we had some great dinners, chartered a long boat to go to Chicken Island and Po Dan Island, and generally had a great time

The biggest scare of the trip was when I was literally run over by a 30-foot, 20-knot 'long boat' off Po Dan Island. I'd been submerged, snorkelling, for about 40 seconds, roughly 100 meters (300 feet) from the beach. When I surfaced I was stunned to see, with no audio or visual warning, the bow of this boat, with a 'bone in its teeth' (frothy waves) literally less than a meter from me and moving at least a meter a second. Fortunately, I managed to fend the bow off from my head (with my right forearm against its starboard bow), and dive. Then I lay prone, 4 feet underwriter, and waited for the props to chop over my legs. When that didn't happen, and after 10 seconds or so of waiting, I surfaced in time to see the bastard driver sitting in the BOTTOM of his boat, not looking up, his view blocked by a dozen passengers.

Angry and scared, I yelled sharply. No response. I yelled again. He was speeding away. But any friends on shore picked up on my alarm and began to swim out to help me. I was really shocked I traced the same boat returning from Chicken Island, got his details, and later that day was able to confront the captain with a Thai interpreter (another skipper), once back at Rai Lay Beach Bungalows.

My travel mates thought it was useless to do so, but I learned in shipping that 'silence is deadly', and that even near misses or 'incidents' (as opposed to accidents) should he discussed and circulated. Perhaps for a few weeks the skippers will be extra vigilant of swimmer; before relapsing to their lackadaisical ways…One hopes…I am quite sure that 1) he came very close to killing me (the bow would easily have stayed in a person's head on impact), and that 2) had I not been raised around boats in Bahamas and worked on them for a living, I might not have (read: an average person might not have) been able to ream as quickly and calmly as I did. It was, after all, a classic 'deer in the headlights' scenario.

After about two weeks on Rai Lay beach I needed a change. Most of my travelling buddies had moved on, and after witnessing three fights, in two nights I got on the next boat out of town to Xo Phi Phi. There I was fortunate to secure a bungalow at Charlie's Bungalows, on the North shore, for Bht350 a night. It had two bunks and was more than I needed, but there was no bar at the place, it was quiet and nice, with movies every night, and a great beach. I was happy there during about a week of serious partying. By far my favourite was Tin Tin's, though Apache gets a good vote, the Reggae Bar was a disappointment for anything other than spectating the kick-boxing or having an early evening beer.

About the only healthy thing I did on Phi Phi was snorkel off Ike islands to the north, visit Long Bay, and leave (!). A Swedish dive instructor who has spent 3 seasons there told me that he saw two relationships one 7 years, another 4 crumble in weeks on Ko Phi Phi, and I can understand why. It is hedonism with an edge, though (sister Ann explained) I was there during Scandinavian holidays, during a cold winter, there were lots of happy Swedes there to soften the edge, I felt quite at home, even with my meagre Swedish.

To get a jump on my overland trip to Singapore, I left Ko Phi Phi on 2^{nd}March about 4 days before my departure from there. I spent a leisurely night in Ao Nang, enjoyed dinner in the good company of a pair of Canadian and American travellers, and the next day hoarded a mini-van for an 11-hour trip from Krabi to the Malaysian border at Kota Bahru.

Stayed in a great guesthouse in Malaysia experienced a real scare of having my credit card cancelled, but made it on the

Juvenilia

KMT train to Singapore the following day, overnighted on the train and returned to the Lion City 36 hours before mv flight. Stayed with Greg and Mimi again (they were really helpful and advanced me some much-needed cash while my card took 5 days to clear), and. on 5thFebruary at midnight I boarded my Air France flight to Paris and Stockholm.

Only just made my connection in Paris, and was met at Stockholm's Arlanda airport by big sister Ann and her and Gustaf's two youngest godsons, Wilhelm and Axel (4 and 2). Enjoyed a great 5 days reuniting with the family, meeting up with old friends from days in Sweden, Singapore, and the Bahamas, and helped out as much as I could with looking after the boys during the day.

One memorable night was a reunion with my shipping buddies for a 'maritime' night in Stockholm. That went on to the wee hours and was a lot like "the good old days". It was nice to be able to laugh about some of the little disasters of working for a tanker owner with Erik Lewenhauptand cousins Henryk and Erik Hartzell. Also caught up with cousin Magnus, godmother Aunt Margareta, and Gustaf's Mom Aunt Karna. Ann and Gusty were excellent hosts.

Enjoyed a quick one-night jaunt over to Oslo, where I got a feel for that comparatively small tart bustling city, returned to the *Kon Tiki* museum, saw Amundsen's Northwest Passage boat, and met up with Nassuvian Nicolette and Hans Herman Horn and their growing brood. I was guest of Kristin (we had met at Rai Lay) and had a wonderful stay.

Back to Stockholm for the night of Sunday 11thMarch, then a quick fright to Paris on Monday, a great stay there at my old (*War Baby* voyage, 1991) haunt Hotel St. Andre-Des-Arts. Did my errands (films, attempts at phone calls and entails, post office), had a great dinner laughing with other dinners at a Japanese joint, called in at an Irish pub where I spoke at length with a Finn working for UNESCO, and ended up with a group of

Jim Morrison fans at a tiny French 'discotheque' opposite the hotel called '*Le Chameleon*' till 4 A.M.

Afternoon (light Paris to Boston the next day (still Air France), and I reluctantly decided to make it and end the trip. Old Singapore and Nassau friend Kent Post met me with his colleagues at Akamai, decompressed at our Boston watering hole, caught up with him and Cindy, and the next day rode Amtrak to retrieve my car in Old Saybrook. Amazingly, I had only a small mountain of mail which was 90% bills, an acceptance and a rejection letter from two different law schools, virtually no voice mails (1 had left a good deterrent for a message!), and only a few new entails, as I had been checking them remotely for a month.

Overall and excellent trip, and one I would recommend thoroughly. The only downers was having to witness the fights and a few drunken conversations in Thailand (that's what you get from being awake at 4a.m.).Otherwise it was a thoroughly energizing, restive, and thought-provoking tour of our little world! It is, I feel, still a wonderful world.

About the Author

Eric Wiberg has operated over 100 yachts over 75,000 nautical miles, many of them as captain. A licensed master since 1995, he is qualified as a maritime lawyer, and a long-time member of the Maritime Law Association of the US. He commercially operated nine tankers from Singapore for three years for the firm that lost the tanker *Braer*, and worked briefly for two salvage firms. He studied at five universities in three countries, including at Oxford. He has published seven other books of nautical non-fiction. A citizen of US and Sweden who grew up in the Bahamas, he lives and writes in New York City, where he works in the shipping industry. His son is Felix.

www.ingramcontent.com/pod-product-compliance
Lightning Source LLC
Chambersburg PA
CBHW051750040426
42446CB00007B/295